Poor Millionaires

*The Village Boy Who Walked to the Western World
and the American Boy Who Followed Him Home*

Nathan Roberts
&
Michael Kimpur

For video and additional media content please visit
www.poormillionaires.org

Copyright © 2014 Nathan Roberts and Michael Kimpur
Cover design by Alex Betzler
Book design by Jeremiah Satterthwaite
Editing by Linda Henry and Keith Hanson
Author Photograph by Jeremiah Satterthwaite

DISCLAIMER

ISBN: **978-1502450920**

A LETTER FROM MICHAEL

Sometimes I catch myself thinking about how far I have gone. When I was a small boy, I could have never imagined that my life would turn out as it did. I grew up in nomadic community, a village of mud huts in the middle of the Kenyan desert. Although, at that time, we didn't know about Kenya or Africa or planet Earth. All we knew was the desert. We spent our mornings walking our village cows to the river and our afternoons hunting small animals to eat for dinner. But my life has taken many unexpected turns since then. I was a World Vision sponsor child at a humble village school. I was with a small group of orphaned boys. We learned to read and write. We discovered so many strange and wonderful things that most people in cities take for granted, like television, radios, and refrigerators. But I had an opportunity to go even farther than my classmates. I came around the world and studied at an American university. It was there that I learned the world was full of so many different cultures.

But I also learned many difficult lessons. I learned about the history of colonialism. How the British enslaved Kenya in the name of Christianity. I learned that my tribe's traditional lands were stolen, first by the British and then by the independent Kenyan government. I learned that there are places where sharing what you have with those who are in need is not expected like it is in our villages.

But perhaps the greatest lesson I have learned is that you never know how far you can go. Every time I thought I had hit a dead end, I was given a chance to turn things around. My life is one of second chances. That is why Nathan and I started a school in Kenya, to give children a second chance, just as I was given a chance as a child. We wanted to give orphaned children from my war-torn community an opportunity to see how far they can go.

Nathan and I wrote this book together. We spent three years sharing stories, emailing chapters back and forth, and learning about one another's cultures. When we started, Nathan asked me to write my own story. But I told him English was my third language. My people are an oral people, where stories are told, not written down. So I shared with him my life and he wrote it down for me. And for that I am so grateful. A book written about my life is yet another turn I could not have expected.

Michael Kimpur

CONTENTS

0
LEMON DROPS AND AK-47S

I awoke at sunset to a gun barrel clicking on the tinted passenger-side window of our SUV. A sixteen-year-old held the assault rifle in his hands. He was wearing a fraying green army jacket and what looked like a picnic blanket wrapped as a skirt. After attempting to look through the glass, he motioned for me to roll down the window.

I looked at Michael. "We found them."

"Actually they found us," he corrected. "And now we are their prisoners. Or their guests," he added with a grin. "That remains to be seen. Either way, they will bring us to the camp." He reached across me to roll down my window before shouting at the teenager in his mother tongue. Two more teenagers with AK-47s emerged from the desert thicket. Michael reached out of the driver's side window, shook their hands, and asked them where their camp was.

"So do these guys know who you are?" I asked, trying to sound calm. We were out of cell phone range. The radio stations had buzzed into white noise hours ago. "Oh, no worries, buddy," he said. "These are just some young herdsboys from my tribe, the famous Pokot." He pulled down his lower lip and pointed at a gap where his bottom two front teeth should have been.

The boy at the window smiled with the same missing teeth. "Don't worry." He patted me on the leg. "They are just taking some precautions. In fact, when I was a herdsboy we were always on the lookout for spies. You know so many people out here are trying to steal cows. So they have to make sure. They want to take us in for a bit of questioning." A Pokot elder sat quietly in the backseat, and Michael's teenage daughter Chelimo sat on a 50-pound bag of corn flour in the cargo bed.

"But they know you, right?" I asked, my voice losing confidence with every emerging detail. Michael shouted to the herdsboys and then said to me, "Okay, you shake this guy's hand." He pointed at the teenager who had his gun pointed at me. The boy leaned in the vehicle, and as I shook his hand, he smiled at me for the first time. I could smell the acidic sweat coming from his dehydrated armpits.

"Okay, do they know me?" Michael said. "That is a good question. These boys do not seem to know me. But the older men in their camp will. This I am sure of. Because I am pretty much one of the most famous Pokot in Kenya. Between the bigness of my belly and our work with children, most nomads have at least heard of me. But these are just some young herdsboys and they are being a little bit cautious." We locked eyes and he quickly amended his explanation. "But no worries, buddy. No worries at all."

Everyone in the vehicle started discussing our situation in a language I couldn't understand. But their pointing assured me I was the topic of debate. The boy motioned to a path barely wide enough for two cows to walk side by side. Then he shouldered his semi-automatic, and stepped onto the SUV's running board as Michael pulled off the broken desert road and down the path. As the vehicle navigated the rocky terrain, I could hear the boy's brightly colored beads bouncing around his neck.

One of the boys must have run ahead and warned of our arrival, because at the end of the path, a dozen men stood wearing what I had begun to suspect were Pokot military fatigues: green army shirts and wraps around their waists, each holding the same Soviet-era AK-47. Behind them, thousands of emaciated cows with humps above their necks and ribs like xylophones stood grazing on short greenish-brown grass in a valley dotted with short thorn bushes. When the vehicle stopped, I noticed flies swarming around piles of cow dung. I rolled up the window. The travel nurse had told me to avoid all contact with African insects.

"You better stay in here, buddy," Michael said, stepping out of the vehicle. "These boys told me that they have never seen a white person before, and you people can be a pretty scary thing to behold for the first time." Michael knew the feeling intimately. "Those men up there are cattle rustlers, the people Google refers to as the fiercest warriors in Africa." We had spent hundreds of hours researching the Pokot tribe online, Michael showing me picture after picture in our college dorm in Minnesota, pointing out this or that inaccuracy in the articles, frustrated that the Kenyan media was destroying his tribe's online reputation.

As Michael and the others began speaking to our captors, a group of half-naked kids waddled out of the thicket and rushed to the vehicle. They tucked their hands around their faces and tried to catch a glimpse through the tinted glass. A boy in only a blue tank top and beaded hoop earrings caught my eye. He pointed to his mouth and cupped his hands. I could see big horseflies were drinking the liquid from the corner of his eyes. Then another landed on the snot trickling from his nose. But he didn't seem to notice. I opened the window and handed him a lemon candy as flies poured into the vehicle. The boy laughed, his eyes wide, pointing at his mouth, like he was acting for a TV commercial.

Michael shouted to me, "That's good to give out the candies. The children most probably have never tasted one." At the sight of food, the other kids rushed to my window. Muddy hands cupped one on top of the other as I placed a lemon drop in each palm.

One of the men started shouting and shaking his gun the way terrorists do in the movies. Michael frantically motioned for the men to calm down, pointing at himself, then at me, and then at the children. I rolled up the window and reached into my backpack for my anti-anxiety medication.

I counted to sixty and waited for my neck muscles to relax. I watched the kids, who were now sitting in a circle taking turns spitting the candy into their hand to look at the shrinking yellow dot, their hands getting stickier and stickier, attracting more and more flies. These kids were the reason I was out here. Michael and I were supposed to convince their fathers to let them come live at our school on the edge of the desert.

We had been planning this meeting for three years, sitting on the couch in our small apartment in Minneapolis late into the night, discussing the future of his tribe. He was a foreign exchange student studying global politics. Shortly after coming to Minnesota, Michael learned the sordid history between the U.S. and the Native Americans: the broken treaties and wars and reservations. From that moment on, he was convinced that this history was being reprised between the Kenyan government and his own tribe. Michael had read every book he could find on the history of the Cherokee Nation.

I remember the night he asked me "Do you want to put kids on the moon?" He pointed at the poster of JFK hanging on our wall with the words "It's time for a new generation of leadership...for there is a new world to be won."

"What?" I laughed, looking up from my theology homework.

"I'm going to open a school for nomadic kids on the moon," he laughed. "Anyways, the moon is just about as far from the desert as the modern world. But I need you to help me."

"Why me?" I asked, thinking he might want to find somebody with more experience.

"Because you are teachable, and where we're going you need to be teachable."

1
THE OGRE

Village years aren't collected and ordered into decades and centuries, numbers and letters. There are no clocks or calendars. As Michael reminds me, "There is only an endless series of today. And today goes back to the beginning of time. Our elders sit around the fire to report the day's work, the hills they walked and the giraffes they saw. Mothers talk of the meals they prepared and what will be cooked tomorrow. And when we speak of the past, we say 'this or that rainy season when we got married' or 'When we were children...' or 'Our ancestors used to...'"

And if these days live on, it's not in photographs or dated journal entries, but in the stories that are told by warriors around the campfire or between women during their long walks to the river. And often times the most beloved stories, the ones told over and over, begin to take on a life of their own. They become proverbial warnings in the mouths of the elders, the songs of women, and bedtime stories told to children.

In one small village in the desert of northwestern Kenya, Michael Kimpur's life is one of these beloved stories. Although "small" or "northwestern" or "Kenya" are not the words the villagers would use to tell it. These words were put on them, the way American flags were put on the moon.

In Western time our story begins in the late 1980s, when Michael Kimpur was a small child spending his days milking cows and sleeping in a mud hut with a grass roof, a cowhide blanket for a bed. When he was finally big enough to hold a canteen and walking stick, he got his first chance to herd his family's cows. His small hands wiped the sleep from his eyes as he sat outside his father's hut. His mother emerged from the round clay doorway, trailed by smoke from the morning fire. She filled his cup, made from dried squash, with warm fresh milk. "Kimpur, today you will be herding the cows with the other boys," his father said in a serious tone. His father never called him Michael—that name came later from the missionaries. As a boy, he was simply called Kimpur, named after the Kimpur River where his mother birthed him.

Kimpur could hear the women in the village singing the grinding song. He had awakened to their singing since he could remember, listening to his grandmother chanting the steps for making porridge: planting the seed in the ground, harvesting the plants, milking the cows, and stirring the pot. His older sisters responded to each verse with a melody, their still sleeping babies strapped to their backs.

Kimpur's heart leapt at the thought of going with the older boys. His whole life he had watched the herdsboys leave the homestead. He'd stand next to the mothers, facing Tororot's holy mountain of Mtelo, and listen to the *werkoyon*[1] pray that lions were not hiding in the bushes, hoping that Karamoja warriors had not yet discovered the location of their homestead. He would jealously watch the boys lead the cows through the small wooden door in the thorn fence surrounding the village. Year after year, Kimpur had watched them leave, waving to his best friend, Keu, a teenager who stood head and shoulders above the other boys. He had earned the name Keu, meaning *from the desert*, because he could out-walk the other boys by miles without ever stopping to rest.

But today Kimpur was going with Keu to take the cows on the long hot walk across the valley to the grazing fields and then down to the river. His father looked at him with pride. "I won't be there to protect you, but Tororot will watch over you," he said, pointing at Mount Mtelo. Kimpur had completed his week on Mount Mtelo, seven days with the elders learning how to kill a lion and extract the poison from wild berries. It was his final test. Last year he had been circumcised in front of the entire homestead and he hadn't cried. He had swallowed the pain as the old woman had torn at his flesh. But it was all worth it for the opportunity to join the herdsboys.

"Your mother sacrificed this goat to ensure your safety," his father said, handing him a chunk of boiled goat meat. "Eat some for strength."

---

[1] Traditional Pokot healer and prophet.

Kimpur chewed it and thought about the dangers that waited for him beyond the homestead. "Have you ever seen a lion, Baba?"

"I have met the lion," his father nodded, pointing at two deep scars on his forearm. "But you will not see him today," he said, rubbing Kimpur's head.

Lions weren't the only danger facing the village. Life in the desert was difficult for the Pokot, more difficult than it had been for their ancestors. They were not desert people by choice. Generations ago white men had come to their ancestral lands. The endless chain of rainy and dry seasons was interrupted by foreign guns, gas-powered engines, and a laundry list of European rules. Throughout the 1800s, British surveyors drove into village homesteads looking for fertile land, minerals, or anything else they deemed valuable. And once they found it, they returned a few weeks later with a troop of soldiers and constructed a red brick building. The British flag was raised and the land was declared part of the new British colony of Kenya. And their ancestors were in no place to negotiate.

The khaki-covered officer explained to the village elders that they could only remain on the land if they agreed to produce goods and services for the British as a "tax." This took a bit of explaining because the elders had never heard of taxes and were altogether unfamiliar with the concept of money. And when the elders asked the British officers how they had negotiated the rights to their land from God, their answer came in the form of a firing squad.

The tribes that had farmed the same hills since time immemorial reluctantly agreed to stay, and paid the "tax" to their new occupiers. But the nomads were different. Nomads didn't grow crops. They moved from valley to valley, grazing their cows, camels, and goats. They walked up and down whichever hill they pleased, and built temporary mud huts, staying in any particular valley just long enough for their cows to eat the grass down to the mud.

For this reason Kimpur's great-great-grandfathers refused to pay the British tax. "We can graze anywhere," the Pokot elders said in their meetings with the British officers. So they walked north, leaving behind the graves of their ancestors, and the original mountain of their God, Mount Elgon. They walked north in search of new grazing land, built new huts, and buried the next generation on new hills. But after a few rainy seasons, the British came for those hills too, pushing the nomads farther and farther north, until the Pokot built their huts on the very edge of the desert, grazing their cows on the farthest mountain overlooking the desert's broken earth. The valleys below were dotted with thorns and seasonal rivers, but finally the British came for the farthest mountain and the Pokot were exiled to the desert.

The British renamed the desert "Northern Rift Valley" and declared it a "Wildlife Refuge." They sold tickets to European tourists to see the elephants, lions, zebras, and, if they were lucky, a nomad in their "traditional" habitat.

Life in the desert was hard, much harder than life had ever been: long walks down thorny paths, drinking muddy water from seasonal rivers, their cows grazing on patches of brown grass. And after the first long hard dry season, the cows were already showing their ribs, as were their owners. However, hunger and thirst weren't the only problems facing the Pokot. They soon learned they were not the only tribe forced off their ancestral lands. The British in the newly founded territory of Uganda had forced the nomadic Karamoja tribe off their lands as well. And in central Kenya the Turkana tribe had recently been relocated into this very same desert. By the early 1900s, three tribes were living nearly on top of each other. Thousands of nomadic people became entrenched in an endless war fought with spears and arrows. Generations of men killing each other over the table scraps of the now colonized East Africa.

It was into this war that the young Kimpur was born. But Kimpur had only heard stories of life outside the desert. The elders sang songs about a time when life was easy, rivers were bursting with fresh water, and the hills were green year round. But he could hardly imagine such a place. He had never even traveled outside the valley. His village was a stone's throw from the Kimpur River, which was one of the few desert rivers that were full year round. Heavy rainfall had allowed his family to graze their cattle without moving, residing in a single valley surrounded by hills a day's walk tall.

But the safety of the homestead had also made Kimpur restless. At home, every day was the same. He was ready to start acting like a man. Kimpur sat on the dirt outside his hut sipping his milk as his father explained the directions to the river, which cows were likely to stray, reminding him to keep watch for Karamoja scouts who may be looking to steal cows from inexperienced herdsboys. Kimpur repeated the directions back to his father absentmindedly, rubbing his herding staff, eager to go as he watched the rest of the herdsboys gathering for the morning prayer. Kimpur finally got up and ran next to Keu, beaming with pride as the werkoyon lifted their requests for protection to Tororot's holy mountain.

"Don't cry, *Yoo*,"[2] he said to his mother. "I'll make you so proud. I won't lose any cows." He watched tears roll down his mother's cheeks.

She smiled. "We can find more cows, but there will only be one Kimpur."

---

[2] Pokot children's endearing name for mom. Perhaps the closest translation is "mama."

He hugged her goodbye before running after the other boys, whipping the slowest cows into a trot.

"If you get lost, just stay close to Keu!" his father yelled as Kimpur bounded around a bend in the path. After the boys were out of sight, the women tightened their babies against their backs and began another round of the grinding song.

Kimpur spent the next two years roaming the hills, and running and playing in the valley. He watched elephants and giraffe feast on the few remaining leaves growing beyond the cattle's reach. "But we were still children," Michael would later tell me. "We would hunt dik-dik or rabbits or play games. We had one game that we would play when the parents were away," he recalled, shaking his head at his childhood recklessness. "A boy would shoot an arrow into the sky. Then we would cover ourselves with the small shields we fashioned from tree bark. And we would wait as the arrow flew back down." He put his hands on his face. "We were a bit reckless, but as you can imagine grazing cows all day can get a little bit boring."

"Life went on like this until it stopped raining. One year, the rainy season never came. And there were so many ideas as to what was happening, but finally the elders decided that God was withholding his rain because he was angry with us. So the werkoyon gathered the whole community for a meeting where each man, woman, and child confessed their sins: who had stolen what, who had lied, who had cheated, and so on. And for each sin, the werkoyon sacrificed a goat or a cow or a camel, depending on how serious the sin. But no matter how many animals were sacrificed, God would not send us the rain back. If God was actually angry, or it was weather, or what, I don't really know. But that was the way that the elders explained our situation to me."

But by the third rainless month, the Kimpur River had turned to sand. Soon the men had to dig three body lengths down just to get water enough to satisfy their cows. Scouts were sent out to find fresh grazing land. And when grass was found, the village moved to the next valley, where the women built new red-clay huts, wrapped new thorn fences, and unpacked their camels. But by the time the red clay had dried brown and the women had found new grinding stones, it was already time to move on.

"We walked farther and farther in search of grazing land. I remember walking around the foot of the holy mountain and into Karamoja land. And every day I scanned the hills for Karamoja scouts. We had heard so many stories of their warriors stealing cows and killing Pokot herdsboys." After six months without rain they had moved their homestead deep into Karamoja land. And as Kimpur helped his mother dig up the clay for their new hut, his father and uncles scanned the hills and sharpened their spears.

Mornings in the new homestead were silent. The women didn't dare sing the grinding song for fear of being heard by the Karamoja. The children weren't allowed to go with the women to fetch water. And the men were always dividing up into scouting parties by day and sitting around a pile of embers and talking in hushed voices late into the night. Soon the cows were so thin, there wasn't enough milk left for the older herdsboys after the children had eaten. But Kimpur wasn't considered a child anymore, so he was forced to deal with hunger like the rest of the men.

After three days of surviving on wild berries and a few gulps of milk, Kimpur lay under his cowhide blanket, tossing and turning, his belly growling late into the night. And when he started to moan, he felt his mother's hand on his head and heard her quietly sing the grinding song as he drifted off to sleep.

He woke to the sound of women screaming outside the hut. He was alone under his blanket. The screaming came in painful waves. He crawled to the wooden door of his hut and cracked it open. The light from burning huts silhouetted his uncle's body writhing on the ground a few feet away as a Karamoja man drove a spear deep into his uncle's stomach. Kimpur nearly shouted before covering his mouth with his hand. He quickly crawled back under the blanket. Surrounded by the darkness, he held his knees to his chest and felt hot tears streaming down his face.

The Karamoja men shouted for anyone to come out. His hand was frozen to his mouth as he tried to take in silent gulps of air through his fingers. *I have to run, I have to run, I have to run...* After a few deep breaths, he crawled with the blanket still covering him and peered out the door. He could see men running throughout the homestead with torches, his uncle's now motionless body still lying a few feet from the door. Across the homestead, bodies were rolling in the dirt, shouting for help. Then he saw Keu hiding in the shadow of the next hut. He instinctively threw off his blanket and glanced around for Karamoja before running through the door and scrambling on all fours to Keu.

"They have the gates blocked," Keu whispered as they huddled against the cold wet mud of the hut. "But I saw the other herdsboys jumping through the fence." Keu's eyes darted around, searching the darkness. He pointed away from the cluster of Karamoja men who were busy gathering up cows and herding them out the main gate. Kimpur followed him, crouching low in the shadows. At the edge of the homestead, Kimpur stood up. The fence was twice his height, each thorn as long as his fingers. He wiped his eyes, stepped back a few steps, and jumped as far and as high as he could.

He closed his eyes as the thorns dug into his bare skin. He kept his legs moving as he rolled his way through the tangled branches before tumbling out the other side. His flesh burned as he frantically pulled the thorns from his skin. Across the field, he could see other boys running naked back toward Mount Mtelo. Keu was already halfway to them. Kimpur turned around to see illuminated smoke billowing off the thatch roofs of their burning village before turning to run.

The boys ran until the first rays of sun crept over the mountain. As the orange sky turned blue, they slowed to a walk, their legs burning and sides aching. Kimpur could see that the ten boys were all covered in tiny scabs left by the thorns, the boys waving their arms in a circle to keep the flies at bay. They walked all day without discussing the previous night. "A man should never mention pain that everyone is going through," the elders had told them on the holy mountain. The boys only spoke to discuss where this or that path led, always scanning for Karamoja scouts who were certainly tracking them.

At dusk, Kimpur built a small fire between two tall bushes, rubbing cold sticks into a small flame. He was from the Snake Clan and it was their clan's responsibility to make the first fire at every new homestead. After the sticks had begun to burn, Keu and the other boys emerged from the darkness with a dozen rats. But after the rats were skinned and cooked, there was only enough meat for each boy to have a few bites.

Chewing the tough rat meat, Kimpur looked back across the valley they had crossed and then towards Tororot's mountain. They were still at least four days from safety and none of the boys knew of any rivers along the way. After the rats' bones had been chewed dry, Kimpur laid on his side close to the glowing embers, one hand under his head and the other holding the thorn that was stuck under the skin of his backside. He closed his eyes to sleep, but his mind flashed with a vision of his uncle's body lying outside his hut.

"Are you awake?" he whispered to Keu's back.

"Of course I am," Keu whispered without moving "My legs hurt and flies keep biting my scabs."

Kimpur rolled onto his back to count the stars, blurring through his tears. "Do you think our parents made it out?" he whispered.

Keu turned over and sighed. "I saw a lot of parents lying in the homestead, but I didn't see ours." He forced a smile. "Go to sleep, Kimpur. We have a long walk tomorrow."

One of the boys stayed awake, keeping watch. It was still dark when he woke everyone up.

"What did you see?" Keu whispered.

"I'm not sure," the boy said, scanning the distance, "could be a hyena." The boys all jumped to their feet. They had all grown up hearing their fathers tell stories of hyenas attacking sleeping children. "Or it could be the Karamoja scouts chasing us. Then again it could be nothing. But I'm not waiting to find out," he scoffed, picking up his staff, his bow slung across his naked back. "We won't be safe until we are out of Karamoja land," he said over his shoulder.

By noon they had walked over three dry rivers, each with a dozen barren trees growing along the sandy bed. As they rested in the shade, the younger boys got down on their hands and knees and desperately dug for water. Keu sat watching them. "Save your energy for the walk. You would have to dig twice your height before you hit water."

At the third river, Kimpur stood up and shouted, "What do you suggest we do for water? You don't want us to dig and I don't see any water around."

One of the oldest boys spoke up. "My father once told me that he drank his urine when he got lost. So there's that option."

Keu looked at Kimpur. "I'm not telling you to drink your urine, but I am telling you we can't wait around for you to dig a well."

They walked for the rest of the day, only catching a few rats along the way. After the sun set, Kimpur collapsed in the sand next to Keu. They didn't need a fire because they had eaten the rats as they walked.

"When is God going to stop being angry at us?" Kimpur asked, looking up at the moon.

"When it rains," Keu said, still breathing heavy from the walk. They laid on their backs listening to each other's stomachs growl.

"This afternoon I drank my urine," Kimpur whispered.

"I did too," Keu sighed. By the next night, everyone had.

After four days, the younger boys could barely stand up, their short legs having worked twice as hard to keep pace with the teenagers. "Just keep moving your feet," someone yelled at Kimpur, who was in the back and unable to even keep his head up. They were traveling so slowly, the most optimistic boy said they were still two days from the holy mountain. *Just keep moving your feet, just keep moving your feet*, Kimpur repeated to himself. His head pounded with pain every time his heel hit the ground. *Just keep moving your feet, just keep*—suddenly his head knocked into Keu's back.

"Shhh," Keu said to Kimpur, who collapsed onto the ground.

"I didn't know talking wasn't allowed anymore," Kimpur snapped back, embarrassed that he had been repeating himself out loud.

"Quiet. We found something," Keu whispered.

"Is it water?" Kimpur said, staring at the sun.

"Hey, tell Kimpur to shut his mouth," someone yelled. Kimpur laid in the hot sand listening to them argue.

"I've never seen a trail so long."

"It's way too wide for an elephant to make."

"Maybe it was a herd of elephants."

"They don't walk side by side. They walk in a line, you idiot," Keu said, hitting the boy over the head.

"Hey, don't hit my brother."

"Tell your brother not to be such an idiot."

Kimpur heard a deep growl. "Quiet!" he whispered. "Do you hear that?" It was coming from the other side of a hill. The boys hid behind bushes and pulled their bows taut. Tired as he was, Kimpur crawled on his hands and knees next to Keu. His eyes fixed on the wide path.

"It's a monster," Keu whispered.

"It's shining like the sun," a boy said with terror.

"We are all going to die," Kimpur whispered as the monster rumbled down the trail, lunging its massive body over the rocks in the path.

"Kimpur? Have you ever seen anything that big before?" Keu whispered. For the first time, Kimpur heard fear in Keu's voice.

The monster stopped a few feet in front of them growling. Its two eyes glowed beside its long horizontal teeth. The boys held still, realizing that it must have seen or smelled them. Then the ears flapped open like an elephant. It was the youngest boy who screamed first. The boys scattered back into the thicket. Kimpur tried his best to keep up with Keu, running until he could no longer hear the monster's growling.

"What was that?" Kimpur asked, falling to his knees.

Keu leaned over him. "That big thing was a monster," he panted. "But did you see the ogre that came out of its ear?"

Kimpur had heard stories about ogres. His mother had warned him about pale-skinned monsters that rode shooting stars down to the valley in search of children to eat. It was a story she told whenever Kimpur played outside the homestead after dark. "How do you know it was an ogre?" Kimpur asked, knowing full well it was an ogre.

"It had long hair and white skin!" Keu shouted as he tried to catch his breath.

Another boy ran up. "We are going back to kill the ogre."

"I'm coming with you," Keu said as they ran back down the path.

Kimpur rested his hands on his knees until he could catch his breath. He knew the Pokot rule about snakes. "If you see a snake," his father had told him a hundred times "you have to kill it. Because if you let it go and it kills someone else, their blood is on your hands." The older boys had apparently decided this rule applied to ogres as well.

He rubbed the dirt off his face and made his way back down the trail, making sure to remain covered by the bushes. As he approached the path, he could hear the boys shouting, but it didn't sound like fighting. When he stood up, the ogre was gone. The monster had stopped growling and appeared to be dead. Beside its carcass a man in strange clothing was handing the boys brownish food and cups of water. The man shouted and motioned for Kimpur to join them. One by one, the boys dropped their bows and started shoveling handfuls of the brown food into their mouths, pausing just long enough to take another drink.

"Thank you for killing the monster," Kimpur said to the strangely dressed man after his first drink from the man's jug. He could feel the liquid coursing through his parched body.

"And the ogre!" Keu added, his mouth full of food. The man smiled and started talking in a language the boys had never heard. Then the monster's ear opened, and the ogre stepped out.

The boys scrambled to their bows and arrows and soon were shouting for the ogre to get back. But the man in strange clothes ran over and put his arm around the smiling ogre, motioning for them to sit back down. For a moment, no one moved, the boys' arrows pulled tight. Then Kimpur pointed his bow at the ogre and asked what everyone was thinking, "Are you going to eat us or not?"

The ogre smiled, but didn't say a word. Then opinions started flying back and forth.

"Maybe he's not an ogre," one boy shouted to Kimpur.

"I've never heard of ogres feeding children."

"He looks like a man."

"But look at the skin!"

"Maybe his dark skin got burned off," Keu shouted above the rest. The others looked at him. "His whole body looks like the bottom of my feet," Keu said, pointing to the light skin on the bottom of his feet. The boys released their bow strings to examine the bottoms of their feet. As Keu was the oldest, it was assumed he was also the wisest. And as everyone was eager to eat more food and drink more water, it was decided that the ogre was indeed a man, and that his dark skin must have been burned off.

***

"Many years later," Michael told me, "I found out these two men were missionaries from World Vision, and they were coordinating famine relief. But it was a good thing the black man was there. You can imagine seeing the ogre was so terrifying. I had already lost my family and now I thought I was going to be eaten alive. But when I saw the black man hug the ogre, it changed everything. In fact, it was their friendship that helped us trust the white man."

The boys stayed with the ogre and his friend that night. And as the strangers seemed to have an endless supply of brown food, Keu decided that it was as good a place as any to wait for their parents to come find them.

In the coming weeks, more trucks came over the hill and soon a village of army-style canvas tents was set up to house the nomads who had begun pouring in from across the desert. Kimpur heard from the incoming nomads that the drought had plunged valley after valley in a state of chaos.

Raiders were stealing cows, entire villages were starving, and lost families were wandering the valleys looking for water and missing children.

Within a month, the missionaries' feeding camp was a working nomadic homestead. During the day, Keu led the herdsboys out to hunt for meat, the women tended to the orphaned children, and the men dug deep wells for water. Day by day, new missionaries came with trucks carrying bags of beans, rice, tents, and blankets.

Keu and Kimpur soon found their role in the camp as informal ambassadors between the nomads and the missionaries. Each morning they woke up and raced through the maze of tents to greet new families that had emerged from the desert overnight. And as the missionaries lined up the new arrivals, Kimpur, Keu, and the lost children scanned the crowd for their missing family members. Every few weeks a lucky child would race to hug his or her mother or grandfather, only to learn that the rest of the family had not survived.

But Kimpur and Keu's families never came. As the missionaries handed out food and water to the new arrivals, Keu and Kimpur would stand in front of a group of tired nomads listening to stories about villages they had never been to, and some they had never even heard of. After the new arrivals had eaten, Kimpur would take a deep breath, smile, and introduce them to life in the camp, each time beginning with the story of the herdsboys meeting the Ogre as Keu acted out the scene. Then the children would stare wide-eyed as Kimpur climbed into the front seat of one of the trucks. Poking his head out the window and smiling, he'd say, "See? There's nothing to be afraid of."

2
OF FIREFIGHTERS AND CAMP COUNSELORS

While Kimpur was adjusting to life with the ogres, I was spending six days a week in the basement of a suburban church in Minnesota. My feet dangling from the small, red plastic chair, as my Sunday-school/pre-school teacher, Mrs. Mayfield, loomed over me in her huge denim dress. One Sunday, I was sitting at a short table drawing a picture of Jesus that I saw painted on the wall of my classroom. The church moms had spent the summer of 1988 covering the basement walls with murals depicting Bible stories. The bottom half of our classroom was covered with ancient bricks, as if we were living inside a Roman city. And behind the painted wall, a pink-skinned Jesus stood alongside his disciples, all wearing bleached white robes as they fed bread and fish to a crowd of people.

As I colored the picture, I felt Mrs. Mayfield standing behind me. "You know, Nathan. Jesus is always with you even though you can't see him." When I looked up from my drawing, she was smiling down at me. She knelt down and put her hand on my shoulder. Up close, I could see she had grey hairs under her dyed-brown hair, but I didn't say anything.

I knew it was dyed because my mom got her hair colored every month. Dad told her we couldn't afford a membership at the country club, and Mom had responded by insisting she would at least get her hair done at the salon the country club ladies went to. After waiting in the salon's lobby for one full rotation of the long hand of the clock, I would stare at Mom's new reddish-brown hair. She told me, "Women don't like it when their grey is showing." I looked away from Mrs. Mayfield's grey roots and down at her eyes.

"You can invite Jesus to live in your heart whenever you're ready," Mrs. Mayfield said, pointing at my tiny chest.

I looked down at the picture of Jesus I had drawn. His face was crisscrossed with pink crayon. "How's he gonna fit in there?" I asked.

"He can fit anywhere, sweetie."

I looked back at the mural of Jesus feeding the people. In all the pictures, Jesus seemed like a very nice man, and I could tell that it would make Mrs. Mayfield happy if I said yes. So I put down my crayons, folded my hands, and invited Jesus to live inside my heart.

When I opened my eyes, Mrs. Mayfield's hands were stilled folded, her elbows propped up on her denim-covered knees. I watched as she whispered a few more words before saying "Amen." Then she opened her eyes wide. "Now you never have to be alone because Jesus is always right here with you." She smiled, patting my chest. And from then on, I thought Jesus really lived inside me, like the Indian in the cupboard. I remember talking to him and hearing him answer me in my head, his voice always kind and fatherly, reassuring me there was nothing to be afraid of as I lay in my bedroom afraid of the dark.

When I was six years old, I remember waiting in line after church to ask my pastor how Jesus could talk to so many people at the same time. The pastor was standing at the back of the massive church sanctuary shaking hands. He wore a dark suit and tie and his white hair made him look old, older than he was. When I asked him, he looked down at me through his glasses. "Well, Nathan," he said in the voice adults use to talk to other adults, "the Bible assures us that because Jesus is God, he is not bound by the laws of space and time, which makes it possible for him to speak to the angels in heaven and every single person in the world at the very same time." He paused, looking at my blank face. "Isn't that cool?" he added.

But before I could answer, my mom cut in, "Thank you, Pastor."

I was seven when my dad was cast as Satan in the church play. Opening night I was sitting between my mom and brother in the front row, my feet unable to touch the carpet under the pew. I watched him whisper insidious plans about betrayal and murder into the ears of Jesus' friends. Strutting around the stage under a red spotlight, dressed in a gold and red robe with a long black cape, his maniacal laugh echoed through the sanctuary.

I stared at my dad in disbelief. The man who cooked me dinner and coached my soccer team had been replaced by someone every bit as diabolical as the super-villains on TV. My mom must have sensed my fear.

Mike Roberts cast as Satan in the church
play in 1991

She grabbed my hand. "Your dad's just pretending to be Satan," she whispered in my ear. Even if he was pretending, I still couldn't believe he was even capable of laughing like that. Then he started telling the disciples that they were going to join him in hell. "Why does Satan hate Jesus so much?" I asked my mom. "And what's hell?" The story of Jesus seemed more complicated than just a nice man living inside my heart. "Don't worry about it, honey." She patted my hand. "It's a place you don't have to worry about." She was right. I didn't have to worry about it for a few more years.

In high school I sat in the youth room of our church, posters of Christian rock bands taped to brightly painted walls. "Telling someone they are going to hell is never easy," my youth pastor said as she tucked her shoulder-length hair behind her ears. "But it's easier than watching them burn in hell." She paused for effect, looking out at forty tenth graders seated on folding chairs in the church basement.

I raised my hand. "How many Christians are in the world right now?"

"Great question Nathan, about one billion." She paused with her index finger in the air. "If you count Catholics," she said, more to herself than to me. "But even if you don't count Catholics, there are more Christians than any other religion in the world."

We had just finished watching a made-for-church movie about four teenagers who died in a car crash. The driver was a Christian about my age who had never told his friends about Jesus. But after he dies, he is sent on an elevator ride from heaven down to hell and sees his friends shouting at him. *Why didn't you tell us what would happen?* Flames danced behind them as their faces melted like plastic toys under a magnifying glass. I had heard about hell before. It was a regular topic of sermons, but it had always been in the abstract—pain, weeping, and gnashing of teeth. But watching teenagers' faces melt off was when hell became a real place, a fire-prison where my non-Christian friends were going to get fire-tortured.

I left church that night determined to save as many of the five billion hell-bound souls as I could. But at sixteen years old, my options were limited. I tried to tell a few of my non-Christian classmates that I was concerned they were going to hell, but they were less than receptive. And after a couple interventions, non-Christians started avoiding direct eye contact with me. So I decided to enlist as a Bible camp counselor in the north woods of Minnesota the next summer.

I was able to convince my best friend, Brad, to come with me. Brad and I had sat next to each other in Sunday-school classes since we were old enough to hold a crayon. Brad was taller and funnier that I was, and by tenth grade he could already grow a beard and play guitar. "You said Julie and Stacy are going?" Brad said, sounding interested for the first time. Julie and Stacy were the prettiest girls at our church. Brad had already been playing guitar at Youth Group for the last year and it was rumored that he serenaded girls with secular music when their parents weren't home.

"Yeah, my mom already talked to their moms about car-pooling," I assured him.

I knew the rumors about Brad were at least half true. He told me he serenaded them, but I had heard from several of the girls that he also made out with them, something everyone found out after he got caught with a church elder's daughter. After that, Brad got a reputation for seducing skinny blonde church girls. And while I strongly disapproved of his behavior, I didn't say anything. The first reason was that Brad would have never listened to me. But the second was that the summer after ninth grade, our pastor gave us a sex talk where he said kissing was okay as long as you kept your hands off the girls *swimsuit areas*. And Brad had promised me he never touched their swimsuit areas.

"Okay, if Julie and Stacy are going, I'm in." And the next day he signed up to play guitar in the camp worship band.

In June 1999, Brad and I drove into the north woods to Bible Camp. We spent every Sunday standing in the camp gym with nametags on, waiting for parents to drop off their kids, Brad smiling in his plaid flannel shirt and cargo pants. And when the moms showed up with four duffle bags of clothes per kid, the tension on the corners of pursed lips released as Brad gave them his canned introduction. "Hi, I'm Brad. Nice to meet you. I'm the worship leader here at camp," he'd say, firmly shaking the mother's hand. "And I'm super excited to be your son's counselor this week..." I could almost hear them thinking, *He is just the perfect male role model for my little guy*.

I stood next to him in plaid bellbottoms and a ripped t-shirt, my Mohawk sticking four inches into the air. I had recently discovered Christian punk music and promptly began wearing my own version of the punk uniform. "Hi, I'm Nathan," I'd say, introducing myself directly to the campers, as their mother scanned the gym for a camp administrator who could arrange for their child to be reassigned to Brad's cabin. But after looking back at the registration line and checking their watches, they would reluctantly succumb to the reality that their son was going to be cared for by a mohawked punk with safety pins stabbed through his ear lobes. I swear I could hear their mumbled prayers that despite all appearances, their child would meet Jesus that week.

And the Bible Camp didn't fail. Each night Brad would sing for hundreds of jumping and shouting kids inside a dimly lit theater built of hundred-year-old cedars. Sweaty kids would hunch over, arms out, singing "dead man's float" as they re-enacted the Egyptians drowning in the Red Sea. The next minute, their arms would shoot into the air as they sang about Jesus rising "up from the grave." After thirty minutes, the kids would be covered in sweat and nearly out of breath. Sitting shoulder to shoulder with Holy Spirit goose bumps running down the backs of their necks, the cement floor wet from the heat.

We spent the first three days of camp swimming, climbing, and feeding the campers pound after pound of candy. And after three days of uninhibited bliss, I'm pretty sure the kids would have believed anything we told them. But that was the point of the camp. Win over their stomachs, and then win over their souls. After Tuesday night's taco dinner we would march our kids to the chapel for Salvation Night, where a local pastor was brought in to tell our campers about Jesus' love. "God loved you *so* much that he sent his son Jesus to die for you," the pastor would shout with excitement.

"He loved you so much that he died on a cross for you," the pastor pronouncing "cross" as if it were a haunted house. Then he would proceed to tell the children the story of the betrayal of Jesus by his friend Judas. He would re-enact the Roman soldiers whipping and punching Jesus, and the nails being pounded into Jesus' wrists. The now horrified children watched, as R-rated violence flickered through their imaginations. And if the pastor did his job, the kids would be crying by the time he shouted "It is FINISHED!"—his arms outstretched like Jesus on the cross.

After that, the room would go silent save for the stifled sobs of the kids drowning in tears. "And he did this so that you wouldn't burn in hell forever." The pastor pointed at the kids. "So I want you to bow your heads and pray these words silently after me. Remember this is just between you and Jesus." Hundreds of children's heads bowed into their folded hands. "Jesus, I realize that I am a sinner and I can't save myself. I want you to come and live in my heart. Thank you for saving me, and help me to follow you with my entire mind, body, and soul. Amen."

After my first Salvation Night, I realized it was a far cry from Mrs. Mayfield's Sunday-school class. I asked the camp director about the need for such a graphic retelling of the crucifixion. He said the Bible camp ran on a tight schedule. "We only have five days to save these campers. Then we have to send them back out into the world, and who knows if they'll ever hear about Jesus again?"

Tuesday night, as I tucked the campers into their bunks, I would ask each of them if they accepted Jesus into their hearts for the first time. The next morning, the counselors would get any new Christians up on our shoulders and parade them through the camp shouting, "Look everyone, we got a new brother in Christ!" to wild applause.

That was how it was supposed to work.

But one week, the camp invited a local pastor who had spent the lion's share of his life as an actual firefighter. The first night, he took the chapel stage in a Jesus t-shirt and red swimming trunks, his Technicolor Ray Bans perched on top of his balding mullet. The second I saw him I knew we were in trouble. He had dark, Kentucky-fried skin that made him look like he had just walked off beach duty alongside Pamela Anderson and David Hasselhoff.

"I'm Pastor James. And what am I excited for this week?" he shouted too loud into the microphone, sending fuzz through the speakers. "I'm excited to share the love of Jesus with you. And I am gonna do whatever it takes to show you how much Jesus loves you. Seriously, whatever it takes."

I looked at Brad on stage. He was devilishly smiling at the pastor. I pointed at Pastor James and mouthed the word "Baywatch" from the first row. We grew up seeing a lot of youth pastors like this guy, middle-aged men who tried to stay "relevant" into their forties. We called them *forever teens,* adults who related to kids because they had never grown up. But we had always hated them. Most of our problems were caused by teenage immaturity, and we didn't want a pep talk from an overgrown forever teen.

Brad and I walked back to our cabins laughing about Baywatch, as Pastor James came to be known. That night, after I made sure a dozen sets of teeth were brushed and bladders emptied, I tucked each camper into their bunk beds and turned out the lights. As I lay in my bed, my headlamp illuminating the Bible verses I had to teach my campers in the morning, I heard someone softly knock on the window. I slid the curtain open to see Brad's face pressed up against the glass, his hands cupped around his face. "Hey, Nate!" he shout-whispered. "You up?" Brad scanned the room. "If you're awake, get some clothes on and meet me outside the bathrooms."

I threw off my sheets and snuck out the cabin door. Brad was in gym shorts and a Mickey Mouse t-shirt, a swarm of mosquitoes circling him under the yellow florescent light. "Nate, you are *not* gonna believe this." He smiled, slapping at the mosquitos on his arms. "One of my little campers Jimmy has shit *everywhere.* I was lying in my bunk and it smelled like a mouse had died in one of the traps. But then I got up and when I walked by his sleeping bag, it was obvious that Jimmy had shit the bed. So I took him outside and he told me he had also pooped in the shower." That's when Brad started laughing. "I mean can you believe that? I went in there and there is a pile of shit on the floor of the shower!" He swatted a mosquito that had landed on his forehead. "So I need you to clean up the shower while I take him down to the nurse. My campers are standing outside our cabin right now because I told them we were going on a super-secret late-night hike. So after I sort out the other campers, I'll be back." Before I could say anything, Brad ran off into the darkness.

I stood on the cold cement porch. I was exhausted from rock climbing all afternoon. I looked down at my What Would Jesus Do bracelet. *Jesus would clean up this poor kid's poop.* I thought. *Judas would go back to sleep.*

For five minutes I waited under the florescent lights, swatting mosquitos. Finally, Brad came running back. "Okay, I got my campers to bring their sleeping bags down to the chapel for the night. But I only have like two minutes to clean this up." He held up two shakers of bleach. On three, we put our noses in our shirts and ran into the bathroom sending white clouds into the air. The smell of bile mixed with bleach brought tears to my eyes. When we opened the shower door, I saw the drain was covered with a dark-brown pile. Brad patted me on the back before turning to run. "Thanks for taking care of this," he yelled over his shoulder.

"No problem!" I shouted back, irritated.

I turned on the shower and the water ricocheted off the solid pile and onto my white shirt, arms, and face. I spent the next five minutes throwing up in the bushes outside. As I sat doubled over waiting for the next gag to ripple through my stomach, I heard Jesus' voice in my head saying. "*This* is how you love people." I looked down at my WWJD bracelet now covered in human feces. I stood up and walked back into the bathroom to finish scrubbing.

I got three hours of sleep that night. The next day I sat on the beach watching my campers wrestle for king of the raft, my mohawk pointed in every direction. As the sun set, I was walking with Jimmy and Brad up the hill to the chapel when a chunky sixth grader waddled up beside us and pointed at Jimmy. "What's that smell?" he shouted. A dozen campers turned around and in unison yelled "Shit pants!" then ran away with their noses plugged. Jimmy stopped walking and stared at the ground. I looked questioningly at Brad. "Someone leaked the shower story to the other campers and Jimmy's been catching hell for it all day."

"Crap," was all I said as we walked through the chapel doors.

"Crap is right," Brad said, stepping onto the stage and shouldering his guitar for worship.

Monday night, Pastor Baywatch gave his pre-Salvation Night sermon, explaining that everyone is a sinner, in case any children in the audience were under the false impression that they were getting into heaven on good behavior. And due to a recent publication surge on books about sexual purity targeted at Christian teens, he decided to weigh in on the topic in front of a hundred junior high kids. Hands on his hips, sunglasses on his balding mullet, he said, "Now I know what some of you are thinking, 'Sex at Bible Camp?'" His voice mimicked that of a thirteen-year-old girl as he waved his limp wrist. "Well, I'm here to set you straight. Everybody struggles with lust, and for those of you who don't know what I mean when I say lust, I mean looking at the opposite sex like this." Then in Bugs Bunny fashion, he bent over, bulged his eyes out, and howled like a wolf, "AAAOOOOOOHHHH!" The boys shrieked with delight, immediately pointing at one another as if to say, "That's exactly what you look like whenever *she* walks by." The girls were unimpressed, folding their arms and furrowing their brows.

"And like it says in the Scriptures," Baywatch continued, "*All have sinned and fallen short of the glory of God.* Romans three twenty-three. Look it up if you don't believe me. So you're not alone. Everyone has sinned, even pastors!" His face contorted into a shocked grandmother, his hand covering his mouth. A quivering elderly woman's voice shrieked "Nooo, not you, pastor, you're too holy to sin!" as the entire chapel erupted into laughter.

"Yes," he responded to his own impression, "even me."

"In fact, I committed the sin of lust today down at the beach." I swallowed my breath and looked up at Brad sitting on stage. He was grinning wide. He loved watching forever teens make fools of themselves. *Please stop talking.* I thought. "Yep, I was lying on my beach towel and I found myself staring at a beautiful lifeguard. And I caught myself. I said, 'Sorry, Lord.' And guess what?" I didn't need to guess what. "He forgave me. And he'll forgive you…"

There was only one lifeguard he could have been talking about, Sally Sheffield. She was the most beautiful girl at camp, a freshman in college with platinum blond hair, an amazing body, and a Colgate smile. There wasn't a male counselor who didn't know exactly what Baywatch was talking about. I had spent my fair share of afternoons trying to avoid temptation by lying on my towel facing away from her stand. "Come on," Brad would nag me, putting his sunglasses on. "Come on Nate, there is nothing in the Bible against window shopping."

"What about when Jesus says if you look at a woman lustfully?" Brad cut me off with a wave of his hand. "Okay, okay, do whatever you want," he shrugged.

I looked back to the section of the chapel where the lifeguards sat. Sally Sheffield was walking out the back doors, her red sweatshirt pulled over her head and her hands over her face. I could see the rest of the lifeguards whispering to one another and shaking their heads. I felt sick. I knew girls like Sally had been dealing with guys staring at them their whole lives. She had probably decided to be a lifeguard at Bible camp to avoid it. And now Baywatch had used her as a cheap sermon illustration.

I looked back up at Baywatch. He had moved on to his next point, completely oblivious to Sally. He was completely engrossed in his exposé on universal sin. He really was an idiot. But I had to give him credit. It takes guts to admit your flaws in front of teenagers, because teens in large groups are always looking for an opportunity to exploit even the slightest weakness in others. Baywatch was opening himself up to a week of taunts from twelve-year-old boys singing "Pastor James and Sally sittin' in a tree…" But it was worth it to him. He wanted to make sure that the kids knew *everyone* was a sinner. Unfortunately, his example had walked out the back of the chapel in tears.

After the meeting, the campers fanned out across the camp woods for a massive game of capture the flag. Jimmy walked between Brad and me all the way back to the cabins. A group of campers wearing their night-game camo-fatigues jogged past us shouting, "Hey, shit pants!"

"No swearing at camp!" I yelled back. It was useless trying to stop camp rumors, so I resorted to enforcing the camp's strict no-swearing policy. "Camp sucks. I wanna go home," Jimmy said, kicking a rock into the woods. Brad knelt down and grabbed Jimmy by the shoulders. "Never say that again. Camp is the best place in the world." I had never seen Brad talk to someone without even a hint of irony. "And I'm gonna prove it to you."

"How?" Jimmy asked, looking up at Brad.

"Promise you can keep a secret?" Brad whispered in Jimmy's ear. Then they darted off into the woods. I later learned that Brad had been tipped off as to the location of the flag by a female counselor he was currently making out with. Brad led Jimmy deep into the woods through a blocked-off trail right to the enemy flag. Twenty minutes later, I sat on a bench outside the dining hall as Jimmy emerged from the woods, flag in hand, before getting hoisted up on shoulders and paraded through the camp. The kids who had spent the day torturing him were now following him around like a celebrity.

Then I saw Brad hobble out of the woods, his smile interrupted each time his left heel touched the ground. I helped him down to the nurse's station where she wrapped his ankle. "That particular trail was blocked off because it was covered in poison ivy and jagged rocks," she scolded. Brad had tripped on one of these rocks and broke his ankle before tumbling into a patch of poison ivy. He spent the rest of the summer scratching his rash under a leg brace with a whittled stick. But it was worth it. Jimmy's rise from shitter to victor became a camp legend, in part because Brad retold the story every time a cute girl asked him what happened to his leg.

The next morning, Brad and I were sitting outside the dining hall. "Could you believe what Baywatch said up there?" I asked. I had spent the last twelve hours worrying about Sally, going back and forth trying to decide if I should talk to the camp director about it. Then I thought about whether or not I should say something to my campers or if they had even noticed.

"You gotta admit, the guy's got guts. I mean he did say, 'I'll do whatever it takes to show how much Jesus loves you.'" Brad put his arms on his hips and adjusted his invisible Ray Bans as he impersonated Baywatch. Then switching to his Richard Nixon impression, shaking his jowls, his arms outstretched in peace signs, he said, "Whatever it takes! And don't forget! Even though I lust after eighteen-year-old lifeguards, I AM NOT A CROOK." I laughed, somewhat jealous of his cavalier attitude. I was always worried about being the perfect Christian role model for my campers.

I thought if I could do everything right, make the perfect counterarguments to their Bible questions, they would enlist in the army of the Lord.

Somewhere along the way, I picked up the idea that the Christian life was the exhausting pursuit of perfection. At the end of the Sermon on the Mount, after Jesus gives this laundry list of sins that are so impossible to avoid that it made me crazy to think about, he ends with, "Be perfect, therefore, as your heavenly Father is perfect." It seemed like an order that stood in direct opposition with Jesus' assurance that, "My yoke is easy and my burden is light."

Nothing about Christianity felt easy or light. I was losing sleep worrying about Sally, and Baywatch, and my hell-bound campers. And then I'd watch Brad light up a Marlboro Red behind the chapel, telling the story of little Jimmy to his latest fling, jealous that he was so unaffected by it all.

Tuesday night, Baywatch began his Salvation Night talk by apologizing to anyone he made "feel uncomfortable" about his confession. "I realize that I should have been more careful to protect people's feelings. I just wanted you to know the Scriptures apply to me too." It was clear he really felt bad. Maybe it was this remorse that empowered him to give the most daring alter call I had ever seen.

Typical camp pastors would spend a few minutes describing the fires and tortured screams of the souls in hell. But Baywatch was not a typical pastor. He was a lunatic ex-firefighter with something to prove. "Everyone has stood around a campfire this week, cooking marshmallows, on long sticks," he said, sounding like a fireman at a school assembly. "Well, we use long sticks so you don't end up like that marshmallow. Standing near the fire is warm, but a little closer is hot enough to brown your skin." He was practically shouting into the microphone. "But if you're in hell, not only is your skin gonna burn. But while you're on fire, the Devil is going to stab you through the guts while he laughs at you." The kids started shifting in their chairs uncomfortably. "As a firefighter, I have seen how hot fire gets. I've seen refrigerators melt inside burning homes!" he shouted. A few chairs ahead of me, I saw Jimmy slip his hand into Brad's before Brad leaned over and whispered something in his ear.

"I told you I'd do whatever it takes to show you how much Jesus loved you. So I want to show you a little of what hell really feels like." He pulled out a plastic red lighter and put his right hand a few inches above it. Brad glanced back at me wide-eyed before turning around and whispering in Jimmy's ear again.

"Hell is a lake of fire where you burn forever. And this is only going to be for one minute with one little flame." He clicked the lighter and a one-inch flame popped up under his open palm. He started counting. "One, two, three, four, five..." When he got to twenty, he yelled, "For you know that it was not with perishable things such as silver or gold that you were saved from hell, but with the precious blood of Christ." At forty-five, he started screaming in pain.

Everyone was silent. Watching him burn himself was beyond anything I could have guessed. I remembered the movie from Youth Group, the teenagers' fake flesh boiling off. Sitting in the third row, I could see sweat beading on his forehead. His hand flinching against his will. At sixty seconds, the lighter flicked off. He raised his burned palm and shouted, "And that's only one minute. Try forever."

That night we had a record number of kids come forward to accept Jesus. News from the camp nurses' office came that Baywatch had third-degree burns. He ended up preaching the rest of the week with his hand wrapped in bandages.

Thursday afternoon I was sitting in the candy shop watching Baywatch tell Bible stories to campers. Brad came in and sat next to me grinning sarcastically.

"What?" I asked.

"Jimmy wet the bed last night," he said, popping Skittles in his mouth.

"He said he was having nightmares about his mom and dad going to hell. He said he wasn't sure they were 'real Christians,'" Brad said with air quotes. "Pretty messed up, if you ask me," he scoffed, drumming his fingers on the table.

"Maybe he should be scared," I snapped back, "you don't know if they are real Christians or not."

"Nathan, Nathan, Nathan," he said, shaking his head like I was a stubborn child. "A little kid shouldn't be wetting the bed because he is afraid God is going to send his parents to hell." Brad put his sunglasses on. Baywatch was sitting at a table on the far end of the candy shop giving kids high fives with his good hand. I waved to him as I left to meet a dozen kids who were waiting for me at the camp skate park. On the walk up the hill, I prayed that no one would find out about Jimmy's bedwetting, and also that his parents were real Christians.

3
THE SCHOOL UNDER THE BIG TREE

Kimpur sat on a rock eating his morning bowl of rice and beans. A caravan of trucks was being parked under a large acacia tree on the edge of the labyrinth of canvas tents. The missionaries unloaded massive, grey plastic sacks of corn, rice, and beans. They handed them to nomadic elders who in turn distributed the food to the hundreds of mothers waiting in a slow-moving line. Months without rainfall had forced more and more nomads to leave their homesteads and word had spread through the desert about a makeshift village that was feeding displaced families.

As the men carried away the last bags, a young missionary stepped out of the truck, her long brown hair flowing from underneath a wide-brimmed hat. Kimpur watched from a distance as one of the missionaries, a man named John, ran across the camp and touched his mouth to hers. He gasped. "I had never seen someone kiss before," he later told me. "In Pokot, mouths are only for eating. And not knowing it to be a western expression of love, when I saw it for the first time it was a little bit disturbing," he chuckled.

The next morning, Kimpur opened his eyes to the sound of a woman singing a melody he didn't recognize. He listened as he lay on the cold sand, his skin already warming from the morning sun. Keu and the other herdsboys were still asleep next to the grey remains of the night's fire.

29

Kimpur stood up. In the alleys between the tents, he saw the woman singing, still wearing her wide-brimmed hat, a colorful skirt swaying just above her ankles. Kimpur watched as a small parade of children gathered around her. Then she led the children to the shade of the large acacia tree and handed each child a stick.

Kimpur felt a tap on his shoulder, and Keu handed him a spear. It was time for the day's hunt. The boys spent most days, spears in hand, bows over their shoulder, wandering the neighboring hills, returning with tired feet and a dozen rabbits, if they were lucky.

For the next few days, Kimpur watched the woman as he ate his beans and rice. He learned her name was Sarah. Every morning just after sunrise he watched as she gathered the children with a song, handed each one a stick, and taught them to draw circles and lines in the sand. "What is she doing with those kids?" Kimpur asked Keu. But he got no response. Keu was sitting with the older boys defending his position as the best archer. Kimpur tapped Keu's dusty shoulder and repeated his question. "What is she doing over there?" he asked, pointing towards the tree.

Keu glanced for a moment at the children under the tree. "What? Who knows?" he shrugged. "Probably teaching them another song." Kimpur watched as the woman crouched in front of a child his age, helping him guide his stick in short lines. She looked up and caught Kimpur staring. She flipped up the brim of her hat and brushed the sand off her hand. Then she smiled and waved at him.

Kimpur wiped the rice off his hand and waved back. Then she motioned for Kimpur to join them.

"Hey, Keu? Do you mind if I learn that song with the other children?" Kimpur asked, nervous that the request would make him look unmanly.

"What?" Keu said, irritated that his meeting had been twice interrupted. "Sure, fine. I'll see you tomorrow morning." Keu stood up to leave. Kimpur put down his empty bowl and walked over to Sarah. He was bare chested, a red and blue wrap tucked around his waist.

Sarah bent down and rubbed his head before taking him by the hand and positioning him between two other boys who were a little shorter than he was. She chose a stick from among those resting against the trunk of the tree and handed it to Kimpur. The stick was recently cut, still green and wet in his hand. .

"When she handed me that stick, it changed the entire course of my life," Michael told me. "I became a student. A few days later, a man from the camp took my picture. And years later, when I was a young man, I discovered that a family in Portland, Oregon, adopted me as their World Vision sponsor child. My photo probably hung on their refrigerator, a small boy in Kenya alongside pictures of their friends and family."

Michael Kimpur's World Vision sponsor child
photograph from 1980

Several weeks later, Kimpur was lying on his blanket humming the ABC song Sarah had taught them, when he heard raindrops begin to fall on the tent. He crawled to the doorway and pulled the canvas aside to see hundreds of nomads. They stood still, watching the cluster of grey clouds blanketing the afternoon sky. Then an old woman cried out the first line to the rain song "Praise to Tororot who remembered us!"

Kimpur held his breath for a moment, feeling a dozen more drops land on his head.

The old woman shouted louder, "Praise to Tororot who remembered us!"

She took a deep breath, but before she could cry out again the sky opened up and rain soaked the valley. And the nomads erupted in singing and dancing, their beads rattling, their wraps hanging down soaked.

Kimpur crawled back into the tent and listened as the hard rain beat against the green-canvas roof.

"Kimpur! We're going home," Keu shouted from outside the tent. "The elders announced that Tororot is calling us home!"

Kimpur had begun dreading this moment. Ever since he started drawing under the tree, he had secretly begun wishing that it would never rain. He didn't want to herd cows anymore. He wanted to stay in the feeding camp with Sarah.

Keu poked his head through the door "Why aren't you smiling?" he asked, shaking the rain from his head. Kimpur rolled over. "Kimpur?"

"I don't want to go home, Keu," Kimpur said, unable to face him. "Sarah invited us to stay here and learn the white man's magic." That's what the nomads had begun calling missionary culture. The nomads didn't have words for so many of the new things they were experiencing. There were not Pokot words for trucks, plastic bottles, letters, bags, glasses, pants, shirts. So the Pokot translator simply used *the white man's magic* as a catchall. "Sarah said we could stay with her." Sarah had repeated this offer several times over the last weeks through the help of a Pokot translator.

"So you don't want to come back home with us?" Keu asked.

"My father told me to stay with you," Kimpur responded, as tears welled in his eyes. "So I *have* to go with you." Keu brushed off his wet arms before sitting cross-legged inside the tent. For a moment they sat listening to the nomads singing outside.

"Then you should stay here," Keu said, rubbing the hair that had sprouted on his chin. Kimpur looked up. Keu stood, and with as much authority as he could muster, he said, "As your father has entrusted me with your care"—he placed his hand on Kimpur's head—"I command you to stay here and learn the white man's magic." Keu stopped to take a deep breath. "And I command you to teach the rest of the tribe this magic once you learn it."

32

"But what about us?" Kimpur asked.

Keu laughed. "The boys and I are going to go get our cows back from the Karamoja." He turned to leave, and with the door flap in hand, said over his shoulder, "I'll tell you all about it when I come to visit."

Kimpur laid back down smiling as the downpour quickly trailed off. Within the hour, the midday sun had already finished drinking the shallow puddles off the hot sandy ground.

* * *

Kimpur spent the next month helping women center tall canvas sacks of cornmeal on their heads, each woman adjusting it slightly before beginning the long walk home. Most women were trailed by a new daughter balancing a smaller sack of flour on her head. The elders had distributed the unclaimed prepubescent girls between the families as parting gifts, knowing the soon-to-be women would fetch 30 cows apiece as a dowry payment.

But Kimpur quickly realized he would have had to stay at the camp, even if he had wanted to return home. Taking a boy his age home was a less-than-attractive offer. He was too small to be much help defending the cows from the Karamoja, and too big to survive on mother's milk. In short, he was a liability. And while Kimpur packed food, Keu spent the rainy afternoons on top of a truck bed rallying any of the boys who could hold a spear. He gave raucous speeches about avenging the dead and taking back the Pokot cows from the Karamoja. When he had rounded up a few dozen men, he led the band of warriors into the bush, back towards the land of the Karamoja.

In the end there were forty boys who hadn't been claimed by an aunt, a neighbor, or Keu. After the families left, Kimpur and the boys began constructing small forts out of sticks and grass. They called their new village Kiwawa on account of the old British hand-pumped well that the missionaries fixed. The name Kiwawa is a Pokot onomatopoeia meaning a place filled with the sound of rushing water. The villagers in the surrounding valleys felt it was a fitting name. From sunup to sundown, there was the sound of water splashing against a slab of concrete as cows, camels, mothers, and sons waited for their turn to drink. The short steel pump provided an endless supply of water even during the driest days.

The boys and the well were all placed under the care of two missionaries, John and Sarah, whom the boys had begun to suspect were married. And for the most part life at Kiwawa stayed the same as before. Sarah spent the mornings with her hand over theirs as they drew numbers and letters in the sand. And when the hot desert sun beat down on them from directly above, they broke for lunch. They watched the dark clouds tumble over the mountains as they chewed their beans and rice.

In the afternoons, the boys huddled under their forts watching their lessons wash away in the rain. As the sun began setting orange over the now-green mountains, the boys spent the remaining hours hunting small animals. They drifted off to sleep with bellies full of the now-plentiful rabbit, huddled around a bonfire for warmth.

"After all the nomads left, and the trucks pulled off, we wondered what would happen to us," Michael recalled. "Each night we would go to bed hoping that the missionaries would be there in the morning to teach class and serve lunch. Because we knew we had no one else. But after the rainy season ended and they remained with us, we knew Kama and Baba Kiwawa, which means mother and father of Kiwawa, were going to stay with us."

Months of rain swelled the rivers and flooded the roads out of the desert preventing the truck from delivering Sarah and John's shiny new hut. When it arrived the boys didn't think much of it. They had seen aluminum trailers before. But John motioned for them to gather around as he pulled the trailer's release lever.

The boys cheered as cloth and metal folded out of the hard metal casing.

John pointed at the 10-foot-tall camper. "Hut," he said.

The boys, now wearing t-shirts and shorts, repeated back, "Hout."

Then a boy pointed at the camper, "Ko."

And John, who was learning Pokot much more slowly than the boys were learning English, responded, "Ko."

John pointed at the date on the side of the pop-up trailer "One-nine-eight-zero, nineteen-eighty." John had attempted to tell them the date before, but time wasn't counted like that in the desert. It was hard to understand how time moved forward. In the villages, time simply flowed back and forth, an endless circle of rainy and dry seasons. "In the desert days are lived, not counted. You are born today, you grow up today, you die today," Michael explained to me. "The past is behind you and the future is in front of you, but how far in either direction is not so important. For example, in Pokot we called it the day John and Sarah got a new hut, but in the west the year was 1980, although I still have no idea the day or month." He laughed.

John turned the door handle and his wife stepped inside their aluminum camper. That afternoon, the boys set to work constructing a thorn fence around the shiny new hut. By nightfall, the fence was high enough that the oldest boys had to toss the final branches atop. The net morning, a small gate was cut into the fence and the boys took turns standing guard, armed with a spear and a bow slung over his now-clothed shoulder.

The guard was given two responsibilities: protect John and Sarah *and* protect the rest of the boys. The guard was charged with informing the boys where John and Sarah were at all times, scrambling to attention and shouting "Sarah OUT!" as she walked through the gate to teach the morning lesson. This was a warning call for the boys to be on their best behavior. The guard then followed her around all day, his spear at his side until Sarah walked back through the gate and he shouted, "Sarah IN." Then boys would wait until they heard John's soft snores before shooting their arrows and dancing around the fire with flaming torches, the way boys do when parents leave them to their own devices.

Eventually the boys drifted off to sleep. Kimpur lay on his side staring at the embers, resting his head on a small pile of sand, his hand over the thorn still lodged in his backside, whispering prayers of protection for his family, hoping Tororot would someday bring them back together.

* * *

At the beginning of the next rainy season, Keu came to visit. The boys all gathered around a roaring fire as Keu told stories of the battles he had fought deep in Karamoja land, just as all Pokot warriors do whenever they return home. Slowly, he recounted the dangerous night he led a herd of stolen cows down a narrow path as Karamoja arrows showered down from above.

Keu felt a keen sense of responsibility to the boys. Tragedy had forced him into the role of father at a young age, not only to Kimpur, but to all the boys, who now looked to him as their connection to Pokot traditions. The boys of Kiwawa were not like their fathers. They were becoming men in a new way. No longer did they earn respect through winning battles or stealing cows. The boys' victories were over letters and numbers, mastering concepts and figures.

But Keu saw the importance of this work. He believed that in time these boys could learn the secrets of the white man's magic. And he hoped that they would return to their villages with cars and radios and endless bags of corn, just as the missionaries had. So he encouraged the boys in their studies, the way Pokot fathers do, smiling as Kimpur showed him the bits of magic that he had learned since his last visit, watching them draw in the sand or pronounce words like "food" or "hut."

After a few days, Keu refilled his squash canteens at the pump and promised to visit again soon. Kimpur climbed up the tallest branch of the acacia tree and watched Keu walk down into the valley until he lost sight of him in the bushes. "As I watched him leave, I hoped the next time he returned he would bring news about my family," Michael remembers. "But Keu never mentioned anything about my mother or father or any people from my former homestead."

As the months rolled on, John and Sarah began to understand themselves less as teachers and more as parents, living into the names Baba and Kama Kiwawa. It was clear the boys needed something Keu couldn't provide, consistent support and affection.

Sarah started giving out hugs and bandages, and John role-modeled manhood by providing food, shelter, and an education. But unlike many parents, John and Sarah didn't dole out punishments. They left that to the council. On his first visit, Keu had appointed six boys with hair sprouting on their chins as the elders of Kiwawa. He spent a week with them on a hill near Kiwawa where he instructed them in the ways of a traditional elder council, showing them how to resolve problems that might arise according to the Pokot traditions. And each night after the guard heard John's snores rumbling out of the camper, the council built a fire and legislated the day's problems according to the nomadic values they had learned, sometimes choosing to defer ruling on more complicated matters until Keu returned.

Stolen writing stick? The elders huddled together in the shadow of the illuminated acacia tree. The oldest returned and pointed at the offender: "Water-fetching duty for a week."

"Oee," the boys would shout, the Pokot version of *Amen.*

"Refusing to share meat?"

"Three rope whippings."

"Oee."

"Crying because you miss your mother?"

"Spend more time with Kama," the oldest boy would say with compassion.

"Oee."

"We were modeling the Pokot elders by becoming the keepers of justice and fairness. You see, Pokot elders can never settle a matter based on anger or some personal retribution. That is so unacceptable," Michael explained. "A punishment is meant to reform the person as quickly as possible so the criminal can be brought back into the group. This is because every single person has a job to do, whether it is to fetch water, herd cows, or stand guard against Karamoja. And if you are gone, then someone else has to work harder in your absence. Nomads do not have prisons like the modern world, which changes our whole entire judicial system. In America you can lock somebody up in prison for two years for just a small crime like stealing a cow. And while in prison they are taken out of the community and are expected to think about what they have done. And then after those two years of isolation, a group of psychologists and lawyers and I don't know who else will examine that person and see if they have changed their stealing ways. If not, then they lock them back up," he said, turning an invisible key.

"In America there is the potential to give up on somebody, to leave them outside of the community. But there are no prisons in the desert, and without prisons the elders are left with two choices: reform you or kill you.

And as I said, if they kill you, they are not only losing a good worker, but also a brother and a son. And the desert has already taken so many of our sons."

"Is there an appeals process if you don't like the council's decision?" I asked.

"Surely you can always speak your mind. But you won't get very far."

"Why not?"

"Because it's a bit difficult to make your case when the elders are whipping your backside," he laughed.

The next rainy season, Tororot squeezed every drop out of the clouds in the afternoon and spent the cool nights refilling them. Soon the puddles sprouted legs and after a few weeks the desert was an interconnected network of ponds, a temporary marshland thick with ravenous mosquitos. And between the itching and swatting, the boys could hardly sleep. Before long, several boys had come down with *the hotness*.

"Pokot don't have a word for germs. If you tell them there are tiny animals living in their blood, they won't believe you. Believe me, I've tried to convince them," he said emphatically. "They just keep asking over and over how an animal could fit in their body. Maybe I should bring a microscope or something," he trailed off. "Anyway, so when somebody gets malaria they just say they have *the hotness*. They don't have medicine, so they pray and sacrifice a goat to Tororot before asking the werkoyon to make a mixture of healing plants for them to drink."

For weeks, the mosquitos swarmed. Eventually so many boys were sick that classes were cancelled. The sound of pumped water splashing on the concrete was paired with boys moaning from their huts. When the eleventh boy fell sick, John loaded the truck with two days' of food and braved the flooded valley.

He returned a few days later with a thorn-shaped object he called "med-i-cine." As John so often did, he introduced this new idea in the form of a one-act play. Sarah held up the syringe with an exaggerated smile across her face. John lay down on the ground, fanning his face, rubbing imaginary sweat from his brow. Then Sarah leaned down and rolled up John's sleeve as she lifted the syringe high in the air for the boys to see. She pretended to stab John's arm, and after a few moments John stood up smiling. The boys nodded along understanding that "medicine" was something that helped sick people recover from the hotness.

"Good?" John asked the council, pointing at the needle and leaning over a sweating boy.

"Good," the boys agreed.

Then he leaned over the first boy who had taken sick. After a week of *the hotness* the boy was barely able to move, sweating faster than he could drink. John pushed the syringe deep into his arm and the boy screamed in pain, trying to shake free. But Sarah immediately sat on the boy's chest, holding him down until the syringe was empty.

The other boys froze, unable to comprehend what they were seeing. Baba and Kama Kiwawa were torturing a sick boy. "The Pokot are a trusting people by necessity," Michael laughed. "If someone says there is a river over that hill, then you believe them. If a scout says Turkana are coming, then you run. We don't have CNN or BBC to confirm or deny or argue the facts of the day, so we have to trust that the messenger is telling the truth. And if we find that he is lying, he knows he will get a beating of a lifetime, which is something that a few Western news people have coming, by the way." He smiled. "We are not as skeptical as people in the West. So if someone tells you medicine will help, then you believe them. That's why we were so shocked that John had hurt the sick boy."

"Good." John stood up. "Next." John pointed at Kimpur, who looked at him with confused fear.

"I was so terrified. But before I could run away, John took hold of me by the arm and Sarah sat on me. I shouted, 'No medicine, no medicine.' I tried to tell them in Pokot that I wasn't even sick. But they stabbed me anyways. But now I know it was my first introduction to what Americans call preventative care." The rest of the boys ran and were lost in the bushes before John and Sarah finished with Kimpur.

That night the elder council built a small fire deep in the valley. And as the fire crackled, they could hear a swollen river sloshing along the sandy banks a stone's throw away. "I have heard of healing plants tasting bitter," one of the elders said angrily, "but never someone being stabbed!"

"Baba said med-i-cine would help them get better from the hotness," one of the younger boys added.

"Then why did they stab Kimpur? He wasn't sick."

"Perhaps we should wait here until Keu comes back." The elders rubbed their hairy chins as they heard the various explanations. Then they retreated into the shadows to talk in hushed tones as the fire died down to embers. The oldest boy returned leaning on his staff. "Baba and Kama Kiwawa have always treated us well and given us good things," he said, swatting a mosquito on his forearm.

All the boys nodded, "Oee."

"So we are curious to see what will become of those who have been stabbed by this medicine. We cannot wait for Keu to return. So we will stay here tonight and send a scout to see how the other boys are in the morning. If they are better, then we will all be stabbed. If they are sick, then each is free to choose to be stabbed or not." And the boys all agreed this was a fair judgment.

The next morning, the scouts returned and explained that two sick boys said they were feeling a little better but the others were still sick.

"What about Kimpur?"

"He said his arm is sore," the scout said.

So they waited another day and another. And on the third day, three more boys said they were feeling better. And the council, who were eager to sleep under a roof, decided that five boys was enough evidence and ordered all the boys to be stabbed.

* * *

John and Sarah had spent longer than usual praying at the table inside their camper. They had been at Kiwawa three years. Most of the boys now had hair on their chins and the youngest boy was able to speak English in full sentences. And as they passed through the thorn fence, the guard yelled "Sarah and John Out!" and the rest of the boys grabbed their sticks and ran under the tree for their morning lesson.

The boys sat crossed-legged in the sand, their sticks resting on their laps, as John stood in front of them holding a picture of a pale-skinned man with a beard and brown hair the same length as Sarah's. "Today's story will be a new story about Tororot's son, Jesus."

"And with one sentence John laid the cornerstone of Pokot theology," Michael explained. "There was no mention of Christianity or the Israelites or the Bible. John told us *this is Tororot's son Jesus* and we believed him, because as I said before, we are a trusting people. We knew Tororot, but we did not know his son. So we were eager to hear the story. We Pokot don't pretend to know everything there is to know about God. In fact, Tororot's name translated into English would be somewhere between 'most high' and 'beyond comprehension.' The Pokot believe that Tororot lives on the holy mountain controlling the rain and thunder, handing us down blessings and curses. But as his name would indicate, the Pokot don't know so much about Tororot. So we are always welcoming new stories about our God."

John held up the picture of Jesus. "Jesus is Tororot's son who lived many rainy seasons ago. He loved all the children in his village. He would heal the sick children and he even raised a child from the dead."

The boys whispered excitedly.

Kimpur raised his hand. "Is he as strong as his father Tororot?"

"Yes. He has all the powers of Tororot but he lived in a man's body." John smiled.

"Can he lift up that tree?" A boy asked pointing at the acacia tree.

"Yes."

"Can he change the direction of a river?" the oldest boy asked.

"Yes."

"Can he make the weather?" Kimpur asked.

"Yes he can," John smiled. "He once stopped a rain storm."

All the boys gasped.

"Why would he stop the rain?" Kimpur asked.

It was Sarah who realized what Kimpur was asking.

"Kimpur," Sarah said, putting her arm around his shoulder to reassure him. "The children in Jesus' village called him the good shepherd because he took such good care of all the children in his village. And when a child would get lost, he would spend the whole day looking for him," Sarah said, sweeping her hands in the air. "He would search under every rock in the valley until the child was found," Sarah said, lifting up a tiny stone and pretending to look under it. "And guess what?"

"What?" Kimpur said, putting his head on Sarah's shoulder. "Jesus is *your* good shepherd. He was with you that night you escaped the Karamoja warriors." Sarah made eye contact with all the boys. They were silently, waiting to hear if Jesus was their good shepherd too. "Jesus led all of you here. To us."

"Finish the story about Tororot's son," the oldest boy said, smiling and leaning on his staff.

John smiled at his wife and continued. "Jesus walked the hills of the desert telling people that Tororot loved them, that they were all children of the same God, no matter if they were Karamoja or Pokot."

"This was a little bit confusing for us," Michael confessed. "Our parents had told us that every tribe worshiped a different god. We worship Tororot. The Karamoja worship *Akuj*. And in fact this was the root of so many of our problems. You see the Pokot have a little bit different version of the creation of the world than the Bible says. Pokot say, 'In the beginning Tororot created one man, one woman, and one cow.' And from this family came the entire world's inhabitance. But the problem is that the Karamoja have the same exact creation story, except Karamoja say Akuj created a man and woman and gave them the first cow. And so a holy war has been raging on for many years with both sides claiming that all the cows in the world are originally theirs. According to their creation story, they are never stealing a cow. You are always taking a cow back. So when they told us that the Karamoja were Tororot's son too, it was so difficult to comprehend."

John continued. "Many people didn't like it when Jesus said God loved everyone. They didn't want to stop fighting. They hated the people from the other tribes. So a group of men captured Jesus one night and hung him on a tree until he died." He pointed at Sarah who was now standing by the tree arms outstretched, her head hanging lifeless.

The boys gasped.

"How anyone could kill Tororot's son?" the oldest boy asked, skeptical for the first time.

"It was because he had a human body," John said, rubbing the skin on his wrist. "But," John said, putting his finger in the air, "after three days, Tororot made Jesus alive again."

"Where is he now?" the oldest boy smiled. It was easier for him to believe that Jesus rose again than to imagine him dying.

"He's on the holy mountain with Tororot. And Jesus' blood became a sacrifice for us, like a cow."

"John was working so hard to use concepts and ideas that we knew. And he did so good a job of making it simple for us to understand." Michael smiled, counting on his fingers. "Tororot we knew, shepherds we knew, and sacrificing a cow we knew. So it was pretty much clear what he was getting at. Then he invited us to be baptized, which he told us was a new way to worship Tororot's son Jesus. And the oldest boys decided that the baptism would be a good time for a naming ceremony. In fact, Pokot have many names throughout their lives. If you cried as a boy when your bottom teeth were pulled out, then you will carry the name *tataka*, meaning crier. And you will bear it until you become the hero of a great battle against the Karamoja. Then you will be renamed *moran*, meaning warrior. And as you look back at your names, you will see the story of your life."

"Like Facebook posts," I said.

"Very good!" Michael smiled. "Perhaps naming is like a traditional Facebook."

John and Sarah had already picked out Christian names for each of the boys. And after Kimpur emerged from the brown river water, John gave him the name Michael.

"What does it mean?" Kimpur asked, eager to hear what John thought of him.

"It means you are a follower of Jesus."

After the boys had all been baptized, they sang songs and danced to celebrate. It was a momentous occasion to get a new name and learn a new story about Tororot. And after John and Sarah went to bed, the boys sat around the embers of the day's fire to discuss their new names. The elder council listened as the younger boys admitted that they had already forgotten their names. Then the older boys complained that their names were difficult to say.

That night seated around the fire, the elders heard dozens of arguments for and against their new names. Finally the oldest boy agreed that the new names *were* hard to say, and despite their different letters, they all seemed to mean "follower of Jesus." So the boys were free to continue using their Pokot names whenever John and Sarah weren't around. And the next day their studies continued, just as before.

4

REAL WORLD ATHENS

I was scanning the highway from the backseat of my father's navy Town Car as my stomach panged with excitement and anxiety, two emotions I have never really been able to distinguish. Next to me was a cardboard box marked "Nathan's Dorm Bedding" scrawled in my mom's handwriting.

I watched a group of high school girls pull up beside us in a rusted-out compact car, their arms flailing to the beat. The teenager behind the wheel looked through the window at my father and turned off the radio. He waved and smiled. With his push-broom mustache and dark aviator sunglasses, he gave off the distinct impression he was an undercover cop.

As their car slowed out of sight, I saw the massive granite sign reading "Transforming the World for Christ." I had driven past it a dozen times on my way to visit my older friends from camp. My father pulled up to the security checkpoint and nodded to the officer as if they were colleagues. We wound around a series of brownstone buildings bordered by wood chips and equidistant shrubs, the lawns dotted with evergreens and the occasional cottonwood. I saw two students standing next to each other on a short bridge over a creek as if they were re-enacting the college brochure for freshman move-in day.

He parked the car in front of a three-story apartment building where a hundred smiling college students in matching blue shirts were lifting cardboard boxes out of trailers and trunks while teary-eyed mothers hugged wide-eyed freshman.

As I picked up the cardboard box from the backseat, my dad walked over to a middle-aged man in a pink polo shirt and khakis. Dad waved me over and I shook hands with the man. "Nathan, this is Bill." He paused, waiting for me to remember. When it was clear I didn't, he proceeded: "Bill—my Bible-study leader from college."

Bill was holding his daughter's school supplies in one hand and had a pillow lodged in his armpit. "It's nice to meet you, Nathan. Your father and I go way back." He said he was the dean of students and his daughter was going to live across the hall from me. "Your dad was quite the rabble rouser when I met him," Bill laughed, putting his hand on my dad's shoulder.

I carried several boxes up three flights of stairs and began unpacking my possessions in the 15-by-15-foot cement dorm room that looked startlingly similar to the prison cells I had seen on reality television shows. "What kind of rabble rousing did you do?" I asked dad, who was busy hanging my clothes in the closet.

"Well, I was a pretty big pot head before Bill invited me to join his Bible study. That was before I became a Christian, of course."

I didn't know he had smoked pot in high school, but I wasn't that surprised. Our church had a lot of people with lost-and-found stories. Every few months, the pastor would set up a microphone and congregants would get up and talk about their former life, before they met Christ. Dad had never shared, but he always made a point of shaking hands with those who did.

The next morning, the boys and girls from my freshman floor were led on a campus tour by a sophomore with perfect teeth and a highlighted ponytail. "Welcome to the best four years of your life," she said, bursting with genuine excitement, her large breasts bouncing under a baggy t-shirt covered in Bible verses. For the next hour, we walked the meticulously groomed lawns as she explained the layout of the campus and the rules, or *expectations* as they were called, associated with each facet of college life. With sweeping hand gestures, she made it clear that we were protected on all sides by forests, swamps, and an internet firewall.

It was a self-enclosed world governed by a "Christian covenant for life together." The covenant was one of the things that attracted me to the college. Before being accepted, all incoming students were required to sign a document promising to live a "biblical lifestyle." On paper, this meant we pledged to abstain from materialism, gossiping, and polluting the environment. And if these rules would have been enforced, our college could have been a beacon of progressive Christianity. But, alas, no one paid much attention to those aspects of biblical living.

Instead, the college administration created a complex web of *expectations* for expunging the big two: premarital sex and drinking.

Girls were allowed to visit the boys' dorm for two hours on Tuesdays and Thursdays, but both people were required to keep at least one foot on the floor, and a shoe was to be firmly lodged in the door. Unwed pregnant women were required to take a leave of absence until their child was born. I was handed a number for the campus exorcist in case I saw any demonic activity, and told to call the school psychologist if homosexual feelings emerged. "And all dorms are subject to inspection for un-godly material..." She said, checking another point off her clipboard.

After the first week, I called Brad. He had decided he'd had enough of sheltered Christian life and was going to study philosophy at the University of Wisconsin. It was 10 p.m. and I could hear dance music hammering through the phone, "Yeah, it's fun," Brad shouted before closing the door to his dorm. "But to be honest it's also kinda gross. Drunk girls just wanna screw at two a.m., not that I'm ungrateful for the offer," he chuckled. "They're just all sweaty and stink like cheap beer. One girl asked me to make out with her and barfed halfway through the offer."

"Did you end up going to the campus Bible study?" I asked. I made him promise me he'd check it out when he got settled in.

"Yeah, I went to a meeting at a Christian frat house. But they just sat around playing acoustic guitar and icebreaker games until I wanted to kill myself. It's basically camp all over again." He paused. "But enough about me. How's Bible college?" He always said "Bible college" with condescension.

I could hear the freshman in my hallway playing acoustic guitar and starting up another Youth Group game. I tried to imagine myself wiping vomit off my shoes, walking home from a late-night kegger.

"It's fine."

"It's camp all over again, isn't it?" I could hear him smiling *I told you so* through the phone. He thought I needed to get out of the Christian bubble. He asked me to come with him to the University of Wisconsin, but moving out of the house was all the change I could handle.

"Basically," I sighed.

The next day, I stood in front of the Campus Life bulletin board with a notepad scanning for activities: "Pray for the World" at Dorm 325, 7:00 to midnight.

Seven to midnight? I read with a mixture of admiration and apprehension.

"Purity Group" at Dorm 413, 7:00–8:30 p.m. Bring your guitar.

"What Does the Bible Have to Say about Free Will?" Campus lounge, 9–10 p.m. I had never even considered that question before.

I jotted down all of the info and spent the rest of my freshman year living like a scholastic monk, hurrying from chapel to class to Bible study to sleep.

* * *

I chose a theological and biblical studies major, basically pre-med for pastors. And by the end of my freshman year, I had filled six spiral notebooks with notes on the history of Western Christianity and as many on interpretations of the Bible.

At home the next summer, I announced I wanted to study abroad in Athens, Greece.

"Oh, that sounds interesting," my mom said looking up from the home décor magazine she was fingering through.

"How much is it gonna cost?" Dad said cutting open his baked potato and taking a long drink of two-percent milk.

"Mike," Mom snapped. "Can't you ask him something a little more encouraging?"

"Okay," he sighed, irritated. "Why Greece?"

Two weeks later my father agreed to pay for my "Biblical field experience" and just after Labor Day I was in an airplane window seat looking out down at the Atlantic Ocean. Hidden under a blanket of clouds, I imagined spending the afternoons walking the streets of Athens, Doric columns flanking the fresh fish markets where the Apostle Paul had preached and Socrates pontificated.

I had not anticipated the four months turning into a season of MTV's *The Real World*. I would be living in a four-story apartment building with twenty students, most of them from Ivy League schools. Exhausted from the overnight flight, I unpacked my Christian books into a small two-bedroom apartment clearly built in the 1960s. The large double doors on my bedroom led to a small cement balcony with a rusting iron railing. Across the street was a florescent-lit daycare center and a dumpster with several bags of trash piled around it. There was a McDonald's two blocks down.

As the smell of garbage floated across the street and into my second-story apartment, I listened to my new roommate Tom explain that he was a law student studying in Washington DC. I didn't know any law students, but Tom wasn't what I would have expected. He wore a Grateful Dead t-shirt and had long curly hair, matted down by a knit hat that smelled like incense, his chubby cheeks covered in beard hair. He continued to rattle off facts about himself as if we were speed dating. I nodded along wondering if he was high.

"I was a camp counselor for a few years at Jewish camp," he said leaning into my room as I made my knee-high bed. "My father runs the Jewish community center in Minnesota." That's why the school had put us together, I realized; we were both from Minnesota. But Jewish Minnesota and Evangelical Minnesota don't cross paths much. However, I knew about camp, so I finally had something to say: "I worked at a Bible camp during my summers in high school."

"Oh, right on," he smiled. Then he walked back to his bedroom and returned a second later with a two-foot, green-glass bong in his hands. "You wanna smoke up?" Brad had given me a tutorial about dealing with *partiers*. "If they offer you some weed, that means they like you, so don't freak out. Just politely say you don't smoke." Brad's voice sounded like he was teaching me to diffuse a time-bomb.

"Thanks, but I don't smoke," I said, just like I had practiced in the mirror.

"No worries," he shrugged. For the next two hours, we sat on the floor in his bedroom listening to Dave Matthews Band, the bong resting between his legs. I told him I was a big DMB fan and had been to a couple of concerts. He told me about the summer he spent touring with the Grateful Dead, tripping on acid. Things must have been going well because he set up a hookah and proceeded to fill it with reddish floral-smelling tobacco. "You want some?" he asked, pointing the mouthpiece of the hookah and offering me a beer.

"No thanks," I said politely. My college didn't allow tobacco use and study-abroad students were only allowed to drink alcohol when cultural decorum demanded it. This rule was added to their strict no-drinking policy after several students were accused of ingratitude for refusing their host family's wine. "Okay," he said, checking his watch. It was three in the afternoon. "It's still a little early." He rubbed his beard and opened the can he had offered me.

We walked to class orientation an hour later. I followed the directions as Tom pointed at small cars parked haphazardly along the winding cobblestone street lined with mom-and-pop convenience stores and restaurants. Through the windows I could see the shelves half empty, the shop workers seated behind the counter reading the paper or playing cards. At dinner, we sat at a long table with twenty students. They looked like the kids I had grown up with—expensive clothes, excellent table manners. During the introductions most mentioned that they had already been to Europe. Midway through dinner, Tom raised his half-eaten grape-leaf wrap and announced he was jet-lagged, stoned, and half drunk, and was throwing a party to celebrate. The table erupted in applause. Then he led a parade of nearly drunk American students back to our tiny two-bedroom apartment. We had no couches, so everyone stood around our living room, a haze of smoke blurring the chandelier. Within a few hours, the professors showed up with more beer and the students began constructing a model Parthenon out of empty beer cans on our dinner table.

The apartment smelled like bodies and weed, with the occasional waft of garbage coming from across the street. Somehow amid the smoke and shoulder-to-shoulder guests, Tom saw that I wasn't drinking. "Hey, Roberts," he shouted, sending a beer flying through the air at me. I caught it and Tom started the whole room chanting, "drink, drink, drink…" I looked around the room hoping that something would happen to distract their attention away from my teetotaling. But the chants amplified until Tom started jumping around, shouting, "drink it, drink it," sweating through his Grateful Dead t-shirt. Somebody in the back yelled, "Drink it for Jesus!"

I started blushing. Obviously they had figured out I was a Christian. "Okay, okay," I said, assuming their insistence qualified as cultural decorum. I lifted the beer and tried to shotgun it like in the movies. But I ran out of air and sent froth tumbling down my shirt. Somebody shouted, "First blood!" as the crowd cheered and then went back to their conversations. I wiped off my shirt and finished the final swig before placing it atop the Parthenon.

"Nice work, Roberts," Tom said, his hand on my shoulder, a mix of beer and weed on his breath.

"Thanks." I forced a smile and then squeezed my way through the crowd and into my bedroom. I lay on my bed looking up at the spackled ceiling. *Jesus, what did I get myself into?* Then I turned off the lights and listened to the creaking wooden floor and the din of conversation from the living room until I fell asleep.

The next morning, I woke up to Tom asleep on the floor next to me, a smudged joint resting on his lips. My door was open and I could see a chubby goth with pink hair was sitting in the kitchen sipping coffee and rubbing her head. She must have heard me roll over. "Oh, sorry if I woke you up," she whispered with a smile. "I'm Jane. I just came over to score some weed from Tom to get rid of my hangover."

I threw on a t-shirt and pajama pants and poured myself a cup of coffee. I introduced myself, trying not to stare at the pale breasts pouring out of her tiny black tank top. "Oh, *you're* the Christian everyone's been talking about," she said, sizing me up. "Tom's been saying you're so," she paused, "*nice.*"

"Yeah, I try to be," I said. *Nice, yeah, Christians are supposed to be nice,* I thought.

We sat there silently sipping coffee until Jane looked up. "Um, there's really no good way to ask this so I'm just gonna say it. Have you ever thrown a Bible at someone?" she laughed uncomfortably. I looked at her blankly. "Let me explain," she said, talking with her hands, miming the words. "Last night, after you left, some of the students and I were talking about you. And Sarah, the girl from Cornell, said a Christian threw a Bible at her head after she called him a…a…" Jane paused, trying to remember. "Oh yeah, a hateful bag of shit." She chuckled. "And then Tom started taking bets on whether or not *you* had ever thrown a Bible at someone's head."

This was not the direction I was expecting the conversation to take.
"And *I* said, 'there is no way he has' because I grew up knowing a few of *those* types and I can just tell. Plus you live with Tom, and you two get along right? And he smokes pot like all the time and he said you were cool with it."

I forced a smile. "Nope, I have never thrown a Bible at someone's head." I took another drink of coffee noticing that my shirt smelled like beer and smoke. "I can honestly say I've never heard of anything like that happening."

I was beginning to sense an underlying hostility for Christians among my classmates—a mix of suspicion, resentment, and admiration. In line at the gyro shops, the student I was with would order a beer and then quickly ask me, "Oh, is it okay if I drink?"—the way one might second guess ordering a ham sandwich when in the company of a rabbi. "No, no, you go ahead," I'd say, trying to be accommodating. Another student swore after class and quickly covered her mouth. "Woops, sorry, I forgot you were here," as if I was a child she was babysitting.

I had never spent much time around non-Christians. I went to a private Christian school until eighth grade. When I did finally go to a public high school, I mostly hung out with kids from my church. My friend choices were limited in that I didn't drink or smoke, and I thought all non-Christians were going to hell.

When we signed up for classes, Tom talked me into studying ancient Greek religion taught by a British professor, Dr. Bradford. "It'll be awesome," he said. "You can teach the class about your pastor stuff." "Pastor stuff" was Tom's way of summing up my faith.

Professor Bradford was a three-season professor who spent his summers excavating ancient ruins along the Mediterranean. I found this hard to believe as he strolled into our small classroom wearing a smug grin and tight stonewashed jeans. His pale skin was almost corpselike under his black turtleneck. He took his seat at the end of the table looking like the kind of man you would expect to double-cross Indiana Jones.

He was a terrible lecturer, unable to hold the attention of the dozen students seated a few feet away from him. It was clear he resented having to teach at all. "Those seeking a vision from the Oracle of Delphi would be lowered into a tunnel by the priests of Apollo," he explained as the class sent text messages about which club they were going to that night. The overhead projector showed the columns of an ancient temple, translucent against the blackboard. I could hear him breathing through his nose over the humming of the projector.

"Underground they would wade through rushing water up to their knees surrounded by a sacred mist. Then they would ask their question of the gods and receive fantastic visions of the future. Oedipus was told he would sleep with his mother, and Socrates was told he was the wisest man in the world." He paused dramatically, looking around the class, despite the fact that we both knew I was the only one still listening. "Historians used to attribute these experiences to mere myth and legend, but scientists have recently discovered the tunnel was filled with hallucinogenic vapors released from underground gas deposits." He smirked. "So it turned out yet another religious mystery was just smoke and mirrors."

I jotted the words "Delphi Oracle = hallucinogenic vapors" into my notebook. Staring down at the words, I thought about the biblical visions of Joseph in prison, Ezekiel's dry bones, and John's angels breaking the seven seals. I raised my hand.

"Professor Bradford," I said, trying to sound smart. "I'm not meaning to deny your theory about hallucinogenic vapors at Delphi, but I get the distinct feeling that you think all religious visions can be chalked up to smoke and mirrors, as you called it." I looked around at my classmates, who still weren't paying any attention. "As historians shouldn't we remain open to all possibilities including supernatural ones? I mean there are plenty of intelligent people who believe in religious visions. Take William James, for instance."

Professor Bradford scoffed with a single "ha!" as if I had fallen right into his trap. The class looked up from their cell phones noticing for the first time that Professor Bradford and I were in some kind of staring contest.

Professor Bradford smiled. He was fond of making large air quotes. "Okay. Americans sometimes take issue with this, so I'll advise the rest of the class in the name of 'intellectual integrity' to maintain 'open' to the off chance than any of this religious hocus pocus is actually real." The way he said "hocus pocus" made my blood boil. I tried to hold it together, but I felt my face turning crimson. He continued with the lecture and I excused myself to the bathroom to take some deep breaths.

Jesus, what am I doing here? I prayed again. I didn't hear an answer. I hadn't heard Jesus' voice since I got here. I thought maybe I was doing something wrong, that some hidden sin had blocked our line of communication. Isaiah 59:2 came to mind. *Your iniquities have separated you from your God; your sins have hidden his face from you, so that he will not hear.* I decided to institute five minutes of mandatory morning and before-bed Bible readings. And no more beer.

After a week or so, Tom and I settled into a routine. We cooked dinner together in our small kitchen standing elbow to elbow as I chopped vegetables while Tom pontificated about legalizing marijuana and the summer he toured with Phish. After dinner, I spent most nights practicing the Greek alphabet and watching a nearly constant plume of various-colored smoke float out of Tom's room and disappear into the spackled ceiling. The weekends were spent watching my fellow classmates stumble in and out of bars and taxis.

Before heading out for another night of drinking, Tom sat cross legged on the floor showing a group of girls how to roll the perfect joint. I was sitting in my room when I heard him shout down the hallway, "Hey, Roberts! Jane wants to know how come you never tell any stories?"

I closed my textbook and leaned my head into his room, which was thick with the smell of pot. Four girls were sitting on the floor, red eyes, the Beatles on the stereo. I thought about telling the story of cleaning up Jimmy's poop at summer camp, but after a month of listening across the hall, I knew they liked stories that ended with someone blacked out or getting laid, preferably both.

"I don't know, Tom. I guess I don't have a wealth of experiences to draw from." I shrugged and turned to walk back to my room.

"Wait a second. Wait a second!" Tom shouted back at me. "Are you telling me you have *never* had sex?"

I turned around to the wide-eyed stares of everyone in the room. A brunette from Stanford asked, "How is that even possible?"

Jane took her lips off the bong. "Yeah, seriously. What the hell, Nate?" I stared back at them. By this time they had come to realize that every cultural abnormality about me was related to my faith. I had stopped explaining why I did what I did. Any serious attempt on my part to explain my religious convictions fell on deaf, or worse, resentful ears.

Tom raised his glass towards me. "Ladies, ladies," he shouted. "We have to do something about this," as if a crime had just been committed. "I propose that the first woman to deflower this wholesome, STD-free young man wins an all-you-can-drink trip to the bar."

Tom's proposal was confirmed with a round of cheers. I blushed and walked back to my room, shut the door and hoped no one would remember his call to arms in the morning.

I called Brad. We hadn't spoken since I left for Athens. "Hello?" He yawned. I remembered it was morning in Wisconsin. I told him about Tom and the bet. Brad was silent on the other end. After I finished, he laughed. "That's it? Your big problem is that girls are trying to sleep with you?"

"Well, yeah, I guess." I was a little irritated he wasn't taking me seriously.

"You gotta lighten up, bro. You are wound *way* too tight, probably because of your sexual frustration," he said, trailing off. "But seriously, Jesus is not gonna strike you with lighting if you screw a hot drunk girl. Hell, you could screw a couple. Jesus has better things to worry about, like war and famine and shit like that. Listen, I gotta get some more sleep, but seriously don't freak out about this. Okay?"

"Okay," I said.

"I love you, man." Click.

"I love you too," I said to the dial tone.

The girls didn't forget Tom's challenge. And much to my chagrin they took it on with the fervor of a reality TV show cast. Every few nights, I would wake up to the sound of a drunken classmate shouting at my window from the street, or someone knocking on my door as they left Tom's room, baked out of their minds. Most weekends, I went with Tom to the bars, dancing with a jug of bottled water in my hand. But the clubs became a sexual war zone, with girls dancing up on me, hoping their upper thighs against mine would break me.

So I started staying in the apartment with Jane watching episodes of the *X-men* cartoon, Tom's bong resting between her legs. As a goth, she was used to being unpopular, and she gave me survival tips, as I was still new to it. "Just say you're sick, or you have homework," she shrugged her pale shoulders. "Or tell them you're expecting a call from Minnesota," she said with absolute confidence. I watched Magneto flying over buildings while robots shot lasers from their eyes. "The important thing is to mix it up, so you're not relying too heavily on any one excuse. They'll catch on after a while and stop inviting you out," she said, a billow of smoke erupting from her mouth.

A few weeks later, we were lying on my bed watching TV. "You know why people hate Christians like you?" She didn't wait for me to answer. "My sophomore year of high school I didn't have many friends. There weren't many goths at my school, plus I'm fat." I tried to interject with a comment about her not being fat, but she put her hand up. "Just don't. I know I'm fat and I've dealt with it." She grabbed a roll clearly visible through her tight V-neck shirt. "So when I started dating this preppy kid, I immediately fell in love. I mean when you don't have any friends, it happens, right? It might not have been real love, but whatever." She took another drag from the bong and I noticed tears gathering under her eyes.

"Ah, shit. I hate crying," she said, smearing her heavy eyeliner down her cheek.

"Well, neither of us were very religious or whatever, so we start fucking, right? No problem right?" She looked at me. I wasn't sure if she wanted me to answer. She wiped her face and took another drag from the bong. "Then one weekend he decides to go on a church retreat up at this Christian camp and comes back an *entirely* different person. I couldn't believe it. I mean, we used to go to concerts and smoke pot all the time. But he came back and told me that it was all over. He was a *born-again* Christian and that I was a bad influence on his *walk with the Lord*." She took a deep breath before grabbing my wadded up t-shirts at the end of the bed.

"I mean, God!" she said looking at me. "Am I really that horrible of a person that I'm gonna destroy your faith? He made me feel like I was the devil incarnate."

I didn't know what to say. My youth pastor had convinced me to break up with a girlfriend I was completely in love with because she wasn't a Christian. "I'm sorry," I said, putting my arm around her shoulder.

"Whatever, it's over," she said. She rested her head in my elbow and turned up the volume on the TV as Wolverine slashed through a metal door.

Two weeks later, we left Athens to spend a weekend at a Greek Orthodox monastery. Jane sat next to me on the bus ride, pointing out buildings cut into the landscape, their walls made from the stones in the mountain. The trip may have taken a couple hours on an American highway, but it was an all-day trip after slowing each time the modern paved highway turned into ancient brick. The small-town roads were lined by white-washed cement buildings with red clay roofs. Our driver resorted to honking several times at the old men in tweed coats herding sheep across the road without concern for modern right-of-way.

It was sunset before our fifteen-passenger bus tottered a mile up a mountain on a gravel switchback. We parked outside a thirty-foot-high white stone wall, which was cut in half by a medieval-looking gate topped with decorative spears. Through the gate, I could see the monastery was comprised of several short stone buildings with pockmarked walls where the modern stucco had fallen off the ancient stone.

The two-story-tall rod iron gate was opened by a woman in her fifties with dyed-brown hair, black tights, and a floral top showing off her cleavage. I was expecting the gatekeeper to be a solemn man donning a brown burlap cassock with a perfectly shaved bald spot. She waved at us with a manicured hand as the bus pulled through the gate. On the other side of the stone walls, three middle-aged monks waved at us, looking like homeless guys in navy-blue bathrobes, smoking cigarettes and laughing. Jane pinched me on the cheek and pointed at the monks, "Oh Nate, now you'll get to hang out with your own kind."

"I'm not Orthodox. I'm Evangelical," I snapped back. "That's like pointing at that lady over there and saying, 'Now you get to hang out with your kind' because both of your boobs are on display."

Jane sat down and pulled her black sweatshirt over her tank top. "Whatever. It was just a joke, asshole."

It had come out meaner that I had meant it to, but I was sick of everyone's commentary on my religion. I especially didn't like my faith being compared to the Orthodox. For starters, they baptize babies, which I considered a serious strike against any real faith. On top of that, they seemed a lot like Catholics, which was strike two. And looking out the window of our bus at three smoking monks and their gatekeeper, I had serious doubts about the monastic wing of the Orthodox Church.

The next morning, the monks put us to work dusting the monastery's collection of ancient books. And after a sandwich lunch, Tom and I were given metal scrapers and told to chip away at the white paint covering up a twelfth-century mural of Jesus and his disciples. Brother Kalistos, who had introduced himself as the head monk, sat on a lawn chair amid the long, unkempt grass. He wore sunglasses and his grey hair was tangled up like Don King's. It was unclear if he was silently praying, sunbathing, or asleep.

When the bell rang at three o'clock, Tom looked at me. "How come Jews are always building shit for other people's religions?" He threw down his scraper. "Frankly, I'm sick of it." He sat down and started rolling a joint.

"Well, word got around that you guys did a great job with the pyramids," I smiled, picking up his scraper and starting to work with both hands. After two months of hearing him take pot shots at Christianity, I had finally built up the courage to joke about Judaism.

"Ha, ha," he said, fake laughing with a deadpan expression.

Brother Kalistos walked over to offer Tom a light. "That's enough," he said, "time for dinner."

We followed him through a wooden door into a narrow, windowless stone dining room lit by candles. We took our seats around a chest-high, dark wood table that filled three-quarters of the room. The gatekeeper, now wearing high-waisted jeans and a tank top, navigated the narrow room ladling red-bean soup into clay bowls in front of each student.

Another bell rang and Brother Kalistos stood up, put his palms out, and led us in the Lord's Prayer in English. He stood for an extra moment, arms outstretched, mumbling to himself with his eyes closed. Tom looked at me to see if he should start eating, assuming I knew about every ritual in all of Christianity. After a minute, Brother Kalistos opened his eyes and picked up his bread, tore a chunk off, dipped it in the red-bean soup, ate it, and motioned us to do likewise. "I want to welcome you to this place of God," he said through a heavy accent, his voice deep and measured. "We here are simple monks who live and pray for the world. And we are glad that you have been studying the history of Greek people. We are happy to see that young people of the Christians, Jews, and Atheists have come together today for our meal." Tom looked at me and nodded.

"I want to open with words from Gandhi," Brother Kalistos said, taking a drink of water. Quoting Gandhi was definitely strike three. I had grown up hearing my father scoff at liberal Christians, whom he referred to as *feel-good Christians*: "They don't have an ounce of backbone," he'd scoff.

"They cast aside biblical truth and just hug everybody."

There was a feel-good Christian church by our house. From the highway the feel-good church looked nearly identical to our Evangelical church. Both buildings were made of immaculate red brick with white shutters and a three-story-high white steeple. But inside, the feel-good pastor was preaching on evolution and tolerance, while we were listening to sermons on creation and the straight and narrow.

Brother Kalistos opened a small hardcover book and read loudly, as if he was addressing a large congregation: "Gandhi said, to me God is truth and love, God is ethics and morality, God is fearlessness." He paused, running his hand through his long curly hair. "God is the source of light and life and yet he is above and beyond all these. God is conscience. He is even the atheism of the atheist." I put my head down on the table. I didn't care if anyone saw. My face was red and the muscles in my neck were taut. I couldn't handle any more. The room started to feel smaller and smaller.

Tom elbowed me in the side, snapping me back into the moment. "Sit up. You need to hear this shit," he shout-whispered.

"At this monastery, we welcome everyone to come and pray," Brother Kalistos continued. "We have found God in the Orthodox church. But the church has never officially declared if God is with the Muslims or Jews." He stopped for a long drink of water. "But I myself believe that God is to be found in the chants of the Buddhist monks, the songs of the synagogue, equations on the chalkboard of science laboratories, and He is here even now, with us." He sat down.

Tom golf clapped, hitting me on the shoulder. "This guy's good. You should take some notes or something. You know, for your pastor stuff." Then he motioned to Jane.

"I could seriously listen to this guy all night," he said, standing up. "Except Jane and I already planned on smoking up five minutes ago."

"But you just smoked before dinner," I said.

"Yeah, but churches weird me out." He looked around at the golden icons of Mary and baby Jesus staring at us from the walls. "Maybe it's the 2,000 years of anti-Semitism." He shrugged. "So I like to keep a decent buzz on." And they disappeared out the door. I looked at the monks, eating their soup, smoking, and chatting in Greek at the other end of the table. I decided to wait for the other students to leave before I accused our host of being a heretic. I didn't think they would understand the nuances of our hermeneutical struggle.

"Ah, excuse me, Brother Kalistos," I said when I was the only student left in the smoke-filled room. He tapped his cigarette, matted down his hair, and smiled at me. "Yes?"

"I want to thank you for hosting us." I said with a practiced tone of respect.

"Oh, it is our pleasure," he said and began chatting again with the other monks.

"But Brother Kalistos, I have an issue with the theology you were proposing at dinner."

He put down his cigarette and walked to the seat across from me.

"What do you mean?" His smile was gone and I could taste his ashy breath.

"Well, I think that we as Christians need to take the Bible seriously, and…"

"You think I am a monk who does not take the Bible seriously." He laughed. Then he pointed at me and yelled to his fellow monks in Greek. They shook their heads laughing.

"Well, not necessarily, but what about John 3:16?" I said, wiping the sweat that was beading on my forehead. My internal temperature was spiking and the room started to feel oppressively small.

The monk pulled another cigarette out of his bathrobe. "Americans are always going on about John 3:16." He lit it and puffed twice into my face. "I'll tell you what. Americans can believe that only Christians are going to heaven because you have a continent full of Christians. But isolation has made your faith a bit small."

He tapped his cigarette on the floor. "Greece has been in the middle of Muslims and Jews and Christians fighting 2,000 years of wars over who is God's favorite." He chuckled with derision. "And we watched both of their soldiers burn down our villages on their crusades, watched them both thank God for defeating us and them condemn each other to hell. And you know what?"

"What?" I wasn't used to arguing theology through history lessons. For me it had always been about Bible verses.

"They all used the same torches to burn down our houses, and prayed on their knees, and made the same speeches." He smiled, showing rotting teeth. "The details were different, but their hearts were the same, the same mistakes and the same faith." He paused to take a long drag before extinguishing his cigarette and exhaling into the air I was breathing. "And you know what? God loves them all the same."

I wiped my forehead, opening the miniature Bible I kept in my pocket for just such an occasion. I pointed to a highlighted verse. "Jesus says he is the Way, the Truth, and the Life and *no one* comes to the Father except through him." I flipped to the next highlighted verse.

"Here in Romans it says that you must confess that Jesus is Lord to be saved."

Brother Kalistos put his hand on my pointer finger. "Young man, I appreciate your fervor for truth. But I am telling you, the God of love is not going to send his children to hell. And if a Muslim child prays to Allah, God will answer him. That is the Gospel. It is that simple." He patted my shoulder, stood up and returned to his seat by his fellow monks.

Why does everyone keep treating me like an ignorant child? I thought as he resumed his conversation with the other monks. I walked back to the monastic guest room, to find Tom and Jane smoking a joint on a wooden bench next to the roaring fireplace. Tom looked up at me blurry eyed, "Hey, Roberts. What did you think of that monk guy?"

"Not now, Tom," I said as I crawled into the lumpy bed.

We drove back to Athens the next morning, Tom lying with a pillow over his eyes, drinking juice boxes to rehydrate. I watched the villages roll by while Jane slept with her head on my lap.

When we got back, Tom swore off weed and switched to hard alcohol. Two hours after he started drinking, I was sitting on my bed studying Greek mythology. He leaned into my room, his cheeks were red and his beard was dripping sweat.

"Hey, Roberts. What did you think of that monk guy saying that everyone prayed to the same God?" His speech was slurred. "That's what they taught us at Hebrew School but I'd never heard a Christian say it before."

"Tom, let's not talk about this now," I said, hoping he'd forget about it in the morning. He stumbled into my room and stood cock-eyed in the center. "No. It's cool. We can talk about it." He smiled, pointing at me with a glass of golden liquor in his hand. "You're not one of those Christians who think people like me are going to *hell?* Are you?

"You know, Tom, let's talk about this later when we're both thinking clearer."

He stepped back and put his hand over his mouth with theatrical surprise. "Wait, are you?"

"Ah, Tom." I was trying to think of something to change the subject.

"Jesus Christ! Just tell me already," he shouted.

I froze for a moment wondering if he was going to punch me. "Tom, you have been a great roommate and you are a *really* nice person, and I hope you don't go to hell, but..." I paused. I didn't want to say it, but it was too late. He already knew my answer. "I do believe the only way to heaven is to accept Jesus as your Savior."

"Fuck you," he yelled, pointing at me with each word. He turned to leave. "*Seriously*. Fuck you," he shouted, slamming the door. I could hear him stumbling down the hallway to his room.

"I wasn't the one who brought it up," I shouted at the door.

Then he burst back through my door. "You know my dad runs the Jewish community center!" He shouted at me before slamming the door again.

A few minutes later, he yelled from his bedroom, "I hope Jesus can sleep at night."

Tom wouldn't make eye contact with me after that. I avoided the apartment as much as possible and ate out at the corner store when he was cooking. I didn't know what to say to him. No one had ever taught me how to apologize for condemning someone to hell.

Word got around and my classmates stopped treating me like a curiosity and started treating me like a Nazi. The next week was a steady flow of patronizing "How could you say that?" and "Aren't Christians supposed to love everyone?" from my classmates. Within two days, Jane was the only one who would still talk to me, so I spent every night sitting on her bed watching TV and doing homework.

Two weeks before the end of the semester I flipped through a stack of Greek vocabulary words trying to memorize elementary level verbs and nouns. Jane sat on the other side of the bed watching a superhero movie. We had hardly spoken the whole evening. She was higher than usual. She turned to me, "I can't decide if I'd like being a superhero." She put her head on my shoulder.

"I would, definitely."

She sat up and looked up at me. "Nathan. We only have two weeks left in the semester and you and I are probably never gonna see each other again." I was about to tell her I was hoping to visit her at school when we got back, but she put her hand over my mouth. "Don't say anything. Talking has gotten you into enough trouble on this trip." The corner of her lip curled into a smile as she tucked her pink hair behind her ear.

"Look, I haven't made out with someone in months, so I'm gonna kiss you, okay?" She pushed me down onto the bed, pressed her breasts against my chest, and filled my mouth with the taste of watermelon Chapstick. My stomach clenched with excitement and anxiety.

I lay on my back trying my best to keep up with her lips, with my hands on her shoulders. Then her legs wrapped around my body. After a few minutes, she reached under her tank top and unclasped her bra. I responded by moving my hands from her shoulders to the square of her back, giving her now-exposed swimsuit areas a wide berth. Then I felt her hand move from the back of my head, down my neck, across my chest, and down my boxers.

I bolted upright grabbing her by the wrist. "Whoa, whoa, whoa. I can't do this," I said, pulling her hand out of my underwear.

She sat up. "Fine. Then you can leave." She rearranged her hair and pointed to the door.

I sat up, red-faced. "I'm sorry, but..."

Jane stood up, dug her black fingernails into my shoulder and walked me towards the door of the apartment. "Nathan, the *last* thing I want to hear is an *explanation*." Her nails dug deeper before she pushed me into the hallway. I stood there with my shoes in my hand looking at my last friend in Athens. She made eye contact with me for a moment. "God!" she shouted more to herself than to me, "I am such an idiot, it's happening all over again." And she shut the door.

I walked down the hall and into my apartment. Tom and a few girls were smoking a hookah in the living room. "What's up, Hitler?" one of the girls said, not looking up from her magazine. I closed the door to my room and called my dad.

"Hello?" he answered casually, as if I was calling him from the neighbor's house.

"Dad, I need to come home early," I said. His casual tone made the request seem smaller, like I needed him to pick me up from a sleepover. I hadn't adequately prepared an explanation as to why or when. I just wanted to go home.

"You know, I figured something like this was gonna happen," he sighed. "Brad was over for dinner last week and he told us it wasn't going well for you." He paused, waiting for me to confirm Brad's comments. But I couldn't say anything. "Nathan?"

"Yeah, I'm still here."

"Pat!" he shouted away from the phone to my mom. "Nathan's coming home!" I could hear her shout something back. My dad responded: "I don't know why. Does it matter?"

"Alright," he said to me. "I'll book a flight for you by the end of the week. Just finish your finals so I don't waste any *more* money on this thing." He paused. "You know, I told your mom we should have *never* let you go overseas with a bunch of Ivy League tree-huggers. But she insisted it would be a good experience..." I stopped listening, relieved to be going back to a place I understood.

5
OVER THE FARTHEST MOUNTAIN

The surrounding homesteads of Kiwawa had begun to see John and Sarah and their village of boys as an important part of life in the valley. John made sure the Kiwawa water pump was always running, a welcome change as the British colonists had often let the pump lay broken for years at a time. And after a Karamoja raid left a nearby homestead cowless, Sarah hand delivered a bag of cornmeal to help the family bridge the gap.

The local elders from the surrounding villages returned the favors whenever they could. A dozen of the strongest men in the valley had recently spent a month showing the boys how to build a traditional Pokot meeting house out of timber, clay, and grass. And for the rest of the dry season, the boys studied their lessons inside the cool red-clay building, grateful to be studying out of the sun. But when the first rains came pouring down, drops began to drip through the thatched roof. A few big drops were all it took to ruin a lesson book, and there were no lesson books to spare.

After a particularly wet and buggy rainy season, John had had enough. In 1990 he took the truck over the farthest mountain and returned with the first corrugated-tin sheets the valley had ever seen. For the next three months, classes were cancelled and John meticulously taught each boy how to secure knotty crooked timbers into the sandy ground. Then, hand over

61

hand, he pounded nails through the wavy metal that reflected the desert sun in every direction. By the first rains, Kiwawa school had three metal classrooms. For months villagers gathered from distant valleys to stare at the shimmering roof, the children holding their small hands against the tin, shocked that it was so hot and bright.

When Keu came to visit, Kimpur gave him a detailed report of the new buildings. As it rained, Keu stood inside, the sound of metallic explosions echoing through the building. "So it doesn't leak?" he shouted, pointing at the jagged holes left by crooked nails.

"It hasn't yet," Kimpur shouted back.

Kimpur knew that Keu had never been all that impressed by letters and numbers. Keu always steered the conversation towards buildings, trucks, and wells, which Kimpur didn't really understand. Upon Keu's orders, Kimpur had spent several days studying John's crude drawing of gas-powered engines and hand pumps, but he couldn't make heads or tails of them.

But Kimpur could see that Keu liked the new buildings, something he did know how to make. "Someday I want a metal roof," Keu shouted, running his fingers along the dry underside of the vibrating metal. "You think you can make that happen for me?"

Kimpur smiled. He didn't know where the metal came from, but he was confident with a hammer. "I think so," Kimpur said. "I'll talk to John and Sarah about it."

"Go fetch them," Keu said, examining a dark brown nail he found lying in the sand. "I have things to discuss."

That afternoon Keu told John and Sarah that it was time for the boys to find wives and build their own homesteads. "They are men now," he said, sitting in John and Sarah's camper as Kimpur translated. His four brass bracelets rattled against the smooth, linoleum-topped table, each bracelet representing one of his wives. "And we have found most of their families," Kimpur translated. Keu was always careful to say *most*. Over the last nine years, he had found most of the boys' parents. And every time Keu walked into Kiwawa with one boy's mother or brother, Kimpur became more and more hopeful that his family was still alive. But Keu would never answer any of the still-orphaned boys' questions about their parents, curtly responding, "When I find them, I will bring them to Kiwawa."

"We are grateful for how you cared for these boys. But they are clearly men now. Even the youngest boy has stopped growing, and these boys' parents want to see them married."

"What if they still want to study?" Sarah asked like a worried mother about to send her child off to basic training.

"That is not for them to decide," Keu said dismissively. "But you may keep this one if you want," Keu said patting Kimpur's dusty hand. Kimpur smiled back, relieved. Before Keu left it was decided that a graduation ceremony would be planned under the big tree, a celebration for the boys of Kiwawa who had learned the white man's magic.

The nearby homesteads were invited to see a demonstration of their new abilities and agreed to bring the largest bull in the valley for dinner. Keu slit the bull's neck, blood flowing down his brass bracelets and into a dried squash. The villagers sat smiling as the werkoyon offered a prayer to Tororot. The squash was blessed then passed around for everyone to drink. "It was the biggest bull I had ever seen." Michael recalled. "But so many people came from across the surrounding valleys that, after everyone was seated under the tree we realized there was only enough meat for each person to have a few bites. But fortunately for us, John and Sarah had bought enough beans and rice that no one seemed to mind. And of course there was plenty of blood, a sort of Pokot delicacy, to drink."

Keu stood in the back of the audience, his still-bloody hands clapping wildly. Next to him were his two oldest wives, and his own parents who had recently been found living in a distant village. Kimpur waved at Keu as he sang "God is so good he's so good to us..." with the Kiwawa boys. After the song, a wrinkled elder stood up, his long stretched earlobes decorated with sun-bleached beads.

"You have cared for these children like your own and we thank you," he said to Sarah and John as Kimpur translated.

"Oee!" the crowd shouted. "And you have not lost one child to disease. And we believe this is a sign of Tororot's favor with you."

"Oee!"

"But you have taught these boys for many seasons. So what do you have to show for it?" the old man shouted. The crowd laughed a deep joyful laugh, excited to see how much of the white man's magic these boys had acquired.

The oldest boy ordered all of the villagers to stand up and form a long line. "Kimpur will stand behind this tree," the boy said. Kimpur waved from behind the trunk of the wide acacia tree. "And I will write down the order you are standing in." he said holding up a pencil and a piece of paper. "Then Kimpur will read it having never seen the line with his own eyes." The villagers, eager to see the magic trick, stood shoulder to shoulder, whispering excitedly as the boy wrote down each of their names on the piece of paper. Then Kimpur came out from behind the tree and read the names in order.

The crowd erupted into cheers. "I told you it would work!" Keu shouted at a few of the students' parents who had refused to believe that their son was learning anything in Kiwawa.

"After the ceremony, most of the boys went home with their parents," Kimpur later recalled. "My fellow classmates went back to herding cows.

63

They soon found wives, became village elders, and settled into life in the homestead. But John and Sarah had other plans for me. They met with a Catholic priest and after hearing my story, he agreed to give me a scholarship to attend the Catholic boys' high school located in a rural city on the very edge of the desert called Kapenguria."

John and Sarah offered to drive Kimpur, but as Keu was curious to see the world over the farthest mountain, he offered to walk Kimpur to the new school. "Perhaps I can discover a place to get metal sheets to roof my home," Keu smiled. It was a five-day walk, stopping for food at Pokot homesteads along the way, up and down the rocky hills, and wading through muddy rivers. All the while, Keu filled Kimpur's imagination with stories of Keu's now-famous raids on the Karamoja.

When Keu had told all the stories worth telling, he asked Kimpur to tell him each and every step required to construct a metal roof. On the fifth day, they stopped talking. Kimpur had started dragging his feet as they made their way up the final rocky switchback, the sandy path lined with long grass on one side and a thousand-foot cliff on the other. Near the summit, they stopped at a small creek to fill their canteens. Kimpur sat on a rock watching the water flow between the grey stones and finally spill over the edge bursting into a rainbow of droplets. "Which one is Tororot's mountain?" Kimpur asked scanning a grey horizon dotted with brown and blue mountains.

"If you squint you can see it there," Keu said, pointing at a light-blue hump. Kimpur's heart sank realizing that he was moving even farther away from the land of his ancestors, the valleys he hoped his family was still wandering.

"Drink up," Keu said. "We are almost there and it would be a shame to stop now." He had forced Kimpur to drink at every river until Kimpur felt like his stomach would explode. "You've been in Kiwawa so long your body has started to expect a drink every other moment," Keu laughed, patting him on the shoulder.

Kimpur responded the way he had all week, "I'll make it." He was about to recount how they had walked three days chased by the Karamoja, but then he remembered the taste of urine in his mouth and decided against it. He took another long drink and started down the path before Keu could finish filling his canteen.

The trail led up through a break in the mountain and as the ground leveled off, the rigid thorn bushes were replaced by bright-green shrubs. The path changed from sand to mud. The air felt wet and cold in his lungs as they walked into the town of Kapenguria.

Kimpur stood at the edge of the path staring wide eyed at the hundreds of buildings all topped with corrugated-tin roofs painted red, green, yellow, and blue. Hundreds of men and women dressed in shirts and pants stood over tables full of small objects like those he had seen inside John and Sarah's camper. Tall trees he didn't recognize loomed over the shops. In the fields behind each shop, he could see clusters of small huts surrounded by cows fatter than he believed possible. Keu was the only man dressed in a robe. They walked slowly through the dusty market, stopping to listen to the music coming from unexpected places. "The elders say that Pokot used to live on this land before they were sent to the desert," Keu said, scanning the market with suspicion.

A man in a pinstriped suit approached them and introduced himself in Pokot as Mr. Rotich. "John and Sarah told me you were coming." He smiled showing his missing bottom teeth. "They said I should take Kimpur to the high school."

Keu looked at the man for a moment. "Thank you," Keu said, trying to mask his surprise at finding a Pokot man in the city wearing pants and jacket. Keu turned to Kimpur and smiled. "It has been a pleasure walking alongside you. I am proud of you. And I wish you Tororot's blessings. We will offer a goat for you when I return to my village."

Kimpur swallowed his sadness. He was too old to cry. "Thank you, Keu. We will see each other again," he said, hoping it was true.

* * *

Michael, the name the Catholic priests insisted on calling him, spent the next year living like a tourist in a foreign land. Everything was different in Kapenguria. It was a town with thousands of water spigots and cars zigzagging across a never-ending web of dirt roads. The cows provided twice as much milk, corn grew out of the ground rather than being delivered in trucks, and there were so many large brightly painted signs: "Fresh Fruit," "Half-Priced Electronics," "Chicken and Beans." Everywhere he went, he was surrounded by words. At night he slept on a raised wooden bed with a pillow under his head and mattress under his body, safely inside a long cement building painted a shade of green brighter than any plant he had ever seen. He spent several weeks wondering around the city looking, smelling, and tasting everything he could get his hands on. Kimpur noticed that there were people from different tribes living right next to one another. He watched as a Pokot man in khaki pants and a t-shirt parked his banana cart right in front of a Karamoja man's restaurant waiting for a fight to ensue. But much to his surprise, when the Karamoja man saw him, they shook hands and appeared to be friends.

In class Michael sat on a plastic chair at a proper desk, his teenage mind expanding with the mysteries of the modern world. It wasn't just the people who were different in the city. It seemed that even the natural world worked in unusual ways. In science class, Michael asked why it rained so much in Kapenguria and hardly at all on the other side of the mountain, expecting to hear the reason why God favored the people in Kapenguria over those in the desert. "There are deserts all around the world," his teacher explained, launching into a lecture on clouds and wind as he pointed at a globe. Michael leaned over and asked his classmate what the teacher was pointing to.

"Pokot, the world is round," the student shot back. "It is?" Michael's imagination was running wild with questions as he tried to take notes on how clouds were formed.

The other students called him "Pokot" whenever he betrayed his ignorance, which was often. "City life took a lot of getting used to," Michael recalled. "Simple things that my fellow classmates took for granted, like money or road directions, were all new to me. You know, we don't pay for things or name our streets. And this practice can be a little bit strange if you are seeing it for the first time." But Michael took his new experiences in stride, embracing his nickname. If he held up the line looking for the right coin to pay for his candy, he would hear a chorus of "Pokot" from the impatient students behind him. Then he would sigh and ask the student next to him for help.

And for the next six months, Michael spent every waking hour studying his lessons and absorbing his new surroundings. He spent his evenings playing soccer, and when the other students went home on holiday, he spent his days alone on his bed reading every book he could find on African history.

Mr. Rotich, the first Pokot man Michael had met outside the desert, turned out to be his history teacher. History was far and away his favorite subject. Mr. Rotich first captured Michael's imagination with a lecture on the history of Kenya, standing in front of a chalkboard full of dates and places, brushing the chalk off his sixty-year-old hands and onto his chalk speckled sports coat, a green plastic rosary hanging around his neck. Mr. Rotich told stories of how villagers were literally stripped of their traditional culture and forced to squeeze into British clothes and churches, becoming Christians at gunpoint. Tribes were offered the opportunity to pay taxes in order to continue farming, and the nomads were pushed into the desert.

It was the first time anyone had explained to Michael the brutal history that forced his people into the harsh and barren desert. The other students took notes unaffected by the history they had heard hundreds of times in newspapers, news reports, and around dinner tables. They had grown accustomed to the legacy of colonialism. It was a fact of modern Kenyan life that Europeans left a wake of architecture and cultural destruction wherever they went. Most of the students had grown up seeing white missionaries or businessmen drive around their town in nice clothes and expensive trucks. They typically lived in large houses in gated communities, often with servants and indoor plumbing.

But it was all new to Michael. He had heard the elders tell legends about a time the nomads lived on green hills outside the desert. But Mr. Rotich's history lessons weren't legends. He had dates and places, cause and effect, colonizers and colonized. Michael listened, nervously tapping his pencil on his wooden desk, wondering how John and Sarah could have come from such a savage race. For the first time he questioned his adoptive parents' motives.

"Are all Christians like this?" Michael asked.

"No, Michael," Mr. Rotich sighed. "I believe some, like the missionaries who taught you, were doing it out of a real love for our villagers. And this is a good reminder for all of you," he said to the class. "It's important we remember that despite these tragedies, we have been blessed to know Jesus." Mr. Rotich smiled, deep lines gathering around his mouth.

* * *

School was in recess for Christmas break as Michael sat bored under a tree watching the school's cows graze on the empty soccer field. Michael startled out of his daydream when Mr. Rotich tapped him on the shoulder. "Pack up your things, Kimpur. Keu has come to take you home." Michael had been hoping that Keu would remember when to visit him next. Keu wasn't used to counting days and it was proving a challenge for him to line up his visits with school breaks. So Michael's heart raced at the possibility of being able to visit Kiwawa as he ran across the campus to fill his school bag with the only change of clothes he owned.

As he ran, bag in hand, he could see Mr. Rotich in pants and dress shirt standing near the wrought-iron gate at the entrance of the school talking to Keu in his blue and yellow robe, his walking stick resting on his shoulder. Michael smiled at the sight of two Pokot men from different worlds talking to each other as equals. It gave him hope that his two lives could reach some sort of harmony.

"Keu!" Michael shouted, running up to him.

"Kimpur," Keu said. His expression was serious. "Your parents have been found."

It was as if he had been punched in the stomach. Michael had stopped waiting for Keu to bring him any news. He had buried the memory of his parents under his lessons. It was easier not to think about them in the city. Life was so different that he was rarely reminded of them. His head was flooded with images of the night his village burned down: men with torches, his uncle's writhing body, his mother's fingers running through his hair. He wanted to know how and where and when and every other type of question about his family, but Keu's tone made him afraid to inquire.

"Good luck, Kimpur," Mr. Rotich said, putting his hand on Michael's shoulder. It looked to him like Mr. Rotich was forcing himself to smile before flagging down a taxi.

Keu and Michael sat in the back seat, Michael staring out the window as question after question flooded his mind. He had replayed this moment a thousand times, but Keu had always been smiling in his imagination.

The taxi drove past the men leaning over rusted-out cars in their small, corrugated-tin repair shop. Past the women sewing brightly colored dresses, past the children playing soccer, and finally parking at the edge of town. Michael and Keu looked out over the desert for a moment. Behind them they could hear shoppers haggling over prices and radios blaring dance beats. Michael scanned the hill for Tororot's blue mountain. When he found it, he smiled and then took the first steps down the farthest mountain.

For the next three days, they seldom spoke. Keu was lost in thought and Michael couldn't work up the courage to ask him for more details on where they were going. On the fourth day, they walked around Tororot's mountain, off the main road and into a valley. When they were through the thicket, Michael recognized his surroundings. It was near his first homestead. As they walked he began to recognize the constellations of trees that had marked his first grazing fields. Michael hadn't been back since his family left all those years ago. He looked up and recognized the hue of the brown mountains that had protected his cattle. He felt a swell of joy from deep inside him, as if his heart was waking up. He navigated the unfamiliar paths realizing that they were heading in the direction of the Kimpur River. Then the path opened up to a homestead surrounded by a thorn fence. Inside were three short red clay huts each topped with thatch. A few goats were grazing just outside the gate.

They had walked past hundreds of huts, but Michael swelled with excitement because he could hear the river flowing a stone's throw away. Keu put his arm on his shoulder, "Your mother searched for you," he smiled for the first time, "and when she couldn't find you, she came back to the river where you were born, hoping you would find her."

Michael swallowed deeply, hoping to keep his emotions inside. He was a small boy when he last saw his parents and he remembered the look of pride on his father's face when he hadn't cried at his circumcision ceremony. He rushed to the edge of the fence waiting for some assurance that it was the right place. From the center hut, an old woman with bright beads encircling her neck and deep lines etched into her long cheeks hobbled through the door. When she saw him, she stopped and dropped the canteen from her wrinkled hand.

"Yoo!" Michael shouted. She looked up and squinted at him, having nearly lost her sight. But when Michael hugged her, and whispered "Yoo" in her ear, she collapsed into his arms, realizing her lost son had found his way home. She wrapped her arms around him and began shouting praises to Tororot through her tears. Then his two brothers, both teenagers, ran out to see what was happening. They stood outside the door not recognizing Michael or Keu.

"Where is Baba?" Michael shouted at them, overcome with joy. That's when he felt Keu's hand again on his shoulder. "Kimpur, your father is—" Keu swallowed hard, choking on the words.

"Kimpur," his mother sighed.

"Where is he?" Michael repeated, concern filling his voice.

She pointed towards the river. Michael ran down the path and stopped on the sandy bank. His father, now crowned with grey, was standing knee deep in the Kimpur River next to a brown-and-white spotted goat.

"Why won't you drink, you stupid goat?" his father shouted, swinging a switch at the bucking goat.

"Baba," Michael shouted. His father looked up.

"Who are you?" his father yelled back, looking at him wild eyed for a moment. "I said who are you?"

"It's me, Kimpur, your son."

His father stood there for a moment, knee deep in the mud, his robe soaked. Then his face screwed up in an angry fit. "Well, whoever you are, get out of here. This is my goat!" He pointed back up the trail.

Michael felt his mother's arm wrap around his side. She rested her head on his shoulder.

"He's been like this since the day we lost you," she said quietly, "always shouting at goats and cows, never making any sense. I told Keu to warn you, but he couldn't bring himself to do it." She sighed. "He's one day here and the next day gone, roaming the hills living on handouts."

Michael stood in silent disbelief, staring at his father, a once-great elder, a man who had killed a lion with his bare hands.

"I went to school, Yoo. I learned the white man's magic," Michael said as he wiped the tears from his eyes.

"Maybe you can teach me someday," his mother said, smiling.

6
PURITY GROUP

My first night home from Athens, Dad made a welcome-back-to-America dinner of steak and baked potatoes. There was a glass of milk in front of every plate and, in the center of the oak table, four candle flames danced under the ceiling fan. "You look terrible," he said, chewing his bloody steak like bubble gum. "Are you depressed? 'Cause you look depressed." I felt the tears pooling in the pit of my stomach. I didn't know if I was depressed; that seemed like a medical term that required a professional examination of some sort. I was tired and my insides felt hollow. Tom, Jane, Brother Kalistos, and Professor Bradford had somehow knocked the wind out of me, and my lungs weren't able to fill back up.

I glanced across the table at Brad and my 15-year-old brother Kellen. They were both staring at their plates, pretending like they couldn't hear my dad.

"Mike, let's just have a nice dinner," my mom chimed in. "He just got home."

Dad put his knife down and wiped his mustache with a white napkin. "Honey, if he's depressed he should just say so."

I sat frozen, like a hostage refusing to give up the code to the safe.

"Your brother started dating a nice girl named Marisa," Mom said, hoping to change topics. Kellen shot me a look that told me not to take the bait.

"Give me a break," Dad said, rolling his eyes as he cut another piece of steak. "Her father's a Democrat," he said. My shoulders released as the weight of the conversation moved across the table and sat on Kellen's shoulders.

"Her father's a police chief," Mom interjected.

Kellen didn't look up. He just cut his entire steak into tiny pieces. "And what difference does it make? She's her own person," Mom shot back.

"Well, she's not a Christian," Dad scoffed. There it was. The real issue. My brother skewered his steak in silence, completely unresponsive to the fact that his dirty laundry was being unfolded on the dinner table. I would have shouted at Dad. I'm not sure what I would have shouted, but something along the lines of "get out of my life." But Kellen had always been better at living his own life, regardless of what my parents thought.

After the air tightened with silence, Brad wiped his mouth with a napkin and threw it on his plate. "So Kellen, as long as we're discussing *every* aspect of your lovely new girlfriend's life, what would you guess her bra size is?" I smirked. Brad had been raked over the coals by my dad before and wasn't going to let my brother suffer in silence.

Kellen looked up for the first time. Then he shoved an entire sourdough bun in his mouth and proceeded to give a very animated and indecipherable description while grabbing invisible boobs with his hands.

"Kellen!" Mom scolded, trying to stifle a chuckle. "Okay, okay, that's enough," Dad laughed, as he turned toward me. "Now, Nathan."

I swallowed hard, hoping he wasn't resuming his inquisition.

"I had a conversation with the pastor last Sunday, and he wants to offer you an internship to work with the Youth Group."

It was a better topic than depression, but not by much. For the last year, Dad had started and perpetuated the churchwide rumor that I was studying to be a pastor. When Mrs. Mayfield found out, she smiled at me through her thick glasses and told me how proud she was that I'd grown into such a nice young man, and always made sure to repeat throughout the conversation that she was praying for me.

I went to church that Sunday and our pastor, his dark suit now in stark contrast to his grey hair, pulled me aside after the service.

"Your father says you're going into the ministry."

"Yes, sir," I said, not wanting to admit to him or to myself that my experiences in Athens had called my plans into question. "Well, as you're a son of this church I wanted to inform you that we have an opening for a *paid* internship. And you're right at the top of our list of candidates." He smiled. "Now this is a *paid* internship. I know how college kids are always strapped for cash. So I hope you'll prayerfully consider joining our staff."

"Yes sir, thank you. I will," I said.

I drove home trying to think of every possible scenario where I turned down the internship, while not having to tell my parents I wasn't so sure about becoming a pastor. I had felt my faith slipping away since I landed in Athens. Some part of me had expected the Ivy League heathens to hold me up as some kind of role model. My sobriety, vocabulary, and militant commitment to bedside Bible reading were supposed to have endeared me to them. It had won me accolades from the world I had grown up in. But for four months I watched them systemically dismantle every aspect of my life. I had come to Athens thinking I was a city on a hill and left with the nagging feeling I was an anti-Semite. And to make matters worse, I hadn't heard one word from Jesus.

That night I laid on my bed praying for forgiveness for every sin I could think of: for allowing things with Jane to go as far as they did, for not telling the pastor about my doubts, and for drinking in Greece. I had heard that unconfessed sins could gum up the lines of communication. Isaiah 59:2 was often quoted at people who were waiting for God to answer their prayers. *But your iniquities have separated you from your God; your sins have hidden his face from you, so that he will not hear.*

I opened my Bible for my nightly devotions. "When all else fails, turn to the Scriptures," a preacher had once said. I flipped through the Gospel of Matthew until I came to the pink-highlighted words, "Therefore go and make disciples of all nations, baptizing them in the name of the Father and of the Son and of the Holy Spirit, and teaching them to obey everything I have commanded you. And surely I am with you always, to the very end of the age." I had highlighted them neon pink when I was in eighth grade. Neon pink was designated for "life verses," the kind you are supposed to come back to. I stared at the words. They felt distant, like an instruction manual for a machine I had never seen. I had tried to show Tom and Jane everything Jesus had commanded. *And how did that work out?* Then I panicked, thinking God had heard my thoughts.

Jesus, I'm sorry. But why won't you speak to me? I got no answer.

For the first time in my life, Jesus was on total radio silence.

I re-read the last verse: "And surely I am with you always, to the very end of the age."

I accepted the internship the next Sunday.

* * *

In the spring of 2004 I attended the first staff prayer meeting. I wandered into the small meeting room five minutes late to find a dozen people seated on baby-blue plastic chairs, their hands folded, eyes closed. I took my seat next to Mrs. Mayfield. And for the next hour I listened as the pastor prayed for everything he could think of: safety for families on vacation, healing for cancer patients, the soldiers in Iraq, the Sunday service, and the missionaries sharing the gospel with Muslims—a whispering chorus of alternated amens and hallelujahs bouncing off the walls.

I sat there waiting for the old feelings to come back, the goose bumps, the fatherly voice of Jesus telling me what to do. I wanted it to go back to the way it was before I left for Greece. But after 45 minutes, I hadn't felt anything—no goose bumps, no heartwarming, no Jesus, nothing.

Then pastor said a definitive "Amen." He took a long drink of water and cleared his throat. "You know, prayer is an incredibly powerful weapon that few people use to its full potential." He said "prayer" with so much confidence, the way scientists on TV talk about gravity or oxygen. I think it was his confidence that made me panic.

Am I losing my faith? I screamed inside my head. My heart was instantly racing, sweat beginning to bead on my face and arms. My throat started to tighten. I sat there frozen as my body overheated like a car in park with the gas pedal to the floor. I looked around the table as people began bowing their heads for another round of prayer. That's when the room started shrinking.

I felt my cell phone buzz with a new text.

WHERE THE HELL ARE YOU? – AMANDA ;)

I stared at the words trying to silence the swirling mass of anxiety that was blanketing my head in a hot fog. *Amanda…from drawing class*, I thought, trying to focus. *I told Amanda I'd go to her boxing match.* Since I had gotten back to school, I had kept my distance from the Christian kids I hung around with before Greece. I had tried to tell a few of the guys at the college Bible study about Tom, Jane, and Brother Kalistos. But they had just stared at me blankly, not understanding what I was getting at. "You do know lots of people out there hate Evangelicals," I ended in a huff.

One of the guys responded, "That sounds really hard, but frankly I'm not all that surprised. That's pretty much what Jesus was talking about when he said, 'Blessed are you when they persecute you for my name's sake.'" I left the Bible study and didn't go back. Every time I tried to explain what had happened I was beaten back with some biblical catch phrase. "The light shines in the darkness and the darkness did not comprehend it," "You are a city on a hill," "…the light of the world…" I could see that they were trying to help. It was like I was telling them that a cancerous tumor was growing inside my brain and people where handing me Band-Aids and telling me to take a few days to relax.

That's when I met Amanda. She sat next to me in drawing class, always in her signature paint-spattered overalls and twin pigtails. She was a large-and-in-charge self-proclaimed artist who insisted on calling herself a feminist artist after she submitted vagina-shaped lollipops to the spring art show. When I told her about what happened in Athens, she nodded along as if the vitriol I'd experienced was commonplace. "Whenever I'm at the bar, people look at me weird when I say I go to a Christian school." I leaned over and said in a whisper, "Most people here don't know what it's like out there." She leaned in and whispered back, "Most people here are idiots." Her paint-splotched index finger pointed at the rest of the class.

I stared down at the text. Another text popped up.

Get your ass to the boxing match. It's behind the sophomore dorms. you promised.

I looked up. The sun was setting through the windows of the staff lounge as the pastor bowed his head and started confessing a long list of sins he had "knowingly and unknowingly committed." In the fog of panic I decided it was better to keep a promise than finish praying. I wiped the sweat off my face with my tie and I leaned over to Mrs. Mayfield. "I have to leave early because I have a big test tomorrow." I was surprised at how easily the first lie came out.

"That's okay, sweetie," she whispered, patting my knee. "God wants you focus on your studies, too." I quietly stood up, walked out of the room, and ran across the church parking lot as the sweat began to show through my dress shirt.

I know I shouldn't have lied, I prayed. The fresh air stopped the spinning enough for me to think in full sentences. *But this whole problem would go away if you'd start talking to me again.*

I sped across town with the windows down, hoping the cool evening air would get my temperature under control. Amanda told me the boxing matches were held at rotating secret locations to avoid the campus security guards. I parked the car behind the sophomore dorms and hurried down a paved path at the far end of the lot. Then I took a wide dirt path lined with evergreens until it opened up to a grassy clearing where two cars were parked, their headlights shining on fifty androgynous hipsters in tight flannels and skinny jeans. The smoke from their cigarettes caught the light like a fog machine. A girl with a crew cut and jean shorts was wedged between two shirtless guys, their bright-red boxing gloves tangled up. One of the guys was clearly an athlete; he was tall and wore the college football team insignia emblazoned on his gym shorts. The other one was thin with curly hair and tight, stone-washed jeans. It was clear he was the favorite.

Looking around I recognized most of the group from the campus war protest Amanda had organized outside the campus chapel. Fifty kids brandished signs decrying America's preemptive strike on Iraq, addiction to oil, and 9-11 conspiracies. I remembered watching as clusters of freshman with furrowed brows wandered past them and into the dark chapel swelling with electric guitars. I scanned the crowd for Amanda. She was sitting on a rainbow-colored folding chair eating popcorn next to a group of the older students who were in my philosophy of religion course. The red haired guy next her made a point of starting every comment with, "As a non-Christian,

I believe that . . ." before going on to spout off some liberal platitude.

"Billy! Channel your inner Hemingway!" Amanda shouted to the boxer in stone-washed jeans as twin punches slapped against Billy's pale abs and scraggly beard.

I tapped her on the shoulder. "Nathan! I wasn't sure if you forgot. But you made it just in time to see Billy get pummeled." Then she cupped her mouth and shout-whispered, "Which is a bit of a relief because I told him I'd make out with him if he won." Sitting next to her in an identical rainbow chair was a beautiful brown-haired girl in a blue hoodie and jeans. Amanda caught me staring and introduced us. "This is Emilie. She's cool because she was born in France." Emilie smiled wide, her cheeks pushing her eyes closed like an anime character.

"Lovely to meet you, Emilie. I'm Nathan."

"So…who are all these kids?" I asked, pointing at the crowd of misfits silhouetted in front of us.

"These are the kids that everyone hates," Amanda grinned. "That's Ian. Everyone hates him because he's gay," she said, pointing at a guy in a purple crushed-velvet sports coat and black coifed hair. "Ian, wave!" she shouted. Ian looked over and gave a wrist-wave that matched his outfit. "He wanted to go to the University of Minnesota, but his parents said they'd only pay for him to go to a Bible college. I'm pretty sure they think it will un-gay him." She fake-laughed a single "Ha" before throwing a few more pieces of popcorn in her mouth.

"Boxing Billy up there," Amanda pointed, "pays his way through school by playing guitar at a mega-church downtown. But he hasn't believed in God for almost two years, not since he started smoking pot." Amanda had a story for everyone. The details were different but there was a common denominator—people who, for one reason or another, hated our school but couldn't bring themselves to leave. Perhaps their cigarettes and bar runs were a token act of defiance, or maybe a coping mechanism, but either way they were all in willful violation of the covenant we had all signed when we entered college, a covenant that explicitly required us to "sacrifice our individual liberty for the good of the community." For one reason or another, they were all living a lie. And Amanda seemed to be the ringleader.

The two boxers danced around the ring for the next five minutes, until the athlete, whom Amanda informed me was a sophomore linebacker, peppered Billy with a barrage of punches and he went down hard. The crowd booed until Billy got back to his feet, tore off his t-shirt, and wiped the blood from his nose. The girl with the crew cut put a joint in his mouth and lit it as Billy motioned for the crowd to quiet down. "This boxing match has opened my eyes to the horrors of war," he shouted. Then he declared himself a pacifist as the crowd exploded with applause.

They were always making declarations like that.

The next week Emilie invited me to the Feminist Bible Study in Amanda's dorm. I opened the door and choked on the mix of incense and lavender, a thick haze of smoke hanging above two boys and eight *women*. I quickly learned that they hated being called girls. I sat cross-legged next to Emilie. Amanda smiled at me, an open journal resting on her paint-covered overalls. I had my Bible in hand, but I could see I wasn't going to need it.

"Hear ye, hear ye," Amanda said as the room hummed with chatter. "Hey, shut up!" she yelled as the room fell silent. "Now before we commence the Zen meditation, I want to read to you a haiku I wrote after last week's meeting.

Dearest Father Church

I'm fine with Mother Earth

So go screw yourself."

As they clapped, I could see all the women in the circle had long curly armpit hair, which Amanda had informed me they grew out to avoid something called the *male gaze*. Emilie leaned over and whispered, "Don't worry. She's doesn't hate *all* men in the church." I assumed Amanda told her about my internship. After Amanda's haiku, we sat silently in the lotus position. I sat there quietly looking at the floor, counting the stitching in the carpet, then the buttons on the TV remote, then the lines in my upturned palms. After an hour Amanda rang a bell "Smoke break!" she sang in falsetto.

I stood outside next to Emilie and stretched my legs. "So what's supposed to happen when you Zen meditate?" I asked.

"I guess enlightenment," Emilie said, flicking her cigarette. I waited for her to laugh, but instead she took a long final drag and let out a long plume of smoke like the women in black-and-white movies. "Well, better get back to it." She tossed her cigarette into the night.

Walking home, I felt strangely calm. Amanda had reminded us to allow our worries to float by us like clouds in the sky. That's when I decided an hour of breathing and counting was better than an hour praying. I didn't expect Jesus to talk to me during my meditations. It seemed like less a conversation with the divine than a relaxing way to spend a Monday night. I went back the next Monday and pretty soon I was spending most of my time with Emilie and Amanda, mostly because they never talked about their faith. They talked a lot about everyone else's faith, making a point to stop and criticize every irrational or absurd phrase or activity they came across on campus. Posters for Bible studies, snippets of conversations in the cafeteria, things they heard their parents say; it was all used as ammunition for their sarcastic holy war.

But they never talked about their own faith. When it came to their own opinions they wanted to talk about art and politics. We would sit in the art studio hunched over charcoal sketches late into the night as they berated

American culture, the only culture they hated more than Evangelical Christian culture. "How could you have elected Bush—twice!" Emilie scoffed, her hands coated in dark dust as she studied a Polaroid picture of a nude male model paper-clipped to the upper-right corner of her charcoal drawing.

"Well, he is a Christian," I said, unable to think of anything else. I'd never heard of anyone *not* voting for the Republican candidate.

"Wow," Emilie scoffed, "great reason to elect the most powerful person on planet Earth. Do you believe Jesus is your personal Lord and Savior? Okay, here's the nuclear code!"

"Ha," Amanda laughed.

Over the next few weeks, I pieced together that Emilie had spent her childhood crisscrossing the European continent as her American parents planted rock-and-roll-style churches across the street from thousand-year-old cathedrals, moving whenever God called their number. She never lived anywhere long enough to learn the language, let alone make friends. But she was the perfect pastor's kid—never complaining, and always ready to pose for fundraising pictures in her Sunday best.

But after eighteen years, she had made every conceivable sacrifice for the sake of the Gospel. And she was done; done pretending she liked living out of a suitcase, done trying to sound out the foreign word for *pencil* or *candy*, done being the weird American, and most important, she was done with Christianity. Well, as done as one can be when they go to a Christian college.

But most of her friends were still keeping up the Christian charade. Not that I was in any place to judge; we all had our reasons. Amanda's parents occasionally called and we'd overhear her say, "Yes, Mom. I'm still praying for God to find me a good Christian man to marry." Everyone would look at the floor pretending we couldn't hear her bold-face lie. By the end of my sophomore year, I was the only full-time Christian left. But after six months of praying without an answer, it seemed like only a matter of time before I joined them.

Going to church had begun to feel like trying to squeeze into a shrunken t-shirt. I walked the church hallways trying to avoid eye contact. I excused myself to the bathroom any time someone would start on some theological diatribe and stared into the bathroom mirror until I was sure it was safe to return, paranoid that someone could smell my lack of faith.

The one place I couldn't avoid getting my hands dirty was the Sunday-morning Bible study. For an hour I gave elaborate explanations to Bible verses I wasn't sure I believed, as a dozen ninth-grade boys in designer jeans and hooded sweatshirts scribbled notes in the margins of their Bible.

Afterwards, I was so exhausted from anxiety I pulled myself up the three flights of stairs and collapsed in the back row of the sanctuary balcony. *Jesus, why won't you talk to me?* I'd pray as a smiling group of middle-aged women sang worship songs alongside teenagers playing acoustic guitars. As the pastor began his sermon, I watched my parents in the front row—my mother feverishly taking sermon notes as my father nodded along, as if he were giving the pastor permission to keep preaching.

Sitting in the balcony, I had a terrifying thought. *Maybe I've been talking to myself this whole time.* That's when my heart started ramping back up to marathon speed. *Maybe prayer is some sort of organized schizophrenia.* Then the sweat began beading under my armpits. I walked down the stairs and out the church doors. The parking lot was full of cars, but no people. So I ran to my truck. I didn't stop sweating until I pulled through the campus gate.

I called Emilie to meet me in the cafeteria.

"Don't worry about it," Emilie said nonchalantly. She had listened to me talk for an hour as she slowly ate her veggie burger and fries."

"So what do you think is happening to me?"

"You're waking up," she said, as if it was obvious. "Everyone thinks of Jesus like Obi-wan Kenobi," she smirked. "He died, and now he's *more powerful than you can possibly imagine*," she said in a spooky voice, her fingers fluttering in the air.

"Don't mess with me right now," I said, running my hands through my sweat-slicked hair. "I'm in a very fragile place. I used to talk to Jesus all the time and now I can't hear him. Like—at all. I never feel anything at worship, and the Bible has *completely* stopped making sense."

Emilie sighed. "Look, I hate to be the one to break this to you, but it's probably all made up," she said, dipping a fry in ketchup.

"What is? Jesus or the Bible or church?"

"Look at the facts. Pretty much everything in the Bible is also in some other sacred book, and have you ever noticed that everything that Jesus says to people is pretty much something they already believe?" I put my head down. I didn't want to hear anymore.

"I've met Christians from every continent—except Antarctica." She stopped for a second to make sure that was true. "Okay, every *inhabited* continent. And I always thought it was *convenient* that in *all* the prayers, in *all* the churches, Jesus never *once* mentioned climate change." She was getting worked up. "Have you ever heard a person say, 'I was praying last night and Jesus told me I should stop driving my car because I'm destroying the Earth he made'?" She pointed a fry at my face before biting off the end.

"No?" I said, looking down at the linoleum table.

"That's because everyone is just talking to *themselves!*" she shouted, "making themselves feel good about their beliefs by saying 'Jesus told me so.' But it's a bunch of bullshit!" She slammed the table with her fist. I looked up and her face softened. "I'm sorry. It sucks."

She put her hand over mine. "I wish it were all true. I really do. I wish Jesus was still hanging around doing miracles. But we're all alone."

I felt like crying. I could feel the last gasps of faith leaving my lungs. Then she tilted her head and smiled wide enough that her warm cheeks pushed her eyes closed. "It's gonna be okay."

"Come on," she said, standing up, "Billy's got a hot tip that the Purity Group is going to hijack the evening worship tonight. And I wanna be there for it." She grinned devilishly.

Billy's roommate was a part of the Sexual Purity Group, which everyone referred to as Purity Group—apparently the Sexual was silent. The group's founder put up flyers around campus boasting that anyone could stop lusting after the opposite sex if they applied his patented three-pronged approach of accountability, prayer, and effort. Billy had gone undercover and reported back to us that their weekly meetings were sort of cross between AA and an acoustic sing-along.

The group gained notoriety on campus for their Old Testament flair for public displays of sinfulness, including wearing red bracelets as penance for each time they masturbated. The Feminist Bible Study group responded by wearing red bracelets whenever they were on their periods.

Emilie and I ran up the chapel's back stairwell and found Billy and Amanda munching on popcorn in the back row of the chapel's movie-theater-style seats. The worship leader had shoulder-length hair, an unbuttoned flannel shirt, and baggy jeans with a large hole blown through the knee. His head rocked back and forth between verses of a traditional hymn set to U2-style guitar. After the song ended, a stagehand set up a microphone and the lights faded from orange to blue. "The singer is in my intro to Bible class," Emilie whispered, her hand cupped against my ear. "He refused to come to class when I made my presentation because he said it was unbiblical for a woman to preach."

The microphone stood under a single blue spotlight, a classic open-mic invitation for students to come on stage and share stories on the night's topic. "There's the purity grouper," Billy said, pointing to an overweight freshman who was walking up to the mic.

"I'm Samuel," he said, staring at the floor. "And tonight I want to admit to you that I'm addicted to masturbation." The air instantly left the room. You could have heard a mosquito masturbating, it was so quiet. I felt a pang in the pit of my stomach. It was normal for people to ask for personal prayers, but never for this. This was too far. "I need everyone to pray for me." He said dragging his palms across his face. "I know I can't quit on my own, and Jesus says 'if you ask in my name, it will be given to you.'"

"This is too much," I whispered to Emilie, getting up to leave.

"Sit down and shut up," Amanda shout-whispered, her finger pointed at my seat. Someone in the crowd clapped as Samuel went back to his seat.

Then a tall guy in gym shorts and a skateboarding t-shirt walked up. "So some of you know my name is James, and I need your prayers too." He paused, pinching the bridge of his nose. "Okay. Wow, this is really hard."

Someone from the crowd shouted. "You can do it." James looked up. "Yeah okay, here goes. So I'm addicted to porn. I'm really struggling with this, and I know Jesus wants me to quit." After a scattered applause, someone shouted "Amen, Brother!" That's when the crowd changed from apprehension to full-on support.

A line formed, and for the next thirty minutes, Billy and Amanda giggled uncontrollably as varsity football players and theater geeks unearthed their secret burdens.

"This is incredible," Amanda whispered, trying to muffle her laughter in her t-shirt collar.

"This is better than I could have hoped for," Billy said, punching me in the arm. I realized this was their consolation prize. After two years of lying to their parents and sitting through classes with wall-to-wall Republicans, they gleefully sat in the shadows of the chapel watching those same Christians publically make fools of themselves.

But Emilie wasn't laughing. Her face looked sad and distant, as if we were at a movie theater watching a romantic comedy and she just realized that the girl and boy aren't getting back together. I looked down at the line of students waiting to step up the microphone, realizing I had switched teams. Before Athens, I would have been the first in line. But there I was, sitting in the shadows, eating popcorn with the faithless. I turned to Emilie, "That could have been me up there," I whispered. "Now I'm just a church intern without any faith."

"I know," she said, putting her arm around me and kissing my forehead. "But we love you anyway."

After that night, I stopped calling myself a Christian—except at church, of course. I couldn't bring myself to tell the pastor. So I raised my hands during worship and continued to dodge any direct questions about my relationship with God.

But then I slipped up. I should have kept my mouth shut, but the new assistant pastor tricked me into it. He was fresh out of seminary and always probing me with theological questions, pushing through my vague answers. Maybe he had sensed my weakness and was picking me off like a wounded antelope.

We were standing in the lobby after Youth Group. He was telling me about two Mormons who had recently stopped by his house. "I invited them in and then I started walking them right through the New Testament, something they were completely unprepared for," he said with a smug grin. At my church, Mormons were not considered real Christians. "They were trying to save me from hell, and I was just trying to return the favor."

I normally would have shrugged and walked away. I was getting good at that. But my current crisis of faith had left me feeling sympathetic toward wayward souls. "Sure, they believe some weird stuff," I said, "but who knows if they're really going to hell? I mean, it's really up to God, isn't it?" I hoped this was true for me too. "They're just doing their best."

It was the cue he'd been waiting for. "So you don't have to believe in Jesus to go to heaven?"

I had already said too much. "No, that's not what I meant. But look, I gotta get back to campus," I said, my face getting flush.

"Hold on there, Mr. Roberts," he said with his hand on my shoulder. "Let's take a ride together. I want to talk a little bit more."

I climbed into the front seat of the church van. It was a cold spring night. He turned on the engine and I heard the heater kick in and the doors lock. I stared down at the dashboard, trying to figure out how I'd gotten here, to be interrogated by the pastor outside the church. I didn't deserve this. I wasn't running away from God. I wasn't drinking or having hot premarital sex. I was going to a Christian college and working at a church.

"What's going on here?" he asked, staring at me from the driver's seat.

"Sorry, I was just confused."

"Confused about what? The Bible makes it *pretty* clear that Jesus is the only way to heaven."

I thought about Tom swimming at Jewish camp alongside a dozen kids in bright swimsuits. His words, "I hope Jesus can sleep at night," ringing in my ears.

"Excuse me," the pastor said firmly after a minute of silence. "*Do you or do you not* believe that Jesus is the only way to heaven? If not, then we need to find you a new job."

A new job?

I imagined a mob of congregants brandishing torches in the dead of night. Some were crying, their faces screwed up into a rage. They poured out of the church that had raised me, my mom and dad shaking their heads in disbelief as I ran for my life, across the parking lot, diving into the lilac bushes.

I wanted to tell him that I wasn't sure. But *not sure* wasn't going to be good enough. So I lied. My dad had always warned me that I would suffer for my faith. And that it wasn't always going to be cool or easy—the camel getting through the eye of a needle. But he never talked about having to suffer for a lack of faith, of being punished for doubting. I stared at the dashboard and thought about Peter standing around the campfire the night Jesus was crucified. The women asked him if he knew Jesus. I tried to imagine his face as he stared into the flames wondering who Jesus really was. Peter lied and said he didn't know him. And here I was, 2,000 years later, about to lie that I *did* know who He was.

I swallowed hard and I recited the verses that I'd memorized as a camp counselor. How Jesus was the only way. "That no one gets to the father except through me . . ." I threw in another lie to seal the deal. "I thought maybe some Mormons were confused and *accidentally* believed in Jesus." The assistant pastor responded with a curt "Good," and unlocked the doors.

I drove home thinking about the first lie I told to Mrs. Mayfield. *I should have told her I was going to a boxing match, and I wasn't coming back.*

7

THE JESUS MOVIE

Michael stood on the soccer field watching John and Sarah's desert-stained jeep pull through the iron gate and park on the field, the school cow grazing unaffected a few feet away. They visited him every time they came through town, taking him out for dinner and offering him a ride to his mother's homestead during semester breaks. Michael smiled as John's sun-browned arm waved for him to get in the jeep. Through the mud spots, Michael could now read the words "World Vision" on the passenger-side door. When he first came to school he expected to see John and Sarah in the front seat of every white jeep he saw tearing down the road outside the school. But he quickly learned to recognize the different logos: USAID, UNICEF, African Inland Mission. Each emblem represented a different tribe of white people. Pokot had missing teeth, and white people had drawings on their jeeps.

They took the gravel road through the center of town. The bustling street was lined with corrugated-tin shops, a mishmash of fraying fabrics sown together as canopies for women selling battery-operated flashlights, and men offering to resole your shoes. Michael had grown accustomed to the market. Although he never had money to buy anything, he still enjoyed walking the streets and examining all the things for sale. Mr. Rotich had told him that if he studied hard and got a good job, Michael would be able to buy whatever the marketplace had to offer. John parked in front of the café that was known for butchering the chicken moments after you ordered it.

They sat on front porch of the café on plastic chairs under the shade of a corrugated-tin awning, John fanning himself with his safari hat. A donkey hauled a cart of cornmeal through a cloud of dust kicked up by a passing car. Michael sat silently next to him, lost in the news report emanating from the radio on the windowsill behind them.

"Michael, we are very proud of you." Sarah smiled at him.

"Thank you," Michael said, turning toward her, noticing for the first time that her hair had begun to grey and creases were sprouting from the corner of her eyes. Michael turned the radio off. It was hard for him to talk while the radio was on. He was still getting used to hearing voices coming from something other than a mouth.

"I am working so hard," Michael said, sipping his tea. "It's a bit of a challenge catching up to the other boys. There was a lot of stuff I had to learn in a short time." As soon as he said it, he realized John and Sarah might take this as an insult to their teaching, so he quickly added, "But I'm so grateful for the opportunity you gave me." He smiled. "The other boys told me how much they are having to pay for school fees."

John laughed. "It's hard to explain what a train is without actually seeing one." He smiled, rubbing his sunken, bristly cheeks.

Their appearances led Michael to believe they had been in the desert for quite a stretch.

"Your teachers tell us you're doing very well," Sarah said as the waiter set three plates of fried chicken on their metal table.

"And the priest agreed to give you a scholarship for your final semester," John added, patting him on the back. "He said you were a student with great potential." The priest had told this to Michael many times since Michael announced his plans to go back to the desert to work as a teacher at Kiwawa.

"And we couldn't agree more," Sarah said. They spent the next few hours sipping tea and eating chicken, a fan blowing the smell of grease from the kitchen into the street. Michael shared stories of learning how weather works and how much easier it was to sleep on a mattress. As the afternoon wore into evening, Sarah checked her watch. "So Michael would you like a ride home? We are going by your family's homestead and it would be no trouble to drop you off." She made the offer as if his family lived at the other end of town instead of a two days' drive up and down mountainous terrain.

He was anxious to see his mother, and had been hoping to see Keu as well. Michael was eager to congratulate Keu on his fifth marriage.

Sarah added: "And while we're there, we were hoping you would help us with a project that we are working on. We want to show a movie about

Jesus to your village and we need someone to translate it from English to Pokot." She tucked her greying hair behind her ear and Michael saw that she was wearing a Pokot beaded earring. "You know what we mean when we say movie, right?" Sarah asked.

He nodded. He had seen a couple movies playing on TVs in local shops, but hadn't ever sat down and actually watched one.

Michael took a drink of tea and glanced out the window as a speckled van sped down the dirt road. He had recently learned the history of the Pokot people from Mr. Rotich. Michael had stayed after class to ask why Mr. Rotich's ancestors had remained outside the desert. Mr. Rotich had explained that his ancestors were one of the few Pokot families who had decided to farm instead of continuing to herd cattle. After that Michael often met with Mr. Rotich to talk about the history of their tribe. Michael had heard the legends, but now he was after facts. He wanted to know why the Pokot were driven off the green hills and into the sand. Why Christian men from across the ocean had forced the nomads into the desert, condemning their women to walk miles for water, and their men into an endless war. "You see, Michael," Mr. Rotich explained, "the Karamoja and the Turkana and the Pokot are in the desert fighting over table scraps because the British stole their traditional lands." It was the first time Michael had considered that he and the Karamoja men who destroyed his village might have a common enemy.

Michael sat sipping his tea thinking of the British Christians who had forced his ancestors into a war that had separated him from his parents for most of his life. "What will you do if the elders don't want to become Christians?" Michael asked.

"Well," John said, scratching his cheeks, "first, we would respect their decision. Keu and the villagers are our friends and they can make their own choices. But I think that they will want to follow Jesus." Then he patted Michael's hand on the table. "You did."

Michael swirled his cup and drank the last sip of tea before throwing the silt in the road. Mr. Rotich's words echoed in his mind: *But despite these tragedies, converting to Christianity turned out to be for the best, because we have been blessed to know Jesus.*

"Okay," Michael decided. "If the elders would like to hear of Tororot's son Jesus, than I will help in any way I can."

"Great!" Sarah clapped. Michael noticed her voice sounded a little relieved. "Then everything else is set. Keu has the elders' approval and they agreed to gather all the nearby homesteads three days from now." That's when Michael realized they had already planned the movie with Keu. They had been banking on Michael agreeing to translate.

Sitting in the back seat of the jeep the next day, Michael watched as the barren bushes blurred by, the vehicle shaking as it rumbled down the neglected road. He had begun to resent the endless heat and sand now that he had seen life in the fertile green hills his people used to roam. He waved at the young herdsboys who trotted beside them, their scrawny cows stumbling along the desert road before disappearing into the dust, trailing the jeep like a cape.

After two days of driving, the jeep crawled up Keu's mountain just before sunset. From above, the homestead must have looked like a giant ant hill, hundreds of black bodies scurrying up and down with pots and bags on their heads. For the last week, families from across the valley had already gathered to hear the story of Tororot's son, Jesus. And Keu's family had been milking every drop from their camels, cows, and goats. Fires were burning across the homestead cooking meat and boiling milk, smoke billowing out of every hut. Hosting the gathering was a great honor and Keu had told his wives to re-mud their huts and milk the camels dry.

As the jeep pulled through the thorn fence, Michael smiled in the back seat and watched the women and children jumping and singing. The smell of camels, smoke, and dung reminded him of his childhood. In the center of a cluster of huts, Keu stood head and shoulders above everyone else, bare-chested, shouting orders in every direction. He looked like a giant as a dozen of his children ran around his feet carrying small pots of water or firewood. As Michael stepped out of the vehicle, Keu stopped shouting and walked to the jeep, his arms open wide. "Kimpur!" He laughed, embracing Michael before introducing John and Sarah to his five wives and twenty children.

"Returning to the village after going to school in the city always made me keenly aware that I was living in two worlds. I had been over the farthest mountain to, as they say in the Bible, a land flowing with milk and honey. Although I would later find that Kapenguria had not so much milk and honey as America. And then I would spend nights back in the desert villages staring into the fire listening to the elders' reports, translating their words to John and Sarah. How the men had to dig two body lengths to get water from the dry river beds, that the Karamoja had begun settling on the edge of Pokot land. And I would poke the fire with a stick, wanting to tell my people everything that I had learned—that the world was round, clouds were made of evaporated water, and what a light bulb was. But it would take so long to explain, if they ever understood at all. I often wondered how John and Sarah had decided what to share about the world and what to keep from us boys under the tree."

"And, finally, when it was my turn to speak, I only shared what I had heard from the nomads along the road. I told the elders who had died from the hotness and how deep the wells were dug on the edge of the desert, always leaving the topics of the modern world for another day."

That night, many of the boys John and Sarah had taught in Kiwawa were gathered at Keu's mountain. Seated around the bonfire, they shared their stories. Most were married and were eager to introduce their wives; some even had small children. And everyone made sure to mention how they had applied their ability to read and write. Some had started small shops along the road; others had decided to send their children to school at Kiwawa. John and Sarah nodded along, glad to see that the seeds of education they had planted were now bearing fruit.

After the stories were all shared, Sarah began setting up an eight-millimeter projector as a crowd of children wandered back and forth, jockeying for a better view of the strange metal box.

"It's a beautiful night for a movie, Michael," John shouted, pulling open the white projector screen. Michael noticed the cool breeze blowing, and looked up at the stars. It was a beautiful night, but he wasn't sure what made it particularly good for watching a movie. Then he stood up to address the 200 nomads who were seated, drinking tea and chatting about life across the valley. Putting his hands in the air, he hushed the crowd to just the sound of mothers soothing their hungry babies. "Thank you for gathering tonight," Michael said in Pokot. "Praise to Tororot for keeping you safe on your journey."

"Oee," the nomads responded, excited for the story they had walked several days to hear.

"You know me, Kimpur, and you know my parents."

"Oee."

"And I have been to the land beyond the farthest mountain where John and Sarah are from." Michael pointed at John and Sarah who were standing behind the projector. "They raised me at Kiwawa when my parents could not be found and they never turned me in the wrong direction. They're word is to be trusted."

"Oee."

"And their people know of Tororot's son, Jesus."

"Oee." The nomads clapped.

"Everyone look here." Michael pointed at his eyes and then at the screen. "People will appear and tell you the story of Tororot's son. And as they speak in their language, I will tell you their words in the language we know."

Sarah flicked on the projector and the electric hum of cinema filled the night air. A white woman wrapped in a grey bathrobe with a red-clay pot balancing on her head appeared on the screen. The crowd gasped at the sudden appearance of a woman out of the darkness. Michael pointed at her. "Mary, Kama Jesus."

The crowd watched wide eyed as sheep grazed in the sun. Grass sprouted amid the grey boulders much like on Keu's mountain.

"Where have you come from?" Keu shouted to Mary.

"Mary can't hear you," Michael said, struggling for words to explain why. "She is…very far away." Then angels appeared to Mary, looking like the spirits of ancestors who deliver the Pokot messages from Tororot.

Michael recalled the night vividly: "The nomads became hypnotized by the film. In fact, it is so hard to imagine such a thing if you have never seen a TV. They have no framework to understand actors or images. To them, the movie was happening in real time, real life played out before them. They began walking the street of Jerusalem alongside the actors."

The people pointed when they saw John the Baptist, shocked that his entire head was covered with hair. Michael pointed, "John the werkoyon of Tororot, and cousin of Jesus." They clapped showing John the same honor they would a prophet from their own tribe. As John the Baptist dunked people into a small stream, Michael explained, "Baptism is a new way to worship Tororot." The crowd whispered to one another, excited to learn a new way to worship their God.

"What if the river is dried up?" Keu shouted to John the Baptist. Michael replied. "It is only done once in a lifetime, like *Sapana*."

"*Sapana* is the Pokot baptism," Michael explained to me. "It's the sacred rite of passage into manhood. A goat is speared and its intestines are smeared on a boy's body. A nomad is covered in death and washed into a new life. He dies to childhood and is given a new name as a Pokot man."

Then John the Baptist began to preach. "If you have two coats, give one away."

"Oee," they responded. This was also true in the villages.

"Whoever has food must share it."

"Oee."

Michael paraphrased John's words to the tax collectors as "Don't steal from others."

And the nomads responded, "Oee."

"They so much liked the things John was saying about helping others who don't have. That is at the heart of Pokot culture." When Jesus walked up to John, Michael pointed, "Tororot's son Jesus." The nomads gasped. "Tororot's son is one of them?" a woman shouted with surprise as she pointed at John and Sarah.

"Many people over the farthest mountain are not dark skinned," Keu responded to her, clearly proud to show his knowledge of the wider world.

Michael added, "Tororot is the God of many people, including the people from John and Sarah's tribe."

"What about the Karamoja?" a woman yelled. But before Michael could answer, someone shouted, "Jesus! Watch out for the snake!" Jesus was walking a stretch of rocky desert trailed by a python hiding among the boulders. Soon the entire homestead was shouting to warn Jesus of the snake closing in behind him. Michael pointed at the python, "Satan, the enemy of Jesus."

An old man with a crown of grey hair stood up, outraged. "How can this be? I am an elder in the snake clan, so why would Tororot's son be the enemy of snakes?" The nomads began discussing the issue, some suggesting that Jesus hated snakes because they had killed so many Pokot children.

"What are they talking about, Michael?" John asked from behind the projector.

"Many of the people here are from the snake clan and they are asking why Tororot's son is the enemy of the snake."

John ran up next to Michael to address the group as Michael translated. "Tororot's enemy is named Satan and *sometimes* he appears in the *form* of a snake."

"Tell us more about Tororot's enemy Satan," the elder from the snake clan shouted back, leaning heavily on his walking stick.

John paused to think how best to explain it. "There was an ancestor named Satan who refused to worship Tororot on his holy mountain, so Tororot sent Satan to live under the ground inside a fire."

Michael translated, pointing at the ground then at a roaring fire across the homestead. "He is a powerful *woi*,[3] the enemy of Jesus and all worshipers of Tororot."

"Has anyone tried to talk to Satan?" the elder shouted back at John.

"Yes, bring him here," another old man shouted, shaking his staff at the ground. "We will convince him to apologize and come back to Tororot." Soon everyone was shouting.

"I will offer a camel to Tororot on Satan's behalf," Keu said, pointing to a nearby pen holding a dozen sleeping camels.

"Yes, Keu," the snake elder shouted. "Then surely Tororot will forgive him. A camel is no small *pution*."[4]

"Kimpur, let us speak to Satan and we will help bring him around to the right path."

---

[3] A woi is a demon from another world; also can refer to the spirit of a deceased ancestor who is cursing the tribe for an offense against his or her honor. An offense may be the tribe not remembering the ancestor in their prayers, or a sacrifice not being offered for him or her.

[4] A pution is a Pokot animal sacrifice to Tororot, typically a chicken, goat, cow, or camel, offered in ascending order of importance based on the magnitude of the offense. The animal will be killed by the werkoyon in a ritual, then the blood will be poured on the ground, and the meat will be cooked and eaten by the community gathered for the ritual.

Michael explained to John, "They want to help Satan make peace with Tororot."

John's brow furrowed with confusion. "Well, what do you think we should tell them, Michael?" John sighed emptying his lungs into the night air. After two decades in the desert he had come to expect misunderstandings like this. He had also realized that it was important to think before he made any knee-jerk theological arguments. "Satan's not going to change his mind." John said to Michael.

Michael thought for a moment. "I think that they are applying the Pokot golden rule: *If someone stands alone, than you must stand with that person as their advocate.* It said that everyone must be given a fair hearing before the elders. Someone must argue the case of those who have done wrong so he can return to the community. And now the elders are saying that Satan should not be left in the fire alone. So they are offering to help Satan make peace with God."

John stared at him confused. Michael racked his brain for another analogy. "Like a modern lawyer. They're trying to advocate on Satan's behalf."

Before John could respond, the movie cut to Jesus standing on a small wooden boat with a short mast and fraying white sail.

"Water!" Keu's first wife shouted. The sight of so much water trumped the nomads' concern for Satan.

"I've never seen such a massive river."

"You can't even see the other side!"

"Jesus is standing on a pile of trees and not sinking."

Michael tried to think of an explanation for a boat, but decided not to distract them from the story. For the next hour, they cheered as Jesus walked from town to town, casting out the woi from the curse, curing the sick, and making the unclean woman clean. They responded "oee" as Jesus told them to turn the other cheek, help the poor, and not repay evil for evil. After the Sermon on the Mount, a young man who had recently had his herd stolen by the Karamoja asked how he would survive without stealing them back.

"I didn't know what to say," Michael recalls. "I told him to pray for Tororot to bring him more cows. Then someone offered that man a cow to help rebuild his herd. It was quite something to see him combining Pokot and Christian values."

When Jesus went in the temple and began pushing over fruit stands and letting all the animals out of their pens, a woman stood up and yelled, "What are you doing?"

"That is holy ground," Michael said, "like the mountain of Tororot. No one is allowed to trade on holy ground." The woman sat down, nodding in assent.

After the last supper, Jesus walked through the dark garden and began to pray near a large rock while the disciples slept on the far end of the hill. "Why are you sleeping? Get up and pray that you do not fall into temptation," Jesus said.

Torches emerged from behind him, illuminating bearded Pharisees dressed in baby-blue bath robes, silver belts, and bleached white turbans. Roman soldiers stood behind them in cardboard helmets spray-painted gold, wearing tinfoil breastplates. When the soldiers pulled out their swords, the nomads shook their heads at the lazy disciples. "You fell asleep and your enemies have snuck up on you!" Keu shouted with disgust.

But the crowd cheered as Peter jumped to his feet, grabbed his short sword, and cut off the soldier's ear. Then the mountain erupted with applause and shouts when Jesus healed the soldier's ear. The nomads had been on both sides of battle; they commended Peter for his bravery and Jesus for his compassion. When Jesus was bound, Michael explained: "They are taking him to the elder council for a trial."

A man stood up, confused. "What has he done wrong?"

"They are jealous of him," Michael replied. "They don't like that people are following Jesus instead of them."

"Well, the elder council will act fairly on his behalf," Keu announced confidently. The other nomads agreed, trusting that Jesus' elders would judge fairly. But before the trial began, Jesus was pushed to the ground by a soldier. And soon the soldiers descended on Jesus, beating his face and kicking his ribs. "What are you doing?" Keu shouted, brandishing his spear in the air. "He hasn't even seen the elder council yet! You cannot beat a man who has done no wrong!" The modern world has grown accustomed to flaws in the justice system, numbed from decades of legal technicalities and jury biases. But this was all new to the Pokot.

The men shouted vitriol as the soldiers took turns raining punches down on Jesus, the women covering their eyes, unable to believe that Jesus was allowed to face this unwarranted punishment. When Peter appeared on screen, the nomads began pleading for him to help Tororot's son.

"Save him, you coward!" Keu snarled. Then he stood up, grabbed his body-length spear, and sent it flying over the heads of the seated nomads. His spear soared directly through the heart of the Roman soldier, tearing a hole in the movie screen. The nomads jumped to their feet with war cries, prepared to finish the fight Keu had begun. They could not sit back and watch Tororot's son be left to suffer this injustice alone.

Michael shouted to Sarah, "Turn off the film!" Sarah clicked off the projector and the images disappeared.

The nomads looked around as if waking from a dream.

"Where have they taken him?" Keu yelled. "We will hunt them down to save Tororot's son."

The nomads stomped, "Oee," a cloud of brown dust rising to their knees.

"Sit down! Sit down," Michael pleaded as John tried to fix the hole in the screen with tape.

When they finally sat down, Michael tried to calmly explain what was happening. "They are taking Jesus to the elder council and you must be seated to see what happens. You cannot help Jesus. As I said before, he is too far away. So put away your spears." The soldiers were gone from the screen. It was a good while before order was restored. Michael shouted for them to calm down and be seated. After the projector was turned off they scanned the mountainside for any trace of the soldiers. But they could find nothing. And while it remained unclear where the soldiers had vanished to, the nomads agreed to sit down and hear how the elder council would punish the soldiers for beating Jesus. As the dust settled, Sarah clicked on the projector. The enraged nomads watched the soldiers carry a bruised and dirt-stained Jesus to the council.

"Surely the elders will punish these men!" Keu yelled with derision.

"Oee!"

But their certainty was cut short when they saw the bearded Pharisees sitting on the council. "You are the ones who arrested Jesus out of jealousy," Keu shouted, jumping back to his feet. "How can you give Jesus a fair trial?"

"Are you the Messiah?" a Pharisee asked.

"Are you the son of Tororot?" Michael translated.

"If I tell you, you will not believe me, and if I ask you a question, you will not answer me," Jesus replied. For the next 30 minutes, the village watched as their values were dismantled piece by piece. The old men hung their heads in shame as the elder council demanded Jesus to be publically humiliated and beaten till his face was covered in blood. The women buried their faces as the thorns Tororot gave them to protect their homesteads were placed on Jesus' head. They were speechless as Jesus was nailed to the cross in front of a crowd who said nothing.

"To see someone punished by mob justice was unheard of. The Pokot had never witnessed a man treated so unfairly for doing God's work. So they wept for him, and for the society that had been so corrupt as to allow their elders to put a man to death because of petty jealousy."

Michael translated the words, "Tororot forgive them for they know not what they do." The nomads shook their heads in disbelief at Jesus' love for his enemies. And as Jesus was laid in the tomb, the nomads began to cry aloud for the death of Tororot's son. "How could Tororot allow this to happen to his own son?" a woman shouted through her tears.

"But the story is not over," Michael shouted back at the woman.

Suddenly a light shone from inside the tomb and two angels appeared.

"The messengers of Tororot have raised Jesus from the dead," Michael announced.

The night erupted in cheers, the whole village electrified with jumping and clapping, the rattling of a million beads drowning out the sound of the projector. It was an outpouring that Michael had not witnessed since the day the rains returned in the feeding camp. The mountain was enraptured with unexpected joy. When Jesus appeared behind their bouncing silhouettes, they began to sing praises to Tororot. A call and response emerged with an elderly woman singing the story of Jesus' miracles, his tragic death and heroic return to life. Michael, John, and Sarah jumped and sang, hand in hand with the villagers, shouting "oee" late into the night.

At sunrise, the homestead awoke to barking goats, bleating camels, and groaning hungry cows. By the time Kimpur rolled off his reed mat and out of Keu's guest hut, Keu's wives had milked the camels and put the porridge to boil. The rest of the women were on their way back up the mountain, humming the melody of Jesus' story from the night before, full water pots balancing on their heads.

Michael took his seat by the fire and scooped out a bowl of hot corn-meal porridge. John and Sarah stood by the jeep unloading another 50-pound sack of corn flour to feed the rest of the homestead.

"Thank you for sharing the story of Jesus with us," Keu said to John, handing him a bowl of porridge. "It was good to hear of Tororot's son."

"Keu, there is more of the story that remains to be shared," Michael said, swirling a cup of fresh camel's milk.

"More?" Keu said, surprised.

"As you know, Jesus was an innocent man," Michael said to the small group of elders seated around the fire.

"Surely," Keu nodded.

"And when his blood was spilt it was a *nyura*."

The elders looked at each other confused.

"This was a new addition to an old Pokot concept," Michael explained to me. "A nyura is a tradition we inherited from the Israelites. You know, Kenya is only a short boat ride down the Nile from Israel. And perhaps the belief goes all the way back to the first murder. In Genesis, God tells Cain, 'Your brother's blood cries out to me from the ground. You will be a restless wanderer on the earth.' And like Cain, any Pokot who sheds human blood is under a curse. So the murderer must be isolated outside of the village, in order to prevent the curse from spreading throughout the entire community. He is unclean. He must be quarantined, as you say in the West. Because his curse could spread, causing crops to die, mothers to miscarry, and prayers to go unanswered. We believe it is the blood that curses you from the ground. So the murderer must spend three full days outside of the village, alone with the hyenas and lions. Then a nyura can be performed by the local werkoyon."

"After the three days are up, the werkoyon selects the best cow from the murderer's herd. Then he meets the man in the desert and prays over the cow before slitting its throat, allowing the blood to fall to the ground. But the killer must also shed his own blood, so the werkoyon takes a dagger and quickly slashes hundreds of short cuts into the killer's torso. And his blood runs down his side, down his feet, and onto the ground. Blood for blood. In this way the curse is lifted. Then the man can return to the village and show the scars lining his body. It is a history of violence tattooed on our skin."

"Jesus' blood was a nyura made by Tororot himself," Michael repeated to the elders, whom he could see were stretching their brains to connect the murder of an innocent man to the cuts lining their sides, each cut representing a life taken in battle.

"Why would Tororot need to make a nyura?" an elder asked. "What has he done? Whom has he offended?"

"That is a good question." Michael nodded realizing they were following his line of reasoning. "It is actually *we* who have offended Tororot."

"How have we done this?" Keu said, a shadow of anxiety in his words.

Michael stood up and walked over to a toddler who was sitting naked in the mother's lap. "Okay. You see this child." Then Michael pretended to slap the boy. "When you hurt this child, do you not also offend that child's mother?"

The elders nodded.

"So it is with Tororot. All people are Tororot's children, and when we hurt them, we offend Tororot. And when you offend Tororot, you offer a goat or cow. But when you spill human blood, you must bleed for the life that was lost."

"This is the nyura," Keu said, putting the argument together.

"But Tororot is too holy to be appeased by a mere cow, or even human blood."

The nomads were surprised to hear this and started to discuss among themselves. An old man stood up and leaned on his long, smooth walking staff. "I have given Tororot my best cows and goats every year." He raised his robe, revealing hundreds of inch-long scars. "I have cut myself for every life I have taken. And Tororot has blessed me with a long life and many children!"

"Oee," the other nomads clapped at the well-measured counter argument.

Michael cleared his throat. "It is good to give your best to Tororot, but it is not quite enough."

The man pounded his staff and shouted. "What more can I give him?"

"It is Tororot who is now giving," Michael smiled.

"He provided the sacrifice. He offered a nyura that was equal to his holiness—his own son's blood. It is Jesus' nyura that satisfied Tororot."

John and Sarah listened to them discuss in Pokot. They had recently discovered the connection between Pokot nyura and the Christian belief in the atonement. They had spent the long ride to Keu's mountain explaining the theological jigsaw puzzle to Michael.

Michael leaned over to John. "They must think this over," he whispered. "It is such a new concept that it will need the approval of the entire elder council."

Keu's first wife filled their cups with steaming milk as the elders walked into Keu's largest hut. When it was clear the public meeting was over, the herdsboys led the cows and camels out of their thorn-wrapped pens and down into the valley for grazing. The women and children followed the herdsboys down the mountain for another round of water.

When the sun was at its peak, the elder council emerged, having discussed the issue until it was too hot to stay in the hut. The young men and women had returned and lay in the shade of a thorn bush, trying to avoid the hot afternoon sun.

Keu stood up to address Michael: "Kimpur, we want to thank you for bringing us the story of Tororot's son, Jesus."

"Oee," the nomads clapped.

"And we also have discussed Tororot's nyura. And this is good to us." The old men all nodded behind Keu.

Michael stood and cleared his throat. "If you accept this story, then let us walk to the river to be baptized, in line with the tradition of honoring Tororot's son, Jesus."

So the elders gathered up every man, woman, and child, and followed John and Sarah down the mountain and across the valley. The women carried empty water pots on their heads, figuring they would kill two birds with one stone.

Two miles later, John stood waist-deep in the river and motioned for Keu to meet him. Then John pushed him under the muddy water, and as Keu emerged, John smiled, saying, "From now on you will be called Augustus Keu, a follower of Tororot's son Jesus."

"Aa-goo-stas," Keu laughed as he threw his soaking red robe over his shoulder.

"What does it mean?" someone yelled from the river's edge.

Michael shrugged his shoulders. "It means you are a follower of Jesus. Same as all the names they give us."

"Why would they give us names with the same meaning?" Keu asked, clearly troubled by his new name.

"I don't know that either, Keu," Michael smiled. "But you will only be Augustus until you defeat the Karamoja again!" Michael shouted, patting him on the back. "Then you will be on to a new name!"

And the other nomads cheered "Oee!" as they waited to receive their new names.

8
COTTONWOODS AND DINOSAUR SKELETONS

"How are things going with the Youth Group kids?" my mom casually asked as she set the dining room table for brunch.

I sat at the table staring over my brother's shoulder out the windows, my back tied up in knots. I fixed my eyes and counted my breaths as I noticed the birch tree in the front yard was still naked in early April, its fallen branches scattered across the dead lawn.

"Youth Group's fine," I said, trying to give Mom the impression it had been just another week. Sunday brunch was the usual place for the airing of congregational gossip, and I had spent the last six days waiting to find out if the assistant pastor had mentioned my interrogation in the church van. So far no one seemed to have heard anything. I assumed my dad would have mentioned it if he had. But when he invited me to come over for Sunday brunch, I knew there was a distinct possibility he was baiting me into a family intervention. Mom set a plate of eggs benedict in front of me, but I waved her off.

"I'll just have my coffee," I said, lifting up the cup of fair-trade coffee I had brought from my dorm room.

The Feminist Bible Study had started weekly screenings of independent films about the secret politics of food, racism in America, and the latest climate change numbers. And for the last month, I couldn't drink regular coffee without seeing visions of Columbian women shaking their heads at me.

"Why's that?" Dad responded curtly from the kitchen. I knew he had made the meal especially for me. Eggs benedict had been my favorite meal as far back as I could remember. But I had sworn off the dish after seeing the documentary on abuses in corporate farms.

"Oh, I saw that the eggs were from a factory farm, and I told you over the phone I'm not eating meat anymore." Over the last six months, I had stopped spouting off Bible verses and had become a fountain of liberal factoids.

"Okay," he sighed, irritated. He stabbed his fork into his perfectly poached egg yolk. Listening to me pontificate seemed to tighten every muscle in his face.

"Mike, you said you would let it go," Mom warned him. It was obvious they had been arguing about how to deal with my new worldview.

"Can I eat in my bedroom?" my brother asked, knowing where the conversation was headed.

"No!" she snapped at him. "We are a family. And families eat together."

I looked down at the eggs and ham. Factory farm or not, I hated seeing my mom yell at my brother for a conflict I was causing. It was clear that her motherly instinct to be de-facto supportive of my interests had reached its end.

"Okay, fine," I said, picking up my fork and taking a bite of the eggs. After a month without meat, it tasted better than I remembered.

"Thank you," she sighed.

For the next half hour, I listened as she maneuvered the conversation around only the safest topics: my brother's math class, the old lady across the street my dad went shopping for last week, and her upcoming trip to visit her family in Iowa. Her voice led us through a field riddled with emotional land mines.

But when Dad mentioned having to work overtime, I cut in. "I just don't understand how you can work for a company that exploits Chinese workers by paying them pennies a day." For the last two weeks, I had barraged him with emails and text messages detailing his company's foreign labor practices.

He slammed his fist on the table, the bottom of the fork banging hard against the wood. "Don't forget for one second that my company is paying for your entire education!"

I could see his fork had chipped the hundred-year-old oak table.

"Mike!" Mom shouted at him. "We agreed that we were *not* going to engage him when he brings up these topics."

I looked at her. Her eyes were pleading with my dad to calm down.

He pursed his lips. "Okay. I'll just say this." He pointed at me with his fork. "Judge not, lest you be judged." And he put a mixture of ham and egg in his mouth, his jaw mashing the bite hard enough to see through his flush cheeks. He swallowed. My brother kicked my shin under the table to make sure I didn't respond.

I drove back to campus, my shoulders taut. Every trip home was ending like this. It was just a waiting game until my dad or I finally poked a tender enough spot.

It usually took me the rest of the day to calm down. I sat under a four-story cottonwood tree on the edge of campus, watching the longest branches hang over a pond that the college administration insisted on calling a lake. I spent hours sitting as close to the lotus position as my untrained knees could get, listening to a few spring birds as the cattails blew in the wind.

I had recently read *The Life of the Buddha*, followed by Saint Augustine's *Confessions* in hopes of finding some trick for summoning divine revelation. And after discovering the Buddha had reached enlightenment under a Bodhi tree and Augustine had been slapped by grace in a garden, I decided my best bet at seeing God would be planted under the oldest tree I could find.

I always brought my Bible, with the intention of reading it. But I could never bring myself to open it. Occasionally, I would glance down at the cracked leather and gold embossed letters. But before I long, my heartbeat quickened and my mind swirled with images of sitting in the passenger seat of the church van, staring at the dashboard, hearing myself say, "I believe in Jesus..." and all the lies that followed it. Then I'd have to spend the next twenty minutes counting my breaths to keep from having, what I had recently learned in my intro to psychology course, was a panic attack.

It was a sunny spring day in April as I leaned against the deep ridges in the bark. The breeze still carried hints of the Canadian winter through the holes in my thrift store sweater. I watched the blue sky reflect off the waves on the lake, the wind pushing them tall enough to occasionally cap white. There were three weeks left in the semester and I couldn't avoid reading the Bible any longer. I had to start writing my final paper on the Gospel of Matthew or I would fail my New Testament class.

I opened to the first chapter of Matthew and read the words, "A record of the genealogy of Jesus Christ, the son of David, the son of Abraham..." Then I re-read each word slowly like a child at the museum staring at a dinosaur skeleton, trying to imagine what it would look like with skin and muscles. The characters no longer reminded me of the pink-skinned cartoons I saw painted on the wall of my Sunday-school class. They felt like the distant relatives of the Iraqis I saw splayed across the cover of the *New York Times*: thick, dark eyebrows; long dust-stained robes; carrying pots of water on their heads.

I turned a few pages until I saw the words, "He saw two brothers, Simon called Peter and his brother Andrew." I imagined Jesus walking into a small middle-eastern town, a dry heat blowing across his sun-beaten face, his sandals sinking into the sandy main street lined with square adobe buildings. And on the edge of town, two unsuspecting fisherman retying the loose knots in their fishing nets, minding their own business as a rabbi begins a conversation that will eventually lead them all to their deaths.

'Come, follow me,' Jesus said, 'and I will make you fishers of men.' And at once they left their nets and followed him. I imagined Peter and Andrew, knee-deep in brown water, looking up at him. But my mind couldn't come up with the expression on their faces. I was at a loss for why they would so quickly agree to follow a complete stranger.

"Come, follow me." Jesus didn't even introduce himself, and Peter and Andrew don't seem to recognize him. Why would they? It was thirty years earlier that the Magi had come bearing gold, frankincense, and myrrh. For all they knew, he was just some rabbi wandering from town to town soliciting unpaid internships.

I re-read the words and tried to imagine if they were smiling, eager to finally get drafted into the rabbinic discipleship program. Or maybe they stared at their feet the way kids do when their grandmother announces it's time for a bath. I had heard a thousand sermons on the faith of Peter. How he had *just followed*. Jesus didn't do a miracle or wax eloquent about his elaborate plan to change the world. No mention of where they're going or what they're doing when they get there. And these two brothers leave the family business to wander out of town with a total stranger. No questions asked. I had always looked down on Peter, his ignorance, bullish plans, always sinking into the water he was supposed to be walking on. But now the whole scene felt strange and tragic. *Just leave them alone,* was my first thought. *Let them go on fishing.*

And week after week the disciples slept on couches and managed crowds of sick and desperate people as Jesus cured leprosy with his hands, scoffed at Pharisees, and shouted a Roman soldier's daughter back to life. All this while he made strange declarations about not building houses on sand, acting like birds and flowers, and cutting your hand off for sinning.

As many times as he repeated his message with different metaphors in town after town, his disciples didn't seem to learn anything. After Jesus calmed the storm, the first sentence out of their collective mouths is, "What kind of man is this?" They're not even sure what *kind* of man he is. Jesus doesn't even answer them. He just stands there, arms in the air on the deck of the ship, clothes soaked through, his hair blown in circles, as if he doesn't even *care* what they believed about him.

I looked out at the lake in front of me, the cattails bent over, nearly breaking from a strong gust of cold wind. I thought about the ten-point doctrinal statement the pastor asked me to sign before my internship. I sat in his office and read "the premillennial return of our Lord Jesus Christ..." I took a deep breath and signed on the dotted line. Every church staff member was required to sign off on the minute details of Jesus' Final Judgment. And here Jesus was 2,000 years earlier, gathering his own interns with not so much as a word about their theological convictions. Just "Follow me."

After the disciples wandered through a dozen more cities, Jesus turned to his deeply loyal and deeply ignorant interns. "The harvest is plentiful, but the workers are few," he said before sending them out, two by two. *You can't do that!* I thought, enraged more for myself than the disciples. *What are they supposed to say when someone asks them to explain the Kingdom of God? Just stand there like an idiot? Maybe try and recite something they heard you say one time? Tell people it's a Jewish insurrection and everyone's invited?* I flipped through the pages, past the parables, past the beheading of John the Baptist, until I saw the red words of Jesus speaking to the disciples upon their return. "Who do people say that I am?" he asked. The disciples rattled off a litany of Jewish heroes to whom the people were comparing him: Elijah, John the Baptist back from the dead.

"But what about you?" he asked Peter. "Who do you say I am?"

"You are the Christ, the Son of the Living God," Peter responded, as if from rote memory.

Peter's words were highlighted neon pink with penciled stars in the margin. But now Peter's words felt like the answers I had given the Youth Group kids. Jesus responded, "I am going to Jerusalem to be arrested by the religious leaders and killed. And then I will rise back to life."

But Peter seemed to have stopped listening after the word killed. "Never, Lord!" he shouted.

"Get behind me, Satan!" Jesus shouted back.

I looked out over the lake, trying to imagine Peter standing there speechless. I resented Jesus for calling him out. Peter had already left his family, his career, touched every variety of forbidden skin disease, and lived on handouts. He'd been chased out of town by Pharisees, only to come back and have Jesus call him his arch-nemesis.

I don't know what else you want from us? I said on behalf of Peter. The next page was the story of the Transfiguration. *After six days Jesus took with him Peter, James, and John the brother of James, and led them up a high mountain by themselves.*

I re-read the words. Jesus took with him Peter. My resentment cracked as goose bumps ran down the back of my neck. Jesus didn't send Peter home. He didn't lock him in a room and tell him to get his story straight or find a new job. That's when I felt an excited pang in my stomach.

Maybe Jesus wasn't going to send me home either. If he didn't give up on a man he called Satan, chances were he wasn't giving up on me.

As I sat there under a cottonwood tree in Minnesota, a dusty van sat parked along a crumbling desert road in Kiwawa. Michael waved at his students from behind a dirt-flecked passenger window. After attending college in Nairobi, he had returned to Kiwawa to fulfill his dream of becoming the first Pokot school principal. He brought a suit and tie back with him from the big city. They were in stark contrast to the clothes worn by the crowd who had now gathered to sing him off. The women jumped, their brightly colored beads rattled like tambourines. Men waved their spears and shouted for Michael to bring something back from this strange place he called America.

Michael smiled as he surveyed the school that had been his home for so many years. Six red-brick buildings now stood where John and Sarah's once shiny corrugated-tin classrooms had rusted and eventually buckled under the heavy rains. It had taken a month for Michael to convince the villagers to fire clay rectangles of dirt into bricks. "This is the way they do it outside the desert," Michael had insisted at meeting after meeting. It had taken two years to finally get them built. The students begrudgingly spent their afternoons stacking bricks one on top of the other until all six classrooms were topped with shiny new tin roofs.

The story of Michael's brick classrooms blew across the desert, slowly making its way across the valleys, up the farthest mountain, across the town on the edge of the desert, and down the winding, 200-mile stretch of road. Finally the story ended up in the form of a letter and two black-and-white pictures on the desk of his college president in Nairobi. And when an American team representing my Christian college in Minnesota came to check on their sister university's achievements, they were taken to Kiwawa. The college administrators nodded approvingly at Michael's work. A month later Michael got a letter offering him a full-ride scholarship to study organizational leadership in America.

Sitting in the front seat of the van Michael felt a surge of regret as he watched his new wife, Angelina, wipe away the tears she had held in for months. It was un-Pokot to cry, but she had spent enough time outside the desert to pick up the habit. He waved a final good-bye as the van lunged forward, kicking up a cloud of dust that blocked out the crowd. The last image of Kiwawa he saw was a cluster of brown and white cows drinking runoff from the steel water pump, their wet noses gathered around a hole in the broken cement. Looking down at his multi-colored plane ticket, Michael wondered if they had cows in America.

9

DIVERSITY DAY

In the winter of 2005, I was stopped in the cafeteria by a thin, balding black man wearing an oversized blue dress shirt and pleated khakis. "Excuse me," he said in an accent I recognized from a documentary about African child soldiers that Amanda had shown the month before. The man's voice brought with it images of kids with bulging bellies speaking in hushed tones about kidnappers stealing them from their beds.

"Do you know where the toilet is?" he asked.

I was balancing a plate of pizza on top of my philosophy text book in one hand, and an ice-cream cone in the other, in no position to give directions. "The *restrooms* are back outside the cafeteria," I said, pointing with my head and annunciating the word *restroom* in hopes that he would catch that *toilet* wasn't the right word.

He smiled, revealing he was missing his bottom two front teeth. "You know, on the campus tour they called them that. *Rest rooms.* So after the tour I went in there looking for some place to lie down. And all I found was toilets." He laughed.

"Yeah, I guess it is kinda confusing," I shrugged.

"Oh, sorry," he said, putting out his hand. "My name is Michael. Michael Kimpur."

I put my pizza down and shook his small, calloused hand. "Nathan— nice to meet you."

He put his suit coat and laptop on the table across from my pizza and walked out the cafeteria door. I sat down. As I ate my pizza, I tried to think of politically correct questions that would prompt him to start talking about war in Africa. After the child-soldier documentary, Amanda had ordered five boxes of orange Save Africa t-shirts for a campus-wide protest march she was planning in the spring. She had told us to try and find some African students on campus to be speakers at the event.

Twenty minutes later, Michael sat back down with a slice of glistening pepperoni pizza and soda.

"You know, I never had cold Coca Cola before I came to America," he said, taking a long drink from the red plastic cup.

"Yeah, it is better cold," I said, unsure how to respond.

Michael sat quietly eating. I couldn't think of anything to say. I just sat there waiting for him to speak again. After a few minutes he was almost done with his food and I finally decided on a question. "So Michael where are you from?"

"I am from Kenya," he smiled, holding up his slice of pizza. The documentary we saw was about Ugandan child soldiers, and I had no idea where Uganda was other than that it was somewhere in Africa.

"The land without pizza," he said triumphantly, lifting his last bite into the air. I chuckled uncomfortably at the odd description. I wasn't surprised he was describing an African country in terms of what they didn't have. The talking heads in the news always spoke with confident tones about what Africans didn't have. *A land without fair elections, without clean water, without modern health-care...* Pizza seemed too small and obvious, as if we should assume the absence of pizza was a necessary outcropping of the continent's other depravities.

"Pizza is pretty good," was all I could think to say.

"So what's the story with your teeth?" I said, pointing at my own two bottom teeth. "That must make it kind of hard to eat?"

Michael laughed. "Most probably it's a bit more difficult for me," he said, rubbing his naked gums. "I got them removed when I was a just a small boy. In fact, all the boys like eight years old or something thereabouts have to stand up straight as an old woman cuts at your gums. Swish swish," he said, his hands sawing the air. "And then she pulls the teeth out and stitches you back up." He knit the sawed air back together. "And no crying is allowed, by the way. You can't cry or everyone will laugh at you, and your father most probably will give you a horrible beating."

"Are you serious?" I said, unable to contain my shock., remembering the day I got four teeth pulled in high school. I was getting braces put in and I remember the nurses leaned over my small reclining body, my white knuckles gripping the blue plastic dentist chair. "A lot of people get queasy at the sight of needles," she said as the prick of Novocain pinched at my gum. I tried to explain that I was still recovering from the deep-seated trauma of my childhood vaccines but her gloved hands brushed my comments aside, "No, no, nothing to be ashamed of." I had cried like a baby before passing out.

"So what happened? Did you cry?" I asked him.

"No!" Michael scoffed. "In fact, if I had cried, my name wouldn't be Kimpur. It'd be something like crybaby, maybe *tataka*."

"Like a nickname?" I said, unsure how someone could just change their name so suddenly.

"No, my nickname is Pokot, which is the nomadic tribe I'm from," he clarified.

"Wait. Now I'm really confused," I smiled.

"Okay. I better start at the beginning. I was named Kimpur because I was born by a river near my homestead called the Kimpur River. That's how we name babies…"

For the next two hours, I sipped Coca Cola as he took my imagination with him to the grazing hills of his childhood and the night he escaped from the Karamoja raiders. I laughed as he explained John and Sarah holding him down for his first injection and Keu launching his spear through the movie screen. It was strange to hear him describe medicine, words, metal, counting, and Christianity as if they were exotic. These were the building blocks of my life, saturating the air I breathed since before I could remember.

"This is my World Vision sponsor picture," he said, pulling a frayed black-and-white photograph from his faded brown leather wallet. "I've kept it with me since I came to America to remind me that the people of this country have been supporting me since I was a small boy." I stared down at the image of him in a dusty white shirt, a prematurely serious look on his adolescent face.

"This is amazing," I said. I couldn't believe that I was actually talking to a World Vision sponsor child. Once a year, a white missionary to Africa or South America would preach at our church, recounting stories of sharing the gospel with *unreached people* as they flipped through a slideshow of children with bloated bellies.

Afterwards the congregants would stand in the lobby hovering over hundreds of brochures, each with a picture of brown-skinned child with a difficult-to-pronounce name, the words "$30 a month" at the bottom in bold letters. Eventually these children's pictures would land under a magnet on a church family's refrigerator door.

"Where was your sponsor family from?" I asked Michael, handing the picture back to him.

"Port-land, Or-e-gon," he said, annunciating each syllable.

"Have you tried to make contact with them?"

"Yes, but World Vision says they don't have a phone number."

"That's a bummer. I bet they'd like to meet you," I said.

The next Sunday the church elders unveiled a plan for a million-dollar church remodel. After worship, a hundred congregants stood around the five-by-five-foot model church with a new gymnasium erected where a dozen trees had previously stood. The Sunday-school kids' noses and fingers smudged up the glass as they pointed out slight inaccuracies in the model: a misplaced tree, the wrong shade of brick, the parking lot missing a row of lines.

I was staring at the price tag. One million dollars. I couldn't help but feel the pangs of guilt as I imagined Michael studying under a tin roof with one lesson book and a hand pump for water.

I returned to reality when I felt the pastor's hand on my shoulder. "Pretty nice, huh, Mr. Roberts?"

"It's an impressive model," I said, not looking up at him. I had been holding my opinions close, keeping a low profile in hopes that I could finish the rest of my internship without any further incidents. I figured if I could make it until my internship ended in July, I would be able to walk away from the church without having to explain anything to anyone.

As about forty teenagers took their seats in the youth room, I stood in the back leaning against the brightly painted cinderblock wall. The pastor, still wearing a suit and tie, stood in front of the teens, giving a stump speech on God's plan for the future of our church. The remodel was going to impact our city for Christ. How the new gym would allow for them to connect with their un-churched friends. I wanted to raise my hand and mention that our church would be building the sixth basketball court in a three-mile radius. But it wouldn't have mattered. The teens were eating it up. After the pastor left, the boys began arguing about who was going to be the first to dunk in the new church basketball court.

I walked to the front of the room, right where the pastor had stood. "Hey, so I just want to add my two cents to the discussion. Because I don't know if this remodel is such a good idea."

The teenagers stopped talking and looked up at me, confused. I looked back out at them. They looked so young, covered in hair product and designer jeans. "We could use that money to help kids in Africa," I said, losing confidence with every word. "They probably need a school more than we need a gym." They stared at me like I was speaking a foreign language.

Then a blonde freshman with a short ponytail and lips lacquered with lip gloss raised her hand. "Nathan? So my dad's on the elder board and he told me God was going to provide the money for the remodel. And so maybe we should start praying that God will provide the money for a school for the kids in Africa, too." I looked at her enthusiastic smile and for a moment I envied her.

"Yeah. That sounds great," I said, sitting back down.

A few weeks later, I got a call from Michael. "It was so nice to talk to you the other day," he said. "I was wondering if you would join me for the Campus Diversity Day Celebration." It was an annual dinner where international students dressed in their traditional ethnic garb and invited their white friends to eat catered food from a local Asian or African restaurant. I told him I would be honored.

Michael was living in the basement of the school librarian's house. I pulled into the driveway of a one-story suburban home with a picket fence wrapped in brown leafless ivy. I checked the clock; we still had plenty of time to get back to campus and find a good seat for the presentation. I rang the doorbell and a second later Michael opened the door in a white undershirt and shorts and quickly ushered me into his downstairs bedroom. For the next hour, I sat on his bed watching him rifle through a dozen canvas duffle bags, occasionally pulling out assorted pieces of what I assumed were part of his nomadic elder outfit. Five minutes after the dinner was scheduled to begin, I stood up. "Michael, let's just go. We're already going to be late."

"Diversity Day will be on African time," he shouted from inside his closet. A second later, he emerged wearing a red embroidered shirt, a red-and-blue checkered blanket tossed over his shoulder, and a tall black fez with a long red plume perched on his bald head.

"How do I look?" he said, beaming with pride. He looked like a Shriner who had just returned from safari. "You look very *African*," I said smiling.

"Very good! And you will wear this," he smiled tossing me a matching red shirt. I looked at the African shirt and prepared myself to spend the entire banquet explaining, "This isn't my shirt. He gave me this to wear. I've never even been to Africa."

I stood on the front step of the suburban home as Michael tried jamming several different keys into the front-door deadbolt before locating the right one. Michael stopped in front of the green Ford Ranger my parents had given me to take to and from my internship.

"Can I drive our truck?" Michael asked.

"*Our truck?*" It came out louder than I expected.

Remembering it was Diversity Day, I took a deep breath and switched to my patient teacher voice, a measured tone I first picked up from my mother and later honed while explaining camp rules to my little campers. "Sorry, Michael, I'm not sure how you got the wrong impression, but this isn't our truck," I chuckled uncomfortably. "Actually it's not even my truck. It's my parents'. They're just letting me use it to go to my internship."

Nathan and Michael Outside the Diversity Day
Celebration in 2005

He cleared his throat. Michael had spent half a decade as a principal in the middle of the desert, and countered with a teacher voice of his own. "Oh, sorry. I don't mean to offend. In Africa, we have a saying, 'I am,'"—he pointed at himself—"'because we are'"—he pointed at me. "We are because I am."

"Okay?" I said.

"Okay, let me put it another way," he said, walking toward the driver's side door. "In my tribe it is impolite to say 'this is my cow' or 'this is my hut.' Instead we say this is 'our cow' or 'our hut.' We don't own things in the same way people seem to here in America. In fact, if I were to drive this truck to the village and say, 'This is my truck,' the elders would get so furious and say something like, 'No, Kimpur, this is our truck because you are one of us.'" He paused for a moment. When it was clear his argument hadn't taken root, he rubbed his chin. "You are a student of theology, correct?"

"Yes," I responded with apprehension.

"So let me put it this way. Jesus said give us *our* daily bread, not *my* daily bread."

"Have you ever even driven a car?" I asked, opening the passenger door with the key.

"I have been in so many cars and it doesn't seem so hard," he smiled.

"Okay," I sighed. "But first I have to show you a couple basic things."

After a painfully slow and anxiety-drenched ride to campus, we entered the campus dining hall an hour late. But despite my initial apprehension about my African shirt, Michael and I blended into the menagerie of ethnic costumes. A Native student stood next to the coffee table wearing moccasins and a beaded necklace talking to a white girl in a shimmering sari. An olive-skinned man in a long white robe stood nibbling on a chocolate-chip cookie just behind them.

Emilie waved us over to her empty table in the back. She was wearing a red floral dress with short sleeves and a single French braid.

"Looks like Michael got you dressed up for tonight," she laughed.

"Uh, yeah. So which of your European countries is this beautiful dress from?" I said, feeling the fabric on her sleeve.

"*This* is from the thrift store. My parents are Americans *living* in Europe," in her *you-silly-American* voice.

"Oh. Well it still looks nice," I said as my cheeks flushed with embarrassment. As soon as we sat down, the white-shirted caterers served us plates filled with deep-fried meats slathered in sweet-and-sour sauce.

"Everyone share a song from their culture," Michael read off one of the Diversity Day cue cards in the center of the table. "Okay, so I'll go first. At the school under the tree I was taught a song called 'God is so good.'" Michael started singing, "God is so good, God is so good…"

I joined in at "He's so good to me." But Michael finished a second later, "...to us."

"Why did you say 'me'?" Michael said, clearly offended. Apparently the singular versus plural pronoun was going to be an ongoing point of contention. "What about *me*?" he scoffed. "Isn't God good to everyone?"

"No, you're supposed to say *me* too," I said, back-pedaling from a cultural difference I was sure was going to end up making me look bad for the second time today.

Michael threw down the card. "That's the same thing I was saying about the truck. Look, in Africa that song would never go with everyone saying *me, me, me, me, me, me*. No way. We accepted many ideas from the missionaries, but never that one of *me, me, me*. In Africa it is always *us*." He folded his arms with finality.

"Okay, sorry," I said with my palms up, hoping it wasn't going to ruin Diversity Day. Emilie elbowed me in the ribs. *Okay sorry* was clearly not a culturally sensitive response.

"No, it's a cultural difference," Michael sighed. "The very thing we are here to celebrate." He said with a smile. "In America everyone has their own stuff. But in the village, we don't have so much things as you have here. So we just have to share everything." Then he started pointing at us as if he was preaching a short sermon to a congregation of two. "In fact, when they paid me for working in the library, the woman asked me if I had a bank account. But in the desert we don't have bank accounts. All you have is your cows and your hut. So if people see you saying *my* hut or *my* cow or *my* car, then when your house is burned down and your cows are stolen, no one will help you."

"Amen," Emilie said.

Michael took this as a cue to keep going. "The problem is that life in the desert is just too difficult to do it alone. You need your neighbor. And when everyone starts saying *I* and *mine*, the community is in big trouble. In fact, I hope Africans never talk like that." He said taking a long drink of tea.

"Happy Diversity Day," Emilie said, clinking her cup of coffee against my empty cup, which still rested on the white linen.

Michael reached for another Diversity Day cue card. "Okay, now everyone share your favorite cultural food." I stared at Michael wondering what had just happened. I still couldn't tell if his speech was meant to shame or inspire me.

I leaned over and whispered to Emilie "What did you grow up singing?"

"I'll never tell," she smiled, taking a bite of sweet-and-sour chicken.

The next day, a phone call woke me up.

"Nathan?" My dad was using his business voice and I could hear the bustle of an office in the background. "This is Mike," he said, introducing himself the way he always does when he calls me from his office.

"Yeah, I know, Dad. What's up?"

"So on Wednesday one of the church elders pulled me aside at Bible Study. He told me something about you criticizing the church remodel to the Youth Group."

I bolted upright, the muscles in my body instantly ready to run.

"His daughter told him you suggested they use the money for kids in Africa?" he paused, waiting for me to confirm or deny the story. Sweat started flash-flooding my forehead and armpits. When I didn't respond he went on. "Anyway, I told him you had every right to speak your mind." Then he paused and softened his voice. "But he didn't see it that way."

"Well, how *did* he see it?" I said, trying to sound calm.

"He thinks that all staff, including interns, need to be in support of the remodel. And I told him you probably weren't going to be comfortable with that."

"Dad!" I shouted.

But he didn't skip a beat. "And he said that you should probably find a new church."

I was speechless.

"He said you should probably finish your internship up and move on. And I just thought you should hear it from me." After a moment his voice re-emerged with a tone I had rarely heard him use since he had stopped thinking of me as a little kid. "I'm sorry," he said.

"Yeah, me too," I said as hot tears ran down my cheeks and on to my pillow. They were the same tears I used to cry at my birthday parties and Christmas, my small body overwhelmed by relief and disappointment as I surveyed the destroyed wrapping paper alongside the long awaited and yet not quite what I had hoped for presents. I was getting fired from the church that had raised me. On the other hand, I finally had a good reason to stop going back every Sunday.

Dad sighed, "Nathan, I also wanted to tell you that I'm proud of you."

"For what?" I snapped back, not yet convinced that lying my way through it wouldn't have been the best option.

"Not many interns would have risked their job for some kids in Africa."

"Yeah, well. It didn't change anything."

"Yeah, I know how you feel."

"No you don't," I said, involuntarily slamming the plastic phone back into the cradle next to my bed. I stared up at the speckled ceiling and wondered if I should go back to sleep for the rest of the week.

A second later the phone rang.

"Hello?"

"After I graduated from college," my father said, picking up immediately where he left off, "your mother and I went to a pretty radical church downtown." Something about the way he said *radical* made me even angrier.

"We would pull homeless people off the street and right into worship. We called ourselves 'Jesus People.'" He paused, apparently waiting for me to be impressed. "Anyway, when I decided to marry your mother, we drove down to Iowa to ask the priest from St. Margaret's for his blessing."

St. Margaret's is the small Catholic church my mother's family attended. It's the type of miniature cement cathedral that visitors are always surprised to find in small Midwestern towns. Whenever we visited, we would sit in the back row as all our Catholic relatives went up for communion. The last time we attended, my brother Kellen was thirteen years old. He had made up his mind on the drive down that he was going to get in line for the Eucharist. But just before the priest handed him the wafer, our aunt Kate told Kellen to cross his arms. So the priest put down the wafer and ran his finger along Kellen's forehead in the shape of a cross. Kellen stood there for a moment, confused, before Aunt Kate motioned for him to move along as the priest handed her the wafer my brother had hoped to consume. Our parents had not taken us back for mass since.

"Your mom wanted to have our wedding down there. I tried to convince her that two radical Evangelical Christians had no business getting married in a Catholic church, but she insisted. So a month after I proposed we drove down to Iowa to get the priest's permission." He said "permission" with a pointed derision. "But when I walked into the lobby of St. Margaret's, I saw this sign on the bulletin board with the list of all the families in town and how much money they gave to the church."

At that moment I could tell the story was not going to end well. "So after the service, which was boring beyond all belief, I went to shake hands with the priest."

I could see my mother's face. It's the face she makes whenever my father causes a scene. She is standing a few feet behind him, usually pretending to examine some mundane object nearby, emotionless, as if nothing is happening. As if she's an innocent bystander who just happens to be standing next to him as she waits for the storm of controversy to pass. "And I told the priest, 'Look, you shouldn't have the list of everyone's tithes on the bulletin board. You know Jesus said don't let the right hand know what the left hand is doing.'"

Then he paused for effect, something he does with all his favorite stories.

"Oh yeah? Then what happened?" I asked out of habit.

"The priest grabbed me by the collar, and threw me down the stairs."

For some reason I felt embarrassed about something my father did before I was even born.

"So you're not the only one in the family to get thrown out of a church," he said with a sense of fatherly satisfaction.

"Yep, that's something we have in common now," I said, hoping it wasn't a sign I was turning into my dad.

"Anyway, I gotta go back to work. But don't worry about it too much. You'll get over it. I did."

I pulled the covers over my head and counted my breaths until I fell back asleep. I tried to let the visions of Mrs. Mayfield shaking her head at me float past my mind like clouds in the sky.

My dad went into church the next Sunday and told the pastor he wanted to be taken off the rolls as a member, that after twenty years of membership he couldn't continue to belong to a church that silenced dissenting opinions. I didn't find this out until months later, because I refused to answer his phone calls and I stopped going home for Sunday brunch.

10
THE SAVE AFRICA MARCH

After the Diversity Day Celebration Michael and I started spending a lot of time together. And almost immediately I began speaking in my college classes with an air of authority about the plight of people of color in America, parading Michael around campus as a testament to my own progressivism. Michael happily played the part, sharing exotic tales from the African desert whenever I wanted to show him off to my fellow students.

It never occurred to me to question why a middle-aged man from a foreign country was so comfortable putting his life into the hands of a naïve 21-year-old kid from the suburbs. I was too enamored with myself to ask any questions. I had a black friend, something few students on campus could say. I had grown up in a wealthy suburb with only a handful of black families, and Michael became the symbol of the fact that I had moved on, that I wasn't some pretend yuppie liberal; I was actually helping Africa. In real life.

It took me quite a while to figure out why Michael went along with it. When I asked him years later, he smiled knowingly. "Well, three reasons: I needed your help. You meant well. And—" he laughed, "I was lonely." Throughout the winter, he relied on me to navigate the strange culture in which he found himself: signing up for a bank account, getting a ride to the grocery store, or just someone to watch a movie with. But this was natural for him. Michael had grown up relying on the kindness of whites.

He had been raised by John and Sarah in Kiwawa. And, now in America, I was just another link in an unbroken chain of white generosity that helped propel him through the modern world.

By spring, he was calling me during class, the buzz attracting irritated glances from my theology professors. A second later, I'd read:

I NEED TO GO TO THE BANK. ILL MEET YOU IN THE CAFETERIA IN 30 MIN. - MICHAEL

I'm in class. Be there in an hour

SOUNDS GOOD BUDDY

On my way out of class, I'd count the bills in my wallet, certain that Michael was waiting around the corner with a pizza and soda that needed paying for. I still hadn't introduced him to Amanda or invited him to the Save Africa March. I was getting a little possessive of him. I liked having a cross-cultural trump card to play when Amanda got on her high horse about politics in Africa. But my friendship with Michael was getting expensive. My parents gave me a few hundred dollars a month for gas and food, which was barely enough to buy organic fair-trade food for myself. My own bills, combined with Michael's, left my bank account hovering in the low double digits. So the week before the Save Africa March, I decided to introduce him to the feminists.

Since my internship had ended, I picked up a minimum-wage job catering dinner for the Friends of the College, a motley assortment of wealthy Christian business people who regularly dined with the president. It was at one such dinner, as I scrambled to refill steaming silver trays of roast beef and potatoes, I spotted Michael at the end of the serving line with a dirty plate in his hand. I presumed he was the token minority for tonight's dinner; there was a rumor going around campus that the president liked to invite a handful of the minority students for fundraising dinners and group photos. This rumor was largely based on the disproportionate number of brown and black students in our campus promotional material. I left the serving line and nudged Michael on the shoulder. "Michael, they give you a new plate every time you go through the line," I said, handing him a fresh plate.

"Oh thanks, buddy,"

"Are you here for the event?"

"What event?" Michael said, looking around. He obviously wasn't the featured student.

"Don't worry about it. Hold on, I'm going to see if I can take my break now."

A minute later, I was in the buffet line filling my plate with salad and potato wedges as Michael loaded his plate with a pile of roast beef.

"Hey, leave some for the rest of us," I joked.

"Oh, sorry. The lady said it was an 'all you can eat' meal," he said. He started putting some of the beef back.

"No, you can't put it back now," I said.

"What should I do?" The roast beef hung in the air, the juice dripping back into the serving tray.

"Just put it on my plate," I said, noticing the couple behind us was beginning to stare.

Michael and I found a table overlooking the parking lot, the street lamps illuminating several fancy cars which I assumed were owned by the dinner guests. Michael took out a book on the history of American quilting and started reading in silence as I sat picking at my potatoes, unsure how to jump-start another conversation about his childhood. The week before at Feminist Bible Study, I had retold Michael's life story, and afterwards Amanda had reminded me three times to invite Michael to come to the Save Africa March.

"It's perfect," she said with a wide smile, "a former child soldier marching to save child soldiers."

I thought about all the token minority students I had served at the president's dinners. They had to know they were props. And here I was about to turn Michael into my own prop. Sure it was to help kids, but wasn't that the same rationale the president used for plastering brown students across the college brochures? I stood up to leave, having made up my mind not to invite him.

"Your friend Amanda invited me to a rally for Africa on Saturday," Michael said as I was walking away. "I told her you could give me a ride."

I smiled. "I'll be there at eight a.m."

It was an overcast afternoon in April when Michael and I showed up in matching orange Save Africa t-shirts. Two hundred kids in identical orange were listening to the student folk band clumsily chunk out a Johnny Cash cover. Between Bono's recent media blitz on AIDS and the mass proliferation of Christian documentaries on world hunger, the Save Africa fever was spreading across campus like malaria. Amanda had decided to capitalize on the momentum by beginning the march with a benefit concert featuring a popular student band in the campus courtyard.

"This is gonna be really something," Michael said, walking into the crowd. By the second song, Michael was dancing in the middle of a hundred cheering white kids in matching shirts. I assumed it was his traditional dance, although it looked a bit like the moves middle-aged TV step-dads pull out to try and look cool: a sort of chicken walk, his head pecking the air, jazz hands shaking beside his bouncing belly.

"This is ridiculous," I whispered to Emilie.

"White kids raising money usually look ridiculous," she smiled.

"But Michael seems like he's having a good time." Michael had started directing a cluster of students to jump straight up and down.

Amanda turned around and glared at us. She had written "This Is What a Feminist Looks Like" in permanent marker across the front of her orange t-shirt. "Shut up," she said, punching me in the arm. "We paid four-hundred dollars to get this band and I want to hear every note." She had swallowed her pride and partnered with the World Missions Bible study leader to put on the event. She'd justified it by saying, "We need the *Christian* kids to show up if we are gonna raise any money."

I leaned over to Emilie. "I voted to give the band money to Michael. His pizza and soda addiction are seriously harshing my cash flow."

"Oh, poor baby," Emilie said, pinching my cheek. "Maybe you won't be able to go on a Caribbean cruise for spring break this year."

Emilie had been criticizing me about my family's money since I'd invited her to meet my parents at an expensive Thai restaurant downtown. I was still stone-walling my father over the internship debacle so my mother had decided we should meet at a public restaurant in hopes that it would keep us from shouting at each other. "And why don't you bring a friend along?" she casually mentioned over the phone. Since I was a little kid she had been inviting guests over to ensure we remained on our best behavior.

"Sure. Fine," I said.

I sat across from my dad, staring at the menu, the painting on the wall, my mom, anything to keep from making eye contact with him. I repeated the words *Dad's just a victim of Evangelicalism, Dad's just a victim of Evangelicalism, Dad's just a victim of Evangelicalism* over and over again in my head. It was my new mantra. It's something I learned from Amanda.

"Liberals blame the system, not the individuals created by that system," she would say. She was always talking about the system that created criminals in the inner city and terrorists in the Middle East. While she never mentioned conservative Christians, I assumed it applied to them too. But eventually my anger would burst through this rhetorical dam and I would have to switch tactics. I tried to convince myself that leaving church was for the best, that my dad had actually done me a favor, that I was better off without the pastors, Youth Group, and praise band forcing me to look both ways before I said what I thought.

When our meals came, my family began its usual round of taste testing, forks reaching across the table, grabbing bites off every plate. Emilie looked at me with furrowed brows, her arms folded as if a murder of crows had just descended on her pad Thai. I leaned over to grab a noodle. "Do you mind?"

"Sure. Fine. Want any of my water too?" she scoffed as half her noodles disappeared in front of her.

As we drove back, I was relieved at having made it through the evening without arguing with Dad. But I had been so focused on avoiding my father, I had missed the obvious signals Emilie was putting out.

"What's wrong?" I said, finally able to think clearly enough to notice she was still upset. Emilie didn't look at me. "You know not everyone gets to go to downtown restaurants all the time—"

"Yeah, I know the kids in Africa…" I said, cutting her off.

"Ahhh!" she shouted, her fists balled up. "I'm not talking about kids in Africa!" She looked at me for the first time since the food had been served. "Growing up *I* only went out to eat *one* time a year." Her index finger in the air. "My parents didn't feel like it was a good use of their supporters' money. So I would plan for months what I was going to order. It was my favorite night of the year." She sounded vaguely nostalgic before getting angry again. "And tonight I realized your family didn't even care what they ordered because they go out every week!"

We drove the rest of the way to campus without talking. I had sort of thought of it as our first date. But as I dropped her off, I realized how stupid it was to expect a meal with my parents to be anything date-like.

I'd been trying to dig my way out of it for the last few weeks. But it was clear she was still mad. Standing at the back of the crowd, we watched the band finish with the crowd singing, "We are marching in the light of God." The final chorus was sung in Swahili. Despite my cynicism about paying the band, I couldn't keep from smiling as Michael jumped up and down, shouting every word inside a circle of students who were clapping to the beat.

After we marched around the campus with signs decrying the plight of child soldiers, we ended in the campus chapel to watch a documentary about Uganda. Michael and I took our seats in the middle of the crowd of students and as the screen came down from the ceiling, the words *Invisible Children* appeared, followed by images of children carrying guns through the African desert.

As I sat next to Michael, the half-naked children, the bullet wounds, the students doing homework by candlelight, they all ceased to be distant tragedies. I pulled my t-shirt over my face and closed my eyes. But the images on screen were replaced with visions of Michael watching his uncle being stabbed to death, running naked across the desert, drinking his urine. It was all I could do to stifle my sobs with my wadded t-shirt as the horrors of war mixed with my shame at having grown up in the heart of American opulence.

"Wow, this movie is incredible," Michael whispered, seemingly oblivious to my emotional state. "Nathan, how did they even make this? You know, somebody should make a movie like this about Pokot."

NATHAN ROBERTS & MICHAEL KIMPUR

Then I felt his hand on my shoulder. "Oh sorry, buddy," he said, his voice softening. "It's so *tough* to look at this stuff." His voice was full of compassion. "I know that."

I pulled my head out of my shirt and looked at Michael through blurry eyes.

"It's okay to cry, buddy," he said.

I stood up and excused myself. In the bathroom, I splashed cold water on my face and wiped my wet hands on the front of my shirt hoping to hide my tears. When I came back, the lights were on. Amanda was standing on the stage facilitating the post-film discussion group with Michael standing beside her. "This *incredible* movie," he said, excited, "is in fact also the story of *my* people. As a boy I walked the hills always looking out for enemy tribesman around every bush..."

Michael enthralled the students with his story. They laughed as Michael acted out hiding behind a bush when he met the pale-skinned ogre, and their concern turned to relief as Michael explained how he reunited with his mother. After he finished, the students cheered and asked him to do his chicken dance one more time. As they got up to leave, several students pulled him aside and shoveled wadded bills into Michael's hand.

Amanda walked up to hug me. "That was incredible." She sang *incredible* in falsetto and waved her hands. "He was amazing." Then Amanda walked up to Michael. "Thank you, thank you, thank you so much for tonight. Your story was so beautifully told." She grabbed him by the shoulders. "Michael, do you need a car? My family is getting rid of my old car from high school."

Before Michael could answer, I cut in. "He doesn't really know how to drive yet."

"Thank you, Amanda," Michael said, brushing me back. "Yes, I very much need a car. And after Nathan finishes teaching me how to drive, I will get the car from you. And again I want to say thank you so much for hosting this event. It is so wonderful to have people talking about the children in Africa. I now see it is events like this that paid for my own schooling with the missionaries in Kenya."

As we walked across the dark campus under the streetlights, I looked at Michael. He was smiling and looking up at the stars. I said, "We should write thank you letters to the people who gave you money tonight. If you thank them, they'll be way more likely to give you something again later."

"Oh, right buddy, that sounds nice," he said, clearly lost in thought.

"And it couldn't have come at a better time. I'm almost out of money."

Michael stopped me beneath a dull-orange streetlamp.

"How much money do we have left?" he said, his face looking concerned.

We? I thought.

"Well, *I* have enough for rent this month." I overstated, still hoping to maintain some distinction between our possessions, "but not a dollar more." This was mostly true. I knew that if I needed more money, my parents would float me after a strongly worded lecture. But I wasn't sure how they felt about floating Michael.

Michael opened his wallet. "I have thirty bucks here," he said, handing me all the bills he had gotten from the discussion group. "You take this for gas. That should get us around for a while."

"No, that's for you," I said. "Keep it for pizza and soda. I'm just saying you need to get a job, especially if you are going to get your own car."

"Oh, right," he said, putting the money back in his wallet.

11
THE EVANGELIST

"Long week?" I asked Joanne as I handed her my student ID. She had been sitting at the entrance to the college cafeteria since I was in diapers. I had seen her thousands of times, but I started to appreciate her after I started picking up lunch shifts refilling the milk and soda machines. Her tight curls and cracked lipstick were conspicuously out of place swiping student ID cards at a liberal-arts college. She seemed more like the woman you'd see dishing out greasy burgers to truck drivers in a family diner.

"It's always a long week, sweetie," she laughed.

"Well, it's already Thursday," I responded. Then I remembered she once mentioned that she works weekends.

"Yep," she sighed, handing back my ID card. She looked tired. This had been an especially long week. Michael and I had gone to the morning chapel service on Monday. The school calendar had said there was a famous evangelist coming to preach. I didn't want to go, but Michael had insisted. I was always suspicious of people who called themselves "evangelists." They tended to conform to one of two models. You had your Mother Teresas, the straight-to-the-point storytellers who usually spent their days ladling soup into bowls held by tired men in dirty jackets. And then you had your Joel Osteens—usually tall men who sold the good news wearing expensive pin-striped suits, their leather shoes reflecting the spotlight to a live studio audience. These guys detailed the benefits of the King of Kings as if he was a new car fresh off the assembly line, selling at a price you couldn't pass up.

When we took our seats, I knew I had made a mistake not doing my standard preacher background check. The evangelist of the day was a tall blonde man in his late thirties wearing a striped-blue dress shirt with the sleeves rolled halfway up his long arms. His hair was slicked back and even from the fifth row it was clear he used tooth whitener. He opened with a story about using airplane rides as witnessing opportunities.

"I mean, they're stuck there for at least two hours. So I figure it's the perfect opportunity to share your testimony."

At camp we had practiced giving our testimonies, retelling the story of how we met Jesus. The camp director required us to memorize two versions, a five-minute one to tell little kids, and a twenty-minute one for teenagers. Apparently this evangelist had a two-hour version, which seemed to include time for questions. I had heard it all before and was getting up to leave when I heard him say, "This morning I spoke to a sweet lady outside the cafeteria named Joanne." I sat back down to hear what he was going to say next.

"And I asked her if she died today, how sure was she that she would go to heaven?" It was the same question from camp. "And her answer may surprise you." He smiled with his pearly whites. "She said she was definitely going to heaven because she went to church every Sunday." I scanned the chapel. The students were shaking their heads *wrong answer*.

Michael leaned over. "I don't understand what was wrong with going to church," he said quietly, as the evangelist rattled off a list of creative ways to create evangelism opportunities.

"No, going to church is a good thing," I whispered behind my hand. "It's thinking that going to church gets you into heaven. This man is saying you have to believe in Jesus, not just go to church."

Michael looked confused. "Why would anyone go to church if they don't believe in Jesus?"

"Maybe their family goes there," I said. That's why I had kept going.

"So it looks like you have a lot of work to do," The evangelist continued. "Even on this Christian campus. I mean," he smirked, "if your cafeteria staff thinks they can get into heaven by going to church, who else might not be a real Christian? Have you even considered asking your roommate about their faith? It would be *horrible* if the person you slept beside for a whole year ended up in hell because you couldn't be bothered to ask."

For the next two days, Joanne was assaulted with invitations to coffee and offered rides to this or that *Bible-believing* church. And Joanne just smiled, politely refused their offers, unsure why and a little suspicious that after three decades everyone was suddenly taking such a keen interest in her.

* * *

It was a sunny May morning, the puddles still gathering around the cracks in the road, as I sat in the cab wearing yesterday's milk-spattered black shirt and khakis. Michael was hoping to get a quick driving lesson in before my lunch shift at the cafeteria.

He stepped into the car wearing an oversized navy-blue suit he had picked out at the thrift store. "Looking good, buddy," I said, dusting off the shoulder of his clearly unwashed sports coat. Michael had decided to stop by every office on campus asking for a job. "Yep, there are so many clothes in this country. Everyone is welcome to be looking their very best," he said, rubbing skin cream on his face.

On the drive back to campus, I sat in the passenger seat, mock interviewing him one more time. "Tell me about your work experience," I said in a professional-sounding voice.

"I have a high school diploma, a bachelor's degree in business, and I have been the principal of a school in Kenya," Michael said from memory.

"And do you have any special skills that we should know about?"

"I can milk the office camel!" He burst out laughing. "Or what do you think I should say?" he turned and asked seriously.

I punched him in the arm. "I told you no joking around. People don't like jokes at an interview," I said trying not to laugh. "You can tell them you have experience in agricultural and hard physical labor."

Three hours later, I stood at the check-out line across from Joanne. Hundreds of students breezed past her with tray after tray of pizza, Chinese stir-fry, salad, milk, soda, fries, and various assortments of tropical fruit. It had been a month since the evangelist came to chapel and I hadn't heard anyone invite her to church in a while. As the lunch rush was dwindling, Michael came through the checkout with a heaping plate of Chinese food, his suit coat hanging over his forearm.

"How'd it go?" I asked, noticing he had missed a belt loop in the back.

"Not so good, buddy," he sighed. "It seems my English isn't good enough to work in any office on campus. It seems the British didn't do a good enough job teaching it to us." He smirked.

"Well, you can probably get a job in the dish room. All of the Latinos back there have pretty thick accents," I said, wondering for the first time what jobs they had done in their home countries. "And if you get a job here, ask for the day shift. Then we can work together." I paused. "I could probably talk my roommates into letting you move in with us. I mean, it'd be easier than me picking you up every day from the suburbs."

"Wow. Okay, that would really be something," Michael said standing up straight.

I took Michael back to the office and introduced him to the manager, explaining that he grew up a World Vision sponsor child and eventually became the principal of his elementary school back in Kenya. Then I added, "He can also milk the cafeteria camels."

The manager laughed and hired him on the spot.

As we left the cafeteria, Michael stopped me. "Why did you tell him I could milk the campus camels after you told *me not* to say that?"

"I don't know. It just seemed like a funny thing to say," and remembered I had told him to not tell any jokes at his interviews.

"Well, I know the manager has a sense of humor. He likes people who can make him laugh." I grasped for an explanation that didn't make me look like a hypocrite. "I guess I just knew how to say it the right way."

"When you come to Kenya, you will see me as I really am." For the first time, I heard homesickness in his voice. "People come from miles to see me," he smiled. "Then *I* will be the one to be telling the jokes."

It was the first time he had mentioned me coming with him to Kenya. "Do the camels come from miles to see you?" I asked, excited at the prospect.

Michael laughed. "The camels know me too."

The next week, my roommates cleared out our living room, hung a dark blue curtain from the ceiling with thumbtacks and placed Michaels short bed and a small bookshelf in his "room". We already had four college students living in a two-bedroom apartment and we would usually wake up to a friend or relative on our couch. So adding a fifth person was surprisingly easy. We were rarely there. We woke up each morning, brushed out teeth side by side, and drove to the cafeteria where we spent our days refilling the milk dispensers, filling the dishwasher, and taking out the garbage nearly bursting with a brown slurry of half-eaten food. We got home each night just in time to watch the ten o'clock news. I'd spend the rest of the night reading books on socialism and eastern religion as Michael watched rebroadcasts of the day's sports. Lying in bed, I would hear through the dry wall the muffled cheers or dull commentators speaking just low enough to make the words indecipherable. I assumed the novelty of having a TV five feet from his bed was enough to keep him awake.

One night Michael was listening to a televangelist well after midnight. The preacher's southern drawl was loud enough to warrant me getting up and telling Michael to turn it down. "Turn off that garbage," I said, standing in the hallway as a grey-haired southern preacher shook his fist against a glass podium.

Michael still had his cafeteria uniform on, a half-eaten slice of pizza and a glass of milk on the carpet by his bare feet. "Hey, Nate. Why are all the preachers on TV so obsessed with saving people from hell?" he said pointing at the screen.

"I don't know, Michael," I said, too tired to discuss theology.

"They talk so much about hell, but they never talk about saving poor people from the hell they are living in?" he scoffed. It was a profound thought that I was too tired to really appreciate.

"I don't know. Maybe they think the hell after you die is worse because it's forever. Just try and keep it down out here. I need to get some sleep," I said, turning around.

"Man," Michael said, turning off the TV in disgust. "Those guys should trying being hungry in the desert. That *feels* like forever."

* * *

The first week of August, the humid air was hanging thick with mosquitos. Michael and I sat on folding chairs on the wooden deck outside our second-floor apartment overlooking a parking lot full of cars. I was feverishly smoking a corncob pipe trying to keep the bugs at bay. "Are you sure there is no malaria here?" Michael said, swatting a mosquito on his forearm.

"I've literally *never* heard of *anyone* getting malaria in Minnesota," I said as billows of white smoke plumed from my mouth.

"Michael, do you know that you started snoring?"

"Oh, sorry about that, buddy," he said.

"No, it's not the noise, although it is pretty loud," I chuckled. "Michael, you've put on like *sixty pounds* in the last six months. You can't keep eating pizza and soda three meals a day." He wasn't big enough for someone to call him fat, but he was well on his way.

Michael looked down at his belly stretching the college t-shirt he was given as a welcome present a year ago. "You know being big is so good in Africa." He laughed shaking his roll. "I always wanted to be fat."

"Yeah, well, now you're in America, and you need to start eating smarter. You can't just eat everything you see or you're gonna have a heart attack or something."

He cleared his throat. "Okay, so here is the problem. It is a good suggestion. I am no longer in Africa and I need to eat *smart* as you say," his index finger touching his temple "but you know I've never cooked anything myself. Only women cook in my tribe. First my mother made me food and then my wife."

"You're married?!" I bolted upright, nearly dropping my pipe, shocked that he had never mentioned his wife.

"Oh yes. My wife Angelina and I have children too."

"You have KIDS!" I laughed in disbelief. "Like how many do you have?"

"Oh, man." He slapped his knee, leaning back in the metal folding chair. "You ask such tough questions!"

"Wait, why is that a tough question?" I laughed, exhaling another cloud of smoke into the florescent lit night.

"Okay, so let me explain something. Surely I told you before, in the villages we don't have bank accounts or stocks or retirement plans as you have here in America. We have cows and children. And that is pretty much it." He clapped his hands together. "And these are such tricky assets to manage. A cow can be stolen one day and then you steal it back and then it dies for no reason the day after. And as for our children, well raising a child is no small thing. New mothers are told not to name their babies until they are strong enough to walk, because about half our children die before the age of three. And the elders say it will only make it harder to handle if the child dies with a name."

We sat in silence for a long time. I thought about all the discussions I had heard between expecting parents as they carefully selected their unborn child's name. Their excited faces flickered through my memory. After a few minutes I remembered my initial question. "I still don't get it. Why is it hard for you to tell me how many kids you have?"

Michael looked at me. He had clearly been lost in his own thoughts. "Oh, asking a nomad how many children they have is like asking an American how much money they have in their bank account." He paused. "It is the measure of a man, and not a good thing to be asking."

"But you ask me how much money I have literally *all* the time."

"But you're not really a proper American." He smiled. I had no idea what he meant by that, but it sounded like a compliment.

"Neither are you," I said, patting his stomach.

He laughed. "Okay, I got you, buddy. I'll start eating *smarter*, as you say. Tomorrow I will go to the market and try and find some beans and rice to eat."

"Grocery store," I corrected him. "We don't have markets."

* * *

Two weeks after fall classes started up again, Michael missed his first shift at the cafeteria. I didn't realize this until I got back to the apartment to find him snoring on the couch with the BBC news blaring on the radio.

"Michael!" I shouted. His bloodshot eyes popped open. "What the hell, man? I vouched for you to get the cafeteria job and you skip without calling in?"

He sat up, rubbing his eyes. "Oh sorry, buddy, I wasn't feeling well. I didn't sleep much last night."

"Fine, whatever," I said, throwing my backpack on the floor.

"Just call the cafeteria if you're not coming in. And make sure you tell them you're sick."

"Right. Will do, sir," he said, saluting me before collapsing back onto the couch.

But Michael didn't show up to work the next day either. At the end of my shift, the manager pulled me into his office and explained that if Michael skipped another day, they were going to let him go. "I know he needs the money, but its three strikes you're out around here."

"I'll tell him," I said, trying to hide my own anger. "He doesn't know baseball, but I'll explain about missing work again."

Standing in the hallway outside our apartment, I could hear our TV through the door. I opened the door and saw Michael in his pajamas watching boxing and drinking a beer.

"Are you kidding me? Boxing? You missed work to watch boxing?" I shouted. "You're gonna get fired and then who's gonna pay for your food? Not me, that's for sure." I stood between Michael and the TV, my arms folded. "You didn't call," I shouted. "All you have to do is call."

Michael stood up, a flash of anger across his face. "You want to know why I stopped going to work?" he shouted back at me. He swallowed and I sensed he was trying to control the volume in his voice. "Why I sleep on the couch all day?"

"Yes, I do," I said, trying to suppress the anger in my own voice. Michael and I had never fought before but it felt a lot like when my dad and I went at it.

"Okay," he said, his finger on my chest. "Every night I go to sleep and have the same nightmare. I dream that I am in my cafeteria uniform." He pointed at the polo shirt on the floor. "And I go to the cafeteria garbage can and it's full of half-eaten food. Then I pick it up to take it outside to the trash." He paused and his voice faltered. "But when I walk out the back door of the kitchen, I am suddenly back in my village in Kenya." He collapsed into the couch and covered his eyes with his forearm. I stood across from him, speechless. "And I start shouting to the people from the nearby homesteads that I have enough food for everyone. I'm standing in the valley with a bag full of food that your people just throw away. And then a line starts to form, moms and their children with their pots and pans." He stopped for a second before looking up at me with watery eyes. "And they line up and I hand them the food from the garbage bag. I tell them to bring their friends because there is enough for everyone to eat, that I will bring another bag of food tomorrow. And then I wake up in the middle of the night covered in sweat. And I can't go back to sleep."

I stood there, thinking of all the times my mother told me to finish my meal and saying, "There are starving kids in Africa." I felt the guilt of

133

American privilege settle in my stomach. I had never missed a meal; I had never even considered eating out of the garbage.

Over lunch I had thrown away two pieces of pizza because the crust wasn't completely cooked.

"I'm sorry," I said, sitting cross-legged on the carpet in front of him. "But Michael, not going to work isn't the answer. If you get fired, then you probably won't be able to find another job on campus. And I can't keep paying for you."

Michael looked up at me. "I have five children," he said.

He threw open the curtain to his side of the living room and pulled out a red shoebox from under his bed. "I've been sending most of my paycheck back to Angelina." He dropped the shoebox full of wire transfer receipts in front of me. "She had to take our youngest kid to the hospital for malaria medication at the beginning of August. Then they had school fees due, then my brother texted me that my mom lost her cows to a Karamoja raid."

I picked through the box. At a glance I could see Michael had sent thousands of dollars just over the summer.

"Michael, why didn't you tell me about this stuff?" I looked at a receipt with the words "cows" and "medicine" written in pen at the top.

"I saw you crying at the Uganda movie. You had so much trouble handling it. So I didn't want to overwhelm you with more pressures."

I took a deep breath and I pulled out a long receipt. "This one says school fees for Chelimo. Now who's that?" I asked.

I watched Michael's shoulders slacken "That's my oldest daughter. She goes to a boarding school in Kampala." He took the receipt from me and sniffled. "Last week she won an award for being the smartest girl in her school."

12
ANOINTED TO PARLIAMENT

Michael started spending more and more time lying on his bed behind the curtain speaking in Pokot to his wife and whoever happened to be drinking tea with her in their living room back in Kenya. I'd sit on the couch doing homework, listening to him speak in a fatherly voice to his children, then he'd pause as the phone was passed, and switch to a serious voice I never heard him use any other time. Occasionally I'd catch an English word amid the sea of Pokot: "Books, helicopter, parliament, election."

When I asked him what he was talking about, he only gave a brief update on his kids. "Not so much," he'd say before telling me which of his kids had a big test coming up in school or who was sick with malaria. I never pressed him about the helicopter or the election. With five men sharing a two-bedroom apartment, our sanity required us to maintain the illusion of privacy.

It was nearing Thanksgiving when the first snow fell. It was too early for a Midwesterner to complain about the cold, but I could tell it was already getting to Michael. At breakfast he would stare down at the dead grass lining the apartment building and tell me the temperature in Kenya, and then repeat it to me again before we went to bed. At first I didn't think anything of it. It's normal for Minnesotans to compare weather. You might be shoveling snow and hear your neighbor shout from the next driveway, "You know, I got a cousin down in Florida and guess what the temp was down there?" Then you laugh and keep shoveling. But Michael didn't laugh after he told me the weather in Kenya.

He started dragging his feet. I hardly ever saw him studying. He stayed up late watching re-runs of classic sports games on cable, slept a few hours, and then drove the car Amanda gave him to get to campus early to clean professor's offices.

I suspected his affect had something to do with his late-night phone calls to Kenya. It had been over a year since he'd seen his family. Over the summer he had nonchalantly asked Amanda and me if we knew where we could find him $2,500 for a holiday flight to Kenya. We both shrugged and said we'd try to come up with something. That was our usual answer when he asked us for any amount over $50.

Amanda and I put our heads together. The weekend before Thanksgiving break, we invited Michael to Amanda's apartment. Michael knocked on Amanda's apartment door wearing a down jacket and a Russian rabbit-fur hat that one of our roommates had given him. Amanda answered the door in a bright-yellow-and-red African floral skirt wrapped around her waist, the smell of curry poured out of her apartment like a fog machine.

"Surprise!" she shouted at Michael as if it was his birthday. Michael smiled from under the rabbit-fur hat and stepped inside her apartment.

"Oh my goodness," he smiled wider.

Amanda and Emilie had spent the last week decorating the apartment with as much African culture as they could find on short notice. They covered the walls with bright fabrics with color combinations that Midwesterners relegate to children's books and kaleidoscopes.

Inside, a dozen students were sitting on the beige carpet drinking chai tea that they pumped from a flower print carafe. Michael walked around the party shaking everyone's hand, thanking them for the food and decorations and wonderful chai tea that tasted "just like my wife makes it." With a plate of curried chicken on his lap, he passed around a stack of photographs he kept in his backpack; always close by in case anyone wanted an impromptu lecture on growing up in Africa. He started with a dozen pictures of his family standing in front of his cement house with its rusting corrugated-tin roof, followed by grainy images of women from his village grinding corn and building huts, and finally men herding cows and sharpening spears. He narrated each picture with a short story about life in the villages or what his kids like to do with their free time.

One sophomore held up a picture of a tribesman in khaki pants, asking Michael about the "lingering effects of British culture on his tribe."

"Oh, yes, the British left quite a mark on us," Michael said offhandedly before issuing another round of compliments on the food. It was clear he didn't want to ruin his party discussing colonialism.

Emilie sat sipping tea in a papasan chair beside Michael, her legs crossed under a quilt as Michael pointed at a college picture of him standing beside his wife "...and Angelina's father asked me to pay him thirty cows for her. But I told him *no way*, that we were a modern Kenyan couple." After hearing about paying for brides, most of the feminists there would have launched into a diatribe about women's rights, but Emilie had grown up in a dozen different cultures and knew better.

"So did he still let you marry her?" she asked.

"That's a good question." Michael smiled. "I was able to convince him we were in love—and that I was broke."

Emilie laughed. "Well you made a good choice. She's very pretty."

"Yes, that's something that people say so much about women in this country," he said, pointing across the room at me. "Nathan is always going on about how women are *looking* at school." He laughed.

"Hey, hey, leave me out of it," I said, not wanting anyone from the Feminist Bible Study to overhear that I'd been rating women's physical appearance.

But Emilie brushed aside the comment. "So people don't say women are pretty in Pokot?" she asked.

"Well, not so much pretty as you say in this country," he said, pausing to think of how to explain the cultural difference. "Being pretty doesn't really get you very far in the desert. You need a *beautiful* woman, which is to say, a strong woman. Someone who will build the family houses and walk so many miles for water without needing to drink it all on the walk back and—" he paused. "It also takes a strong woman to birth a healthy child on the floor of a mud hut."

Emilie took a sip of chai. "Strong women. I like that," she said, winking at me.

Amanda stood up to make a speech. "Now, Michael, we have all really appreciated getting to know you." The room erupted in cheers. "And when we heard you were trying to go back to Kenya for the holidays, a bunch of us called our parents and asked them to use our Christmas money for your plane ticket. And we were able to raise the twenty-five hundred dollars," she sang in falsetto, hugging Michael and handing him an envelope.

"Praise the Lord," Michael said, staring in disbelief at the envelope. He looked up and smiled wider than I'd seen in months. "I want to say very much, thank you. Or as we say in Kenya, *Asanti Sana*."

Five weeks later, Michael was chewing goat fat and drinking boiled milk in Keu's homestead, the smell of burnt fur billowing from a smoking fire. Keu and a handful of village elders sat on short stools, each with a Cold War-era AK-47 resting between their leathery knees. Behind them, Michael's wife, Angelina, sat, legs crossed in a long floral dress and shoulder-length hair. Beside her were three of Keu's bald wives nursing their newborn infants.

"How did you get so fat?" one of the women asked, pointing at Michael's belly. A toothless old woman held her arms wide apart. "When you walked up the hill, we could not tell if you were coming or going." Everyone, including Angelina, burst out laughing.

"Actually, I am not so fat as the others in America," Michael said, shaking his belly. His answers were getting more and more creative, having spent the last week answering every stripe of question about life in America. He ordered three of Keu's older sons to stand side by side, their shoulder bones touching. "Once I saw a woman that big," Michael said, motioning around the three boys. The elders' eyes widened. "How big?" one of them asked.

"I am not joking," Michael smiled. "This big," he said, putting his arms around the three boys.

"You know, in America they have so much food that you cannot possibly eat it all. You can't just eat everything you see before you." He pointed at his eyes and at the steaming pile of goat meat at his feet. "You have to eat smart," pointing at his head.

"Eat smart?" Keu asked confused. If there had been a concept of eating smart in the desert, it would mean eating everything you could get your hands on.

"Yes, Keu. In America, they have so much water that the cows are as big as huts," Michael shouted, pointing at Keu's first wife's hut. "And the corn grows as tall as two men," Michael said, jumping as high as he could. "They even have so much food left at the end of the day, they take the meat and milk left over and put it in a hut that is always cold and save it for later. Because if they eat it now, they are afraid that they will eat so much they will die." At that the whole homestead electrified with excitement and suggestions started flying.

"How can you die from eating?" the toothless old lady shouted skeptically.

"If they are afraid of eating themselves to death, then they could give some to us!"

"We want a hut that keeps our food cold till the next day!"

"Maybe they can mate their cows with ours...so our calves will grow big as huts!" one of Keu's sons shouted, proud of his creativity.

Michael stood in front of the group listening as the homestead buzzed with anticipation. He listened to each new idea, not wanting to kill the mood with a long description of how electricity works and the problems with diverting Minnesota lakes through the Atlantic Ocean. After all the suggestions had been discussed, Keu stood up and motioned for silence, his long red robe and AK-47 slung over his muscular shoulders. "These are good suggestions. But it is not what we have gathered to discuss. But before we send the women and herdsboys off, we want to present you with a gift for your friends from America." The crowd cheered in agreement. "It is obvious from the size of your belly that they have taken good care of you. You have returned to us fatter than we could have ever imagined. So we want to give them a gift to say thank you for hosting you. And before you came we had agreed to send you back with a cow for your friends."

"Oee!" they shouted.

"But now that you have said that more food may be harmful to them, we are uncertain how to thank them," Keu said.

Kimpur stood up. "That is a tricky question," he said, stalling for time to think of something that would be useful to his American friends but small enough to fit in his luggage. "Give me a necklace and a belt made of beads and that will be good for them. Americans really like to dress themselves."

"Then it is decided," Keu shouted, pounding his staff into the dirt. "My wives will begin working on the beadwork today."

"Oee," the three bald women nodded.

"Now, thank you for coming to see our brother Kimpur," he said to the women and herdsboys who were gathered around. "But for the rest of the morning we have important matters to discuss and you have chores to do."

The women nodded as they wrapped their babies on their backs, collected their pots, and walked out of the thorn gate and down the path to the river. The young men shouldered their dark metal guns and whipped the cows down the path and into the valley for their morning grazing. Then the elders stood up and filed into Keu's hut, resting their weapons along the red mud wall, leaving Angelina alone near the fire sipping milk in her floral dress.

Inside Keu's hut, the elders sat packed so tight their knees nearly touched. Michael looked at their calloused feet and black rubber sandals cut from old car tires, the treading worn away, their toenails broken into jagged shapes.

"Museveni has declared war with the desert," Keu said. "That is why we have traded our spears and so many cows for guns." Museveni was the Ugandan Prime Minister who was known for a no-holds-barred approach to foreign policy, a strategy that had soaked East Africa in the blood of men, women, and child soldiers. Michael wasn't surprised to hear about the war. Over the last few months, Michael had been lying on his bed in Minnesota listening as the elders explained how Museveni had burned nomadic villages along the Ugandan border. Keu pointed to the row of automatic rifles resting in the sun just outside the doorway. "Museveni is a suspicious and arrogant man, who believes his soldiers are the only ones that deserve to have guns!" Keu pounded his walking staff into the ground.

"Oee," the elders responded, pounding their staffs and sending a cloud of red dust over their feet.

"Tell me the story," Michael responded. Keu had kept him up to date on the war, walking the five days across the desert to use Angelina's cell phone. But he asked Keu to tell him again. He didn't have time to explain how phones worked and he wanted the elders to know he had heard the entire story.

"It began when Museveni's soldiers held a meeting with some Karamoja elders," Keu began. "The soldiers demanded every villager in Uganda give up their guns." The elders shook their heads at Museveni's demands. "And the Karamoja elders explained that all the nomads in the desert had exchanged their spears for bullets, and without weapons to protect their cows, they would be robbed and surely starve. But Museveni's soldiers would not change their minds and an argument broke out and a young Karamoja man killed several of Museveni's soldiers." The elders again shook their heads at the impetuous young man who had taken the first life. Keu sighed, picking up his cup from the dirt floor and taking a long drink of milk before continuing. "The Karamoja elders knew Museveni would retaliate, and that the war could spill over into Pokot land. So the Karamoja elders sent a messenger to warn us. And the next day, we sent several herdsboys to the main road." Keu pointed towards the road Michael had driven the day before. "Where they traded so many of our cows for these guns."

"And then we prepared for war. Every day we sent out scouting parties as the women wrapped more and more thorns around our homesteads. And after the moon had gone round two times, some began to suspect that Museveni wasn't coming. But I woke up every morning and scanned the horizon." Keu's eyes scanned the faces of the elders. "I knew Museveni would not forget those who had killed his men. I know this as a man who has killed so many." He lifted his robe to reveal hundreds of nyura scars along his torso, atoning cuts for the human blood Keu had himself spilled. "And one day as I sat by the morning fire, my youngest wife heard a rumbling echoing off the hills. We agreed it wasn't a helicopter, or a truck, or a stampede of cows. So I grabbed my gun and ran out of the homestead in the direction of the main road to see if it was some kind of vehicle coming towards us. But before I got to the road, fire started raining from the sky."

Keu clenched his fist. "All the villagers grabbed their guns and began shooting at the vehicle. But our bullets couldn't stop it. It had a long snout like an elephant and it kept shooting fire. But it didn't travel on roads like the other trucks; it could drive over trees and bushes. It went up and over our thorn fence as if it was made of sand. The women and children ran up the mountain and hid among the rocks as our men shot every bullet we had. But nothing could stop it. Soon, choppers were in the sky shooting down at us from above." Keu's voice faltered, and he stopped.

The elders sat sipping their milk, waiting for Keu to compose himself. But after a long silence, Keu stood up and walked out of the hut. Another elder finished telling Michael that the death toll had reached one hundred and many were women and children. For the rest of the morning, they sat in the hut thinking of those who had lost their lives. As the sun moved into the afternoon sky, they heard the cheerful songs of women returning with water, and the elders left the hut, relieved to rejoin their sisters and wives around the cooking fire. But as they sang and danced, Michael felt the weight of the war heavy on his shoulders, sensing that he would be called upon to broker peace between Museveni and the desert.

The next morning, Keu's eight wives were running across the homestead, milking dozens of camels and fanning the glowing embers below boiling pots of porridge. His first wife ordered around the other seven, as people from across the surrounding valleys walked up the mountain and sat down in Keu's homestead. A werkoyon had been summoned for a prophecy and, as his apprentice threw sticks on a roaring fire, the werkoyon picked through Keu's goat pen to find a worthy sacrifice for Tororot.

After the last of the porridge had been ladled out, Keu stood up. "I called this meeting because we are in need of a new leader in our fight against Museveni."

"Oee," the crowd shouted.

"As many of you know, my cousin Potea did not return to bury those who died."

The elders shook their heads in disgusted agreement.

Keu's cousin Potea was the Pokot representative to Kenyan parliament, although even Keu was unsure what the parliament was or how his cousin had gotten there. The elders' best guess was that there was an elder council outside the desert and Potea was the representative for their tribe. But the details of western-style elections, budgets, and constitutional democracy were still unknown to them. And Keu's cousin Potea capitalized on their ignorance.

Like Michael, Potea had been a sponsor child. He went to elementary school in a small city in Uganda. An American family sent $30 a month for Potea's pencils and paper, beans and rice. After graduating from high school, Potea studied politics alongside Michael at the college in Nairobi.

But unlike Michael, who returned to serve as the principal at Kiwawa, Potea returned seeking approval from the elders to serve in the Kenyan parliament.

Michael had watched as Potea promised the elders he would dig wells and bring food trucks during famines. Even after Michael tried to explain the concept of elections and representative democracy, the elders were still confused. But they agreed that more wells and food trucks were needed, so they put an X next to Potea's name on a long sheet of paper.

But Potea's name, like so many nomads, was not originally Potea. That was a name he earned over the last fifteen years. After the second rainy season, Potea stopped returning to the desert to ask for guidance from the elders and he never delivered any of the wells he promised. So the elders had begun to call Keu's cousin *Potea*, which means *the one who disappeared*. And every few years, just when the Pokot began to suspect Potea had died, he would land his new helicopter on top of Keu's mountain and hand out bags of food to whoever agreed to put an X by his name on a piece of paper.

Michael was the only one who really understood where Potea was or what he was doing. Michael followed Potea's political career closely and learned that Potea had become a very wealthy businessman, and upon further research he learned why. Potea was pocketing all the money that the Kenyan government gave him. Each year, the Kenyan government set aside millions of dollars for Potea to build roads, schools, hospitals, and to dig wells. But by the end of the year, all the money vanished into Potea's increasingly substantial portfolio. Potea's largest asset was a new helicopter he had purchased for campaigning. By the time politicians and journalists realized Potea was skimming from the top, middle, and bottom, he was already rich enough to buy their silence. Meanwhile the elders roamed in the desert, oblivious to the ways and means of their "elected" official.

But after war broke out and Potea did not return, it was decided that they would no longer put their X beside his name. So Keu was once again called upon to rally the troops. "Potea did not come home after the war with Museveni," he shouted to hundreds of men and women who had gathered for the meeting.

"Oee," they shouted like soldiers on the eve of battle.

"He did not honor those who died!"

"Oee!"

"He did not use his helicopter to defend our women and our children!"

"Oee!"

"So it is time to choose a new leader!"

"I knew at that moment what was going to happen," Michael told me several weeks later. We were sitting on the floor of our apartment, a box of pizza between us. "It was like Saul and David. Their blessing was taken from Potea and I was to be anointed to be the parliamentarian for Pokot. I tried to explain that I was living so far away in America, that I was a student with no money. But they wouldn't listen. I pleaded with them to choose someone else. But they insisted that I surpass Potea." He sighed. "After hours of discussion, I could see they didn't understand that it took so much money to run a campaign. Nor did they comprehend elections and voting. They just believed that they had anointed me, and that was it," he said, clapping his hands together.

After Michael made his case, the elders called the werkoyon to speak. Throughout the day, he and his apprentice had been squatting silently over the roasted goat carcass, seemingly oblivious to the heated political debate happening behind them, quietly cutting the goat into small pieces as his apprentice handed out handfuls of grey muscle.

After everyone had been served, the werkoyon pulled the translucent intestines out of its splayed open stomach, and unraveling the wet organs like a scroll, patiently ran his fingers up and down the fatty tissue. Michael sat slowly chewing a piece of the roasted goat, hoping the werkoyon would find some reason why God didn't want him to run.

And as the sun set, the werkoyon stood up and motioned for silence. "Tororot is pleased by you choosing Kimpur," he shouted. And with that Michael's fate was sealed.

"Oee!" the elders shouted back.

"He would be a good leader for our people."

"Oee!"

"But I see that there is someone sitting on his head," the werkoyon said, his long, blood-covered index finger pointing at Michael. "I see that someone is sitting on you." The werkoyon paused, going back to the intestines. "On your head," he repeated to himself as if lost in a daze. "Sitting on your head," the werkoyon mumbled to himself as his fingers ran along the goat's vital organs. It was common for the werkoyon to speak in images and metaphors, leaving the work of deciphering their meanings to the people.

Ideas started flying. "Maybe someone has placed a curse on Kimpur."

"Who would do that?"

Werkoyon and assistant preparing a goat for a prophecy

"Maybe Kimpur has the fever, making him sweat from his head."

"It is Potea who will step on his head," Keu shouted, standing up to be heard over the crowd.

"I know my cousin and he will not give up power. He has disregarded the elders before and he will do it again." He pounded his staff. "That is why we must assign our best men to protect Kimpur."

"Oee," the group agreed, pounding their staffs and sending a cloud of red dirt into the air. Several young warriors stood up, agreeing to accompany Michael all the way back to the farthest mountain.

"I felt like Moses being asked to succeed Pharaoh," Michael told me after he had stress-eaten half a pizza. He sounded as if he had already lost the election. "I have no money and Potea has millions of dollars. Each year the government gives Potea money to build roads and dig wells in the desert. But he spends that money on houses and gas for his helicopter." He looked at me with desperate eyes. "I mean, how could I have explained that to them?"

"I don't know," I said, picking up another slice of pizza. We sat there chewing in silence for a few minutes as the absurdity of the situation sunk in. The campus janitor who slept behind a curtain in my living room was running for Kenyan parliament. "So what did you say to the elders?"

"What could I say?" he sighed, walking to the kitchen. "When the elder council decides, then it is decided."

"So you're running for parliament?" I asked. I paused trying to think of something helpful to say. "You can use our living room as your campaign headquarters." Michael walked back into the living room with a beer in his hand.

"Yep," Michael said, grabbing the remote and turning on the TV. "That would really be something," he said, taking a long drink.

13
PROPHETS AND POLITICIANS

As the January snow piled up around campus, I took notes on the Prophet Isaiah. The professor, a tall, thin man with large hands, was explaining the complex relationship between God, the ancient Israelite prophets, and the kings of Israel. I looked around the windowless cinderblock classroom. At every desk, a future pastor sat jotting down every word the professor said. I had signed up for Professor Short's History of Israel class on Amanda's recommendation. "He can speak five extinct languages—and wait for it—," she smiled, mouth open wide: "He got his PhD studying under biblical scholars who don't believe in supernatural events!" She made it sound like it was some sort of special certificate.

It was my final Bible course for my theology degree, a major that was originally supposed to tee me up nicely for seminary but now served as the last remaining vestige of my former career path. Lots of my ex-Christian friends had started as theology majors. But semester by semester they switched to philosophy, art, literature, or any major where they could ignore the subjects of the Lord.

But I knew switching majors would eventually lead to my dad finding out I wasn't a Christian, and that I needed him to pay for another year of college so I could study philosophy. My junior year, I had told Mom I was reading *The Communist Manifesto* in my philosophy class.

"I didn't know this, but Marx was actually one of the first proponents of quality public education," I said. Word by word, I saw her motherly, supportive smile fade into thinly veiled discomfort. "...and he advocated for workers who were often exploited in modern society." I realized I should have told her about the report I was writing on Hamlet.

"Oh, that's interesting," she said, with Midwestern skepticism.

On Monday my philosophy professor called me into his closet-sized office and handed me a sheet of paper. "Can you tell me what this is all about?" he said, angrily rubbing his thinning white hair.

Dear Professor,

I am paying twice the price of a secular university for my son to get a Christian Education. And I am not pleased to hear that he was assigned Karl Marx as MANDATORY reading in his Philosophy course. It is common knowledge that he was an atheist. My son is a very impressionable young man and he doesn't need to be studying Socialism.

Sincerely,
Michael Roberts
Sales and Marketing Coordinator

My face was a deep shade of purple by the time I looked up from the page. "I'm sorry, Professor," I pleaded. "*Please* don't allow this misunderstanding to affect my grade."

My father had also made it clear he was cutting off all financial support if I got a "C" in any class. I left the office casting out any hope of being a philosophy major and I resigned myself to graduating with a theology degree.

I was sitting in the back of Professor Short's class lazily drawing the Hebrew symbols he had written on the chalkboard: King, God, Israel. But when I got to the Hebrew word for prophet, I stopped. I had always thought of prophecy as bearded men in robes, standing in stone throne rooms reading from dusty scrolls. But when I drew the word prophet, I was lost in Keu's homestead, smoke billowing out of a dozen mud huts. The werkoyon was hunched over the charred goat, his hands soaked in blood, the intestines splayed out on the ground. Michael was sitting by the fire anxiously chewing goat meat. By the time I snapped out of my daydream, the lecture was over.

I packed up my things and drove back to the apartment. Michael was there, watching TV on the floor in his janitor's uniform. He was slouched against the couch, a six pack of beer resting against his thigh with two empty bottles rolling around his feet.

"How was work?" I asked, picking up the bottles and tossing them in the recycling. I was in the habit of asking him about work every day, just to make sure he went.

"Fine," he said opening another beer.

"So you finally warmed up to the taste of beer," I joked. He had had the occasional drink with me as we watched the late-night news, but this was the first time he had bought some.

"You know, I never had beer before I came here," he said, looking at the label. "Beer is a western thing and we don't have it in the desert. And in the city I never tried it. I didn't have friends who drank."

"How's the campaign going?" I asked. After he was nominated to run for parliament, I was expecting our apartment to turn into a bustling hotbed of East African politics, our living room full of Kenyans in suits and ties shouting in a dozen languages, and each wall lined with desks and matching green lamps. I imagined posters blocking the windows reading "Kimpur 2007" with Swahili catchphrases.

But since he had returned from Kenya, he was like a ghost of his former self. He wandered around the apartment in a white t-shirt and boxers, nervously answering his cell phone, shouting at someone in Pokot for twenty minutes, then lying on his bed with his head in his hands. Occasionally he'd ask me if this or that person we knew would be willing to give him some money for his campaign. I told him I didn't think it was legal for Americans to make campaign contributions to African politicians.

"What if they are friends with the African politician?" Michael asked, sounding more and more desperate by the day. When he wasn't talking to someone in Pokot, he was watching sports, eating pizza, and drinking cheap beer late into the night. I knew he wasn't sleeping much because our roommates had stopped complaining about his raucous snoring.

That night, Michael and I sat on the floor watching a heavyweight boxing match. I remembered Professor Short's lecture on the Prophet Isaiah.

"Michael, I've been thinking about the werkoyon's prophecy, about Potea sitting on your head. Because I'm taking this class on ancient Israel and we were talking about the prophecies of Isaiah—" I paused, not sure how to phrase my question.

Michael turned off the TV and sat up for the first time since I got home. Teaching me about traditional Pokot culture seemed to be the only thing that distracted him from the election. Having spent the better part of his life in a classroom, it was clear that he was more comfortable teaching than campaigning. "Okay, go ahead. I'm familiar with the Prophet Isaiah."

"So do you think that prophets can actually predict the future? Like Isaiah predicting the fall of Jerusalem?" I asked.

"Okay, that is a good question, buddy." He began pacing in front of me, looking as authoritative as a man can in a white t-shirt and boxers. "Now in America, I can see you don't have so much of these types of people," he said in his teacher voice. "So they might seem a little bit weird. But in Pokot the werkoyon get so many prophecies from God. It is so normal that people are not suspicious of it." It was clear he thought Isaiah and the werkoyon were cut from the same cloth.

"So you think that God actually speaks to the werkoyon?" I asked.

"Why not?" he snapped back, offended. "In fact, even that *question* is colonialism," he said waving his index finger at me as if I were a child who needed to be set straight. "You know so many missionaries are always telling us to stop reading the intestines, calling it witchcraft or devil something or other. But they don't know the first thing about reading intestines." Michael stopped pacing and pointed to heaven. "The Buffalo clans of Pokot are visited by the angels and even God himself. Listen, when I was a small boy, we had an old prophet living in our village. So I grew up hearing so many prophecies. And one night I remember so clearly. A Turkana village had been built close on a nearby mountain. But our scouts didn't find them there. And that night the werkoyon had a dream where he was visited by an angel from God who said, 'Wake up, the Turkana are coming!' So the old man ran out of his bed and woke everyone in our homesteads, shouting 'The Turkana are coming!'"

Michael cupped his hands to his mouth as if he was sounding the alarm. "And so we ran to the bushes. A few moments later, we watched as Turkana men silently snuck through the gate with spears and they went right into our huts," Michael smiled. "But our beds were empty."

I had grown up hearing about traveling faith healers pulling people out of wheelchairs and I had watched televangelists explain how earthquakes were a result of America's sin. But Michael's story seemed more immediate, more Old Testament.

"Prophets are a different kind of people," Michael continued. "Some throw shoes in the air and read the words of God by the way they fall, others read intestines, or see visions in dreams. But the Pokot are no strangers to God." With that, he sat down, assuming he had proven his point.

"What about the drought when you were a boy, when the prophets told everyone to offer goats because of your village's sins? I mean, it was just a drought, that's how weather works in the desert," I said cautiously, hoping that discussing his childhood trauma wasn't crossing the line.

Michael took a deep breath. "Before that one, there was three months of drought. And I saw a prophet pray as three girls poured water on their heads as a rain dance to God. The entire village was gathered, singing and praying for rain." He paused. "And you know what?"

"What?"

"Before we finished praying, the rain began to fall."

He grabbed the TV remote but paused before turning it on. "Okay, let me say it this way, when the Pokot pray, God listens. And God responds in the language of shoes or intestines or rain or whatever language the people use."

I wanted to believe him. It wasn't that I didn't trust him. It was clear Michael really believed what he was saying. But I couldn't believe. I had lost my faith in prophecies, miracles, heaven, and hell.

"So you actually believe the werkoyon's prophecy is a real message from God, that God is trying to tell you someone is stepping on your head?"

"Unfortunately, yes," he sighed, turning the TV back on.

* * *

In January 2006, the president of our college called my name and I walked across the campus chapel stage to receive my diploma. My father clapped as I shook hands with the president, not yet realizing that he paid the equivalent of a summer home for his son to become an agnostic theologian.

The week after my graduation my dad flew the family to Naples, Florida, to celebrate. For seven days we crisscrossed our way through miles of golf courses, canals, and ocean-themed restaurants, the windows up, the air conditioning at full tilt. On day three, I was in the back seat with my brother, who was looking out the window pretending to ignore the discussion between Dad and me.

"So what's next for the big graduate?" he said, adjusting the mirror to look back at me. "Any ministries that you think would be a good fit for you?"

"Ministry" was quickly becoming my least-favorite word. The Feminists call it development, human rights, activism—anything but ministry.

"Yeah, I guess I'm just decompressing from school. I was thinking of just getting a coffee-shop job until the right fit came along."

"Oh, that's sounds like a good plan, honey," Mom jumped in before Dad could respond.

"Well, okay I can see that," Dad said, sipping a hazelnut latte. He was always more amiable on vacation. Having a dozen bosses yelling at him for eight hours a day got him wound pretty tight. "But keep your eyes open," he said, his eyebrows slanted. "I didn't pay $100,000 for you to serve coffee..." We all sensed he was about to launch into a speech.

"Okay! We got the point," my brother shouted, exasperated at having already sat through dozens of lectures on how much my tuition cost. We drove the rest of the way to the Everglades wildlife refuge in silence. Mom had planned for us to spend the day on a walking tour of the swamp, a decision she regretted after we pulled into a parking lot with hundreds of human-size alligators sunbathing on the sidewalk like homeless people.

"Where are the other animals?" my mother asked the tour guide, leaving a wide berth between her and the lizards. The tour guide explained that the reptiles and pythons had eaten most of the cute and fuzzy ground-dwelling creatures that Midwestern folks like my mother associate with the great outdoors. For the next hour, my brother pondered whether the prehistoric creatures were crocodiles or alligators, while my father attempted to investigate their teeth by poking them with sticks.

I spent the afternoon talking on the phone, trying to figure out how to get Michael and me on a plane to Washington, D.C. We had recently been invited as student guests to the National Prayer Breakfast. From the website, it seemed like a fraternity for Christian politicians. And the Prayer Breakfast seemed like their prom, a weekend gala where leaders from around the world sat around and discussed faith and politics over eggs and toast.

"Bono from U2 is scheduled to be the keynote speaker, and he's on such an African kick right now I thought that you and Michael should come on out to the Prayer Breakfast," a college friend turned Prayer Breakfast intern told me over the phone. "If you two can handle the plane tickets, the Prayer Breakfast will cover everything else." I leapt at the first real bit of help I could provide Michael's campaign.

"Hey, Nathan," my dad shouted at me as he leaned over a crocodile. "Hey, Nathan! You dare me to touch it?" he laughed. I looked at the six-foot crocodile splayed out in front of him, clearly not intimidated by my dad.

"Dad, not now," I shouted back. "I've got to make another phone call." I walked around the corner onto a wooden bridge. Sinewy trees grew out of the dark water on either side. I punched in the numbers and waited for Michael to pick up the phone in our apartment.

"Michael," I said. "Good news for your campaign! We got invited to Washington, D.C. to go to an international meeting of leaders called the Prayer Breakfast."

"Oh, man," Michael said. "That is really something. You know Potea is a member of the Prayer Breakfast in Kenya, and in fact he will be there. I am sure of it."

"Wait. How is Potea a member?" I said incredulously. It seemed absurd to believe that two sponsor children from a remote corner of the earth could both be entwined in the same international fraternity.

"Potea is always talking about how he is such a Christian. How he always hangs out with friends of President Bush at the Prayer Breakfast," Michael scoffed. "In fact, just a short while ago, Potea gave a speech in the Kenyan House of Parliament about how his *faith* was *strengthened* by his involvement in the Prayer Breakfast. And the parliamentarian from another

Pokot district was so enraged he stood up and began shouting at Potea. He cut into the middle of Potea's speech, and shouted to the whole Kenyan parliament: 'Does anyone want to know what the devil looks like? He's speaking to you right now.'" Michael chuckled. "It was really something. The police had to escort the Pokot man out of the building because he wouldn't stop shouting curses down on Potea."

"So do you still want to go?" I said, not sure what he was getting at.

"What are you talking about?" Michael exclaimed. "This is the breakthrough we have been praying for! I will meet Potea at the Washington Prayer Breakfast and show him that he can't be standing on my head any longer!"

"Can you find the money for the plane ticket?" I asked. I hated being the practical one, but Michael was continually forcing me into it. I had grown up hearing my mom say "and how are we gonna pay for *that*?" every time my father came home excited to show us the new, as-seen-on-TV gadget he had bought. "It was on clearance, honey," he'd say, looking down at his new toy.

"What about your parents?" Michael asked.

"They just finished paying for your dental work," I reminded him. Mom had spent the last month driving Michael downtown to the University of Minnesota where a dozen grad students had taken turns filling a lifetime of cavities. It had taken twice as long because one student insisted on documenting their work for a paper on the effects of traditional life on oral hygiene.

"Well, God got us this far and He will get us to Washington, D.C.," Michael said.

As a child I heard people say that a lot, as if God would reach down from heaven and destroy the cancer or magically add two zeroes to someone's bank account. But I had begun to realize that when Michael said "God will provide," he really meant "somebody will eventually agree to pay for my ticket."

And sure enough, someone did, and the next week Michael and I were sharing a queen-size bed at the Washington, D.C. Hilton. Michael stared into the closet mirror wearing my father's best navy-blue pin-striped suit.

"It tastes like dirt," Michael chuckled to himself. "Oh man, your brother is so funny," he said, still laughing about the dinner he had at my parents' house before we left.

Michael had offered to make a Kenyan meal as a thank you for paying for his dental work and a celebration of my graduation. I had tried to warn him about my dad on the ride over. "Now Michael, my dad can be a bit hard on people."

Michael gave me a knowing glance. Then he pulled up his pant leg and showed me a three-inch scar left from a stick, "No worries," he said, "My father used to beat me for losing cows."

"No, he never beat me or anything," I said, suddenly feeling embarrassed that I'd brought it up. "He just criticizes me sometimes."

Michael's knowing look broke into a smile. "Oh, well, that's what a good father does to their first-born. It is a way of making sure you stay on the right path."

Michael spent the afternoon in my parents' kitchen taking turns with my brother, Kellen, stirring cornmeal. Steam billowed out of deep pots, turning the entire first floor into a sweat lodge. Then the solid brick of cornmeal was put on a serving dish and topped with a ladle of boiled African greens. The result was a ten-pound dish that looked like sod after a heavy rainfall.

"It tastes like dirt," my brother said, disappointed by the fruits of his labor.

"Kellen!" my mother shouted.

"Oh, man," Michael exploded in laughter, his head rolling back as he gasped for breath. My brother blushed. He was now a freshman at our college, and unsure why Michael was laughing. "Oh, maaaaan," Michael shouted, letting out a final laugh from the pit of his stomach. "No one has ever thought to say that. But you are exactly right! This food tastes exactly like dirt." He pounded the table with delight before swallowing another bite. The rest of my family chuckled along, the way Midwesterners do when they see something they don't quite understand.

"So what are you planning on wearing to the Prayer Breakfast?" my dad asked Michael, hoping to steer the conversation away from Kellen's comment.

"We're gonna swing by the thrift store to pick up suits," I said, having decided that wearing used suits was some kind of political statement.

"You can't wear a thrift-store suit to a dinner with the President," my dad scoffed dismissively.

"Mike, it's *his* thing. He can wear whatever he wants," my mom cut in.

"Mr. Kimpur? Do you want to run for parliament in a thrift-store suit?" he said, trying to reason with Michael in his man-to-man voice. "Why don't you try one of my suits on?"

My dad got up from the table and led Michael into my parents' bedroom. From the dining room, I could hear him slide open the door to the closet. Dad always kept his expensive new suits on the right side. On the left side there was an assortment of suits from the eighties that no longer fit him or the company he worked for. "Take any one you want," he said, his hand surveying the left side of his closet. Michael stood for a moment scanning the options before reaching in and pulling out my father's brand-new navy pinstriped suit, which my mother had hung on the wrong side of his closet. Ever a man of his word, my dad let Michael try on his brand-new suit. As Michael exited the bathroom, my dad said in quiet disbelief, "We are *exactly* the same size."

It was this pinstriped suit that Michael wore when we ran into Potea in the lobby of the D.C. Hilton the morning of the Prayer Breakfast. "There he is," Michael said, pointing at a tall well-built African man flanked on either side by shorter middle-aged white men.

"Who's he with?"

"Those are President Bush's top men for African development. In fact, he is friends with *so* many people from Bush's administration. I took the one on the left on a safari to Pokot back in the nineties. But since then he has been hanging around with Potea," Michael said as we approached them. Potea stood in front of us, towering over Michael. Potea smiled wide, with large white teeth, and shook his hand. I don't know what I expected to happen when they met, but a casual handshake, smile, and a few words in Pokot felt underwhelming.

"What did he say?" I asked Michael as we walked away.

Michael walked briskly across the lobby until we were out of earshot of Potea and the other men. "Potea said he heard a rumor that the elders nominated me to replace him. And that he has a helicopter and a million dollars to make sure I don't win."

"Really? His voice sounded so nice."

"That's because he said it in a very nice tone," Michael scoffed as we walked through the double doors and into the hotel's faux-Victorian banquet hall. We were seated at a white-linen-covered table with three older couples speaking in southern accents about this or that business they ran according to *Christ-i-an* values. Michael and I ate our bacon and eggs in silence as we waited for the twenty-by-twenty-foot screen to begin projecting speeches from the head table located in an adjacent banquet hall. The screen lit up showing President Bush at a long table between King Abdullah of Jordan and Bono. After an opening prayer, Bono stepped up to the podium to speak, his bright orange sunglasses and long, slick black hair complementing his smug grin.

"This guy is a rock star who raises money for Africa," I whispered to Michael.

"Like Bob Marley?"

"Kinda, but not really."

Bono spoke in a lyrical Irish rhythm, punctuating each line with a brief poetic pause. "If you're wondering what I'm doing here, at a prayer breakfast, well, so am I. I'm certainly not here as a man of the cloth, unless that cloth is leather. It's certainly not because I'm a rock star. Which leaves one possible explanation: I'm here because I've got a messianic complex. Yes, it's true. And for anyone who knows me, it's hardly a revelation."

Everyone laughed, and Michael leaned towards me. Michael always wants to understand why people are laughing, so I usually spend however long it takes to explain the joke.

"A messianic complex means that you want to save people, like a messiah," I whispered. "But you mostly do it so other people will think you're a good person." It was the best definition I could come up with in ten seconds.

"Oh man," Michael chuckled. "That is what white people are so fond of doing in Africa."

I turned back to Bono's speech. "Look, whatever thoughts you have about God, who he is or if he exists, most will agree that if there is a God, He has a special place for the poor. In fact, the poor are where God lives. Check Judaism. Check Islam. Check pretty much anyone."

"Check Pokot," Michael nodded to me.

"I mean, God may well be with us in our mansions on the hill... I hope so. He may well be with us as in all manner of controversial stuff... maybe, maybe not... But the one thing we can all agree, all faiths and ideologies, is that God is with the vulnerable and poor. God is in the slums, in the cardboard boxes where the poor play house... God is in the silence of a mother who has infected her child with a virus that will end both their lives... God is in the cries heard under the rubble of war... God is in the debris of wasted opportunity and lives, and God is with us if we are with them."

"That is true, by the way," Michael said, clapping along as the room erupted in applause, "God is with us if we are with the poor."

After the speech, we were led upstairs, through a door with a sign that said "Africa," into a small banquet room. Inside, two dozen politicians and wealthy businessmen from across the continent stood around discussing public policy over coffee and cookies. For the next two hours, I stood by watching Potea make small talk with nearly every African dignitary, as if they were all old friends. Michael on the other hand, spent the afternoon on a floral-print couch telling stories to the dignitaries' wives, sending the plump African women into a fit of laugher every few minutes.

I watched the men move slowly around the room, their short controlled laughter, a look of feigned interest on most of their faces. I wondered which of them had grown up in mud huts like Michael and which had been groomed for power by their wealthy parents. As Potea sipped his coffee from a porcelain cup, I imagined his childhood photo hanging on some American family's refrigerator. They had sent $30 a month for years so he could go to school. And now, thirty years later, their sponsor child was the most powerful man in his tribe, spending his days building mansions and buying helicopters with money that was designated for schools and wells.

That night Michael and I stood side by side in our sweaty t-shirts and boxers brushing our teeth, our suits hanging on the bathroom door hook. "So how was talking to the most powerful wives in Africa?" I asked Michael through the mirror.

"In fact, they are such funny ladies. How they could be married to such men is a tragedy," he said, spitting white minty foam into the sink.

It was clear he was not impressed by the collection of African politicians assembled for the Prayer Breakfast. I had argued that it was the worst politicians who needed to hear Bono's message the most. But he brushed it aside. "They have heard that message one hundred million times from every man, woman, and child in Africa," he scoffed. "And if they won't listen to their own people, they won't listen to Bono. But they will smile for the camera or for Bush or whoever is handing out money that day."

Michael grabbed a bottle of lotion out of his toiletries and squeezed a dot onto his hand. He pointed a finger at me: "If being called the devil before all of Kenya didn't affect Potea, Bono's speech is not likely to change him."

Hearing the contempt in Michael's voice for Potea, I realized I didn't want any secrets that Michael could hold against me. I spit my toothpaste into the sink. "Michael, I probably should have told you this a while ago. But I'm not actually a Christian," I said to his reflection in the mirror, too ashamed to make direct eye contact. Michael's eyebrows bent far enough to fold the dark skin between his eyes. "I know I should have told you before. But I'm what people in the west call an agnostic, which means I don't actually know if there is or isn't a God."

I paused, waiting for Michael to tell me how disappointed he was, how I should have never gone to Greece, how liberal philosophy was rotting my soul, how it was gonna break my poor mother's heart when she found out. But all he said was, "Okay, go on, I'm listening." He hardly seemed phased.

"Okay, well," I said, trying to regain my verbal footing. I hadn't expected our conversation to make it past the word "agnostic." "So the problem is I used to hear Jesus' voice answer me when I prayed."

"Like the Buffalo Clan of Pokot," Michael smiled. "In fact, maybe you are a distant relative of them."

"Probably not," I sighed. "But anyway, two years ago I stopped hearing Jesus answering my prayers, and when he stopped talking to me, I started to think that maybe I was just talking to myself the whole time." I stared at the porcelain sink still waiting for him to change direction and launch into an "Oh ye of little faith" lecture.

I felt his hand on my back, "I don't think you are so faithless as you suggest."

I looked up and saw Michael's understanding smile in the mirror.

"You are a good person. And you live with so much Christian love for people. That's why you cried when you saw those kids suffering in Uganda. And why you let me live in your apartment when there was so little room you had to hang a sheet from the ceiling. I have known so many Christians who are less Christian than you." He paused, thinking. "But as for hearing the voice of God, that is quite a thing to be doing. In fact in Pokot it is really something to hear the voice of God. Most people never once hear a message from Tororot. That is reserved for people like Moses. And in Pokot we have the Buffalo clan who as children are taught to read the intestines, or throw shoes, or interpret dreams." Michael turned and looked directly at me. "If you never hear God's voice that is not so much a problem as you may think. That pretty much makes you just like the rest of us."

I wanted to hug him as two years of repressed tears lined my eyes. Michael turned back to the mirror and opened his mouth wide, examining his teeth to make sure all the new silver fillings were still sparkling. Then he patted me on the shoulder "We are all just trying to do our best, praying, and waiting for something to happen." He walked past me and sat on the edge of the bed to polish his black leather shoes with a massive brush. I sat down next to him and turned on the TV.

After twenty minutes, Michael muted the TV and sighed without turning towards me. "Nathan, when I was in the airplane flying to America, I was so scared." His voice sounded distant as if he was reliving a memory in his mind. "I had already gone farther than I ever imagined, from sleeping in a mud hut to studying in Kiwawa to college in the capital city of Kenya. And now I was heading to a place called Minnesota on the other side of the world." He turned around to look at me, putting his hand on my sock-covered foot. "I prayed that God would send me an American to show me how to survive. And I never heard a yes or no from him. But when I met you in the cafeteria, I knew right away that God himself had picked you to help me." He squeezed my foot and unmuted the TV.

14
PARENTS ARE PEOPLE TOO

Two hard years after we got back from Washington, D.C., I was standing in line at a Mexican restaurant, thirty pounds overweight, dark circles hanging under my eyes. I stared down at a burrito wrapped in shiny aluminum foil. On the other side of the serving line, a Latina was sweating under a florescent light, her fingers tapping the stainless-steel buffet table, waiting as I slowly chose each ingredient. The anti-depressants coursing through my veins had a way of making everything slower. As I pointed at the beans, white rice, and onions, I remembered all the times I had been to this restaurant with Michael. The roasted chicken with rice, beans, and veggies was the closest thing to traditional Kenyan food within a ten-mile radius of campus. I watched the woman as she piled beans, rice, and salted chicken until it I was sure the tortilla would burst under the pressure.

A smile broke through the fog of depression. I imagined Michael back in his cement house on the edge of the Kenyan desert. He was probably sipping tea listening to the BBC with a dozen rural Kenyan farmers, most of whom had probably never traveled more than a dozen miles from their homes. I pictured the old men in dusty tweed jackets and ripped polo shirts nodding along, eager to hear stories from Michael's travels to America, a land they had heard was flowing with milk and honey.

The woman slid my pile of carbs down the steel counter, stopping in front of the lettuce and cheese. "And this one?" she asked.

I nodded. That's when I felt my stomach roll over, sweat soaking my armpits. *They don't have lettuce and cheese in Kenya*, I thought. It didn't take much to set me off. I was walking an emotional tightrope through each day, the slightest emotional breeze sending me tumbling. I watched her grab a handful of greens and shredded cheese. I took three deep breaths, hoping she wouldn't hear me and misinterpret my early-onset panic attack as customer dissatisfaction.

By the release of the third breath, my mind was already racing with images of half-naked children running around thatched huts, thirty kindergarteners with bloated bellies standing outside Michael's cement house shaking their heads at me. I watched her wrapping the ingredients in aluminum foil, like a mother changing a diaper for the thousandth time.

I paid for the burrito and sat in the chair between Brad and Kellen. They were in charge of taking care of me. I couldn't go anywhere without someone who could drive me home if I broke down, which was a weekly occurrence. My heart was racing as I picked up the burrito. I could feel sweat gathering on the edges of my hairline. I took several shallow gulps of air. By my first bite, I was already in the middle of a full-blown panic attack.

I can't live like this. I can't even eat in public without sweating through my shirt, I thought. My next thought was. *Does "I can't live like this" count as a suicidal tendency?* I was completely incapable of answering that question in my current state. I called my therapist.

"I gotta make a phone call," I said to my brother louder than I meant to. I stood up and felt the blood drain from my face and pool in my intestines. These emergency phone calls were happening twice a week and my brother knew the drill. He watched me pull out a bottle of pills and shake a small, white circle into my palm before washing it down with his water.

"Sure, take some of my water," he scoffed. He never said anything outright, but his patience was fraying. Brad looked up from his half-eaten burrito, the aluminum peeled back like a metal banana. The therapist had explained to my parents that I was supposed to take medication whenever I started to feel *out of control*. It's the pill the nurses give to patients when they wake up after surgery. One pill lowers the heart rate; two will numb the vision of tubes erupting from your vital organs.

I stood outside the restaurant and called my therapist, Paul. He had given me his home number in case I ever thought about hurting myself.

"Paul?"

"Yes? Nathan?" He was already using his calming voice.

"Yeah. I'm having trouble breathing and you told me to call you if I ever thought about hurting myself."

"Did you take your medication and try and control your breathing?"

"Yes," I said as hot tears rolled down my face. "Paul? I'm sick of this. Why can't I just sit there and eat a burrito like a normal human being?" I was almost shouting. I probably would have shouted if I hadn't been standing outside a restaurant.

"Is anyone else there?" I could hear the concern breaking through his usual calm voice. I had seen him every Thursday for the last year and never heard him sound the least bit worried.

"I'm with Brad and Kellen," I said, pacing back and forth through a patch of grass lining the parking lot.

"Good," he said, audibly exhaling. "You know, Nathan. You have experienced a lot of disappointment, and it's a long hard process sorting through the emotions." He paused. "Remember we talked about this on Thursday."

"Yes," I sighed, wiping the sweat from my forehead.

"Okay, tell you what. Why don't you come in tomorrow?"

"Okay. That sounds good."

"Do you mind if I talk to Kellen?"

"Sure. Here he is." I walked back inside and held the phone between Kellen's face and his half-eaten burrito.

"Paul wants to talk to you."

Kellen sighed and took the phone. Paul was becoming a part of the family. If I called in sick to watch re-runs of Seinfeld in my parent's basement, I only had to mention "Paul" and everyone would leave me alone. I spent the majority of my time sunk deep in their musty couch watching TV as anti-depressants coursed through my veins. The medication slowed my body down: my metabolism, my sex drive, but primarily the voices that circled my mind like vultures, telling me I was letting everyone down, reminding me that Michael and I hadn't spoken in a year, asking why I couldn't get my life back on track.

Kellen handed me back the phone. "He said not to leave you alone." I could hear the exhaustion in his voice. "Let's just finish our burritos and go home," he said. I felt my heart rate settle down to a light jog.

"It's not a big deal," Brad said, with one bite of soggy tortilla left in his hand. "We'll grab a movie on the way home." He forced a smile.

As we drove the long stretch of highway back to the suburbs, I noticed the Minneapolis skyscrapers towering over the Catholic cathedral, the skyline silhouetted by light pollution. I didn't know if there were any skyscrapers in Kenya. I had never thought to ask Michael. All he ever talked about was life in the village: thatched huts, cooking fires, and cows.

The next day I sat in Paul's office, on the brown-leather sofa across from him. Every Thursday morning I went to his office. The walls were painted the color of sunflower petals, and there were matching bronze lamps and an end table. I assumed such a strong home-away-from-home vibe was intentional. Paul sat across from me, a yellow notepad resting on his khakis, an impressionist painting just above his head. I knew every detail

161

of the green and brown landscape. It was where my eyes escaped to when I started to cry. Paul would hand me the first tissue, telling me how strong I was, encouraging me to "trust the process." I could look away, but I couldn't escape the self-imposed humiliation I felt from crying in front of any man my father's age.

My first visit, my family had filled the entire sofa. My mom had called a family intervention when my dad and I started shouting at the dinner table. Every Thursday afterwards, I sat in that same spot. I had been staring at the budding cottonwood tree for almost five minutes with a piece of paper in my hand, trying to hold back the tears that had begun to swell under my eyes as soon as I pulled into the parking lot.

"What do you want to talk about today?" Paul asked. His eyes were naturally large and soft, but the reading glasses increased them to an almost cartoonish size. I looked at his salt-and-pepper hair and cornflower-blue sweater, avoiding his eyes as I handed him the paper with two emails.

May 16, 2008

Nathan

It's Michael. I'm in Kenya. I lost the parliamentary election. But after the votes were counted there was an outbreak of violence and so many people were killed. I have 30 orphans from my village living in my house. Their parents are dead and I don't have money to feed them. How much money do you have in your bank account?

Sincerely,
Michael.

May 21, 2008

Michael,

Sorry about the election. I have $250. It's yours if you need it.

As always,
Nathan

After reading the emails, he tried to make eye contact with me, but I looked out the window to avoid his patient smile.

"How did you feel after reading Michael's email?"

"I started having a panic attack," I said, watching the small cottonwood leaves flicker green, jasmine, and then green in the spring wind. "So I took the anti-anxiety meds. And I've been taking them three times a day like you said, until I could come in and process it."

That was my new routine. Wake up in my childhood bedroom, swallow enough anti-depressants to turn a basset hound into a rodeo clown, go to my substitute teaching job where I spent my fifteen-minute breaks doing breathing relaxation exercises, come home, eat dinner with my parents, and watch TV until bed. And if anything set me off, I was supposed to take extra anti-anxiety meds until I could come in and *process it* with Paul. "But then when I was getting the burrito with Brad and Kellen, I just snapped."

"You emailed him back two days ago. How have you been feeling since then?"

"Remember when I emailed my friend Tom, the Jewish guy from Greece, to tell him I was sorry for saying he was going to hell, and that I wasn't a Christian anymore? So, Tom emailed me back a few months later telling me not to worry about it. But I had forgotten about the email I had sent him. I wasn't expecting to ever talk to him again, and so when his email came it took me by surprise."

But that was in college. These days I was a lot more fragile than I used to be. Unexpected events, even small things like an email that brought up some past failure, and I would lie on the couch for the entire weekend with no appetite, afraid to look away from the TV until I could talk it over with Paul.

"Hearing from Michael was like that, except I realized I was still angry. But then I imagined Michael sitting in a mud hut somewhere, thirty hungry little kids sitting around, and I felt ashamed for still feeling angry at him. And then my head started going back and forth between being mad at Michael and ashamed for not helping. So I took meds and tried to relax my breathing. But I couldn't stop thinking about those kids."

I started crying. "And then I remembered the night we were driving back to our apartment." I grabbed a tissue and covered my face. "I promised Michael that whenever he needed money, he should just ask and I'd give him as much as I could, that my money was his money."

"Do you still feel that way? You're allowed to change your mind," Paul said.

That was something Paul did a lot. Give me permission to feel something I was desperately trying to repress. He was right though. I could have changed my mind.

After we got back from Washington, D.C., Michael started drinking a six pack every night. And for the next two weeks, I'd wake up before the other roommates, turn off the TV, and pick up the empty beer bottles as Michael lay asleep on the couch, his hand touching the thorn that was still lodged in his butt cheek from his childhood jump through the fence. I had decided not to talk to him about the drinking; it had only been two weeks. Plus, I had no idea what to say "Cheer up, Michael. Losing an election's not that bad. You're just going to disappoint everyone who put their faith in you, with no real way of explaining why you let them down." I had let enough people down to know speeches didn't help anything.

One early Sunday morning in February 2006, I woke up and saw I'd missed three calls from Michael's cell phone around two in the morning and a call from Amanda a while later. I figured they went out for late-night pizza and decided to wake me up and tell me about it. But when I called Michael, I only got "This is Michael Kimpur from Kenya. Leave a message."

So I called Amanda.

"Hello?"

"Amanda, what's up?" I said, stifling a yawn.

"I'm down at the police station with Michael."

"What? Why?" I said, shouting myself awake.

"Calm down!" Amanda shouted back. "I'm gonna let him tell you. I picked him up a few hours ago and we've been filling out paperwork. I'm dropping him off at your place in a half hour or so. And Nathan? Go easy on him," she pleaded. "He's had a long night."

I got up and ate breakfast at the dining-room table, watching the sunrise reflect off the bluish-white snow piles. An hour later, Michael walked in the apartment and lay on his bed with his hands over his face.

"Amanda said you had a long night," I said standing over him. Then I noticed his ear lobe was puffed up and bleeding.

"Yep, buddy," he said through his hands.

"Wanna tell me what happened?" I tried to use the most patient and understanding voice I could muster.

"Last night I went out to a bar with a few Somali guys. I got drunk and then I tried to get a ride home from them, but they refused me. So I started driving home and when I woke up my car was on a frozen lake a hundred feet down a hill."

I felt as if Michael had just pushed me out of an airplane, my stomach free falling. But a second later the righteous anger set in. When I was two years old my oldest cousin was killed by a drunk driver and I grew up hearing drunk drivers spoken of with a derision that most people reserve for child molesters.

"I tried to find a hat and gloves but I couldn't see any in the car. And I was getting so cold. So I ran up the snowy hill and tried to wave down a ride." He looked up at me with bloodshot eyes. "I called you several times, and then I called Amanda. And no one was stopping to help me. Car after car went by and my ears were so hurting. The only one who stopped was a police officer. I asked him to take me back to our apartment but he brought me to the police station instead. He had me blow in a bottle and then he said I had a driving while intoxicated ticket."

He sat up and looked at me for the first time. That's when I noticed his jeans were muddy and his boots were soaking wet.

"What are we gonna do?" he said, pleading with me.

Most of the time, Michael's biography led me to give him a pass on whatever problem he had. If he was late to a meeting, I'd chalk it up to African time. If he didn't clean the dishes, I'd assume it because of his of Pokot maleness. But not this time. There were no excuses for this. I wanted to shout at him. *You totaled the car Amanda gave you! You're gonna lose you license! You're probably gonna get deported! YOU are lucky you didn't kill someone!*

But I swallowed it all down. As matter-of-factly as I could, I said, "Michael, this time there is no *we*." I tried not to let my building rage seep through my words. "You have to deal with this on your own."

"What?" Michael stared at me in shock. "You can't leave me standing alone under this," he said desperately. Then he sighed and firmed his resolve, putting his index finger in the middle of my chest. "You *have* to help me. I am in a foreign country and I am a *guest* in your home. I am under your protection and if you never want to see me again after this is over, then fine." He clenched his fist. "But you *must* stand beside me until this is over."

"Why?" I said, as if he was a common criminal pleading for bail.

"Because that is what tradition says should happen," he explained as if it were common knowledge. "No one stands alone." Then he kicked off his boots, lay down, and pulled the covers over his head.

Paul pulled me back to the current reality. "What are you feeling right now?" he asked. I thought about his question. *What if I changed my mind?* I didn't have to answer Michael's email. I didn't even have to open it. He was a million miles away. If he called, I could just let it go to voicemail. Sure the kids at his house might go hungry, but there were hungry kids all over the world. Why were *these* kids my problem?

And then I realized they were my problem because their faces were haunting me. Standing in line at the grocery store, at the dinner table, ordering a burrito—I saw their faces every time there was food in front of me. I started sweating and wiped my eyes. "I was thinking about cutting ties with Michael," I paused, "but I knew the kids' faces would haunt me," I said.

"Why would they haunt you?" he asked.

"Because I let them starve—to get back at Michael."

"Let me stop you there," he said, putting his hand up like a crossing guard. "I hear what you're saying about the kids starving. And I agree that it's important to feed hungry kids. But I want to focus for a moment on the anger you feel towards Michael."

"Okay," I said. Paul was always redirecting my train of thought, diverting the tracks into some untapped cavern of my mind.

"Why do you still feel so angry at him? You seem to be able to forgive your other friends for making stupid and dangerous decisions. What's different about Michael?"

I had agreed to stand beside Michael until his court date. The morning of the sentencing, both of us stood in front of a judge wearing the same suits we had worn at the National Prayer Breakfast. Michael told the judge he was sorry and that he had learned his lesson. In response, the judge gave him a small fine and let Michael keep his license.

For the next two months, I couldn't stand to make eye contact with him. I chauffeured him to and from campus in an awkward and angry silence, the BBC playing at a nearly inaudible level. Around that same time, the panic attacks started becoming a regular part of my week.

The last day at the apartment, Michael and I sat on the carpet of the empty apartment in silence. I was fingering the deep dent left from the couch leg when I heard Amanda's horn blaring from the parking lot outside. "That's Amanda." I said, looking down at her car in the parking lot. Amanda stayed in the car whenever she picked Michael up; she had decided to stonewall me for stonewalling Michael.

"Yep," Michael said, looking out the window and waving down at her.

"Goodbye, Michael," I said, extending my hand to him.

"Okay, buddy. Thank you for hosting me," Michael replied, shaking my hand as if he was checking out of a hotel. He brushed off his campus janitorial shirt, picked up his duffle bags, and left my life.

I looked at the impressionist painting above Paul's head, afraid that my next statement was going to bring on more tears. "I guess I thought Michael was different than other people," I said. "I mean, he grew up in a mud hut and went to school with a stick under a tree. He had overcome every human obstacle and then threw it all away in one night."

"He threw *what* away?" Paul responded incredulously. "A lot of politicians get DWIs. Then they pay the penalty and move on. He *still* ran for parliament in Kenya."

Amanda had said the same thing; that I was overreacting.

When I didn't respond, Paul continued. "I think we need to explore why you started having panic attacks when Michael let you down," Paul said. He leaned forward. "Now, feel free to tell me if I'm wrong here." His palms were up as if he was approaching a wild animal. "But do you think you were looking to Michael as a father figure? Someone who understood the direction your life was going? A father figure who encouraged you in ways that, perhaps your own father couldn't?"

I thought about brushing my teeth next to Michael in the Hilton bathroom, confessing my faithlessness through the mirror. I had shown him my darkest secret and he had found a spark of hope tucked inside it. Paul read my face and continued. "It's called transference. People who have a psychological void left by a parent often try to fill that void by transferring others into the role of father or mother." I made eye contact with him for the first time. He put his palms back up. "I'm not saying that's what happened, I'm just suggesting a possible explanation."

"So let me see how this would have played out," I said, more comfortable to be back in the realm of theory rather than feelings. "I felt unable to connect to my own father, so I looked to Jesus as a surrogate father and spent my childhood talking to the Jesus in my head. And when Jesus stopped talking to me in Athens, I crashed into depression as if I had lost a father." I counted the steps with my fingers.

"That would be one way of reading the situation," Paul nodded.

Then connections started clicking, "Then came Michael, someone who saw me as something other than a faithless church intern. And my subconscious latched onto him, even though he was basically a complete stranger."

Paul smiled. "You see, the problem with transference is that we aren't really in control of it. We have a built-in psychological need for a father figure, a strong, supportive person in our lives who role-models manhood to us. But when our biological fathers cease to be that person, we look to other men to fill in the gap. And our subconscious brains do this without our really knowing it. It's not like you *decided* to make Michael your new father. It just happens because of the nature of the relationship. I mean, how long did you actually know Michael?"

"Just over two years."

"And have you ever met anyone who knew Michael from before?"

"No. Well, I met Potea, but I didn't really talk to him," I said.

"So a relative stranger becomes your friend and then your roommate. Then he gets a DWI and your entire life falls apart. That suggests to me that something deeper is going on."

My three fathers were hanging in the air on my index, middle, and ring finger: Dad, Jesus, and Michael. I put up my pinky. "And now I have you. No offense, but my subconscious must be scraping the bottom of the barrel if I've resorted to paying for fathers," I smirked.

Paul sat back, and pushed his glasses up his nose, magnifying his eyes. "You're paying for the quality time with me." I assumed that meant he knew he had taken on the dangerous mantle of father.

"Well, I can't argue with that." I smiled, feeling like I had reached some kind of breakthrough.

"Nathan, what you need to remember is that parents are people too." Paul almost never said the word *need*. "Your father gave you what he could. He worked a job he hated so you could spend your summers at camp. He put your college tuition on his credit card instead of buying a bigger house or driving a new car around town. I know he probably wasn't the father you would have chosen, but I believe he did the best he could." He paused. "He gave you everything he had to give."

"He's paying for us to have this conversation," I conceded.

"And I know it's painful that Michael didn't work out the way you wanted. But you are going to have to start to see these father figures in your life for who they really are, not who you need them to be." He pointed at himself. "I would venture a guess that the only reason you haven't rejected me is because you don't actually know anything about me." He picked up his note pad and checked his watch. "Okay, let's leave it there for this week."

The hour was up and I pulled out my checkbook to pay him with my father's money.

Was that all my friendship with Michael was? I thought driving home, *just some subconscious need for a father?*

It was an unusually warm night for May and after dinner my dad and I drove down to the lake to watch the sunset and eat ice cream. We sat on the park bench watching the massive yachts float by. The orange and purple sunset reflected off the lake and onto the windows of the lakefront mansions. It was the kind of view most people only see in paintings. "So what did you and Paul talk about today?" Dad asked, a bit of vanilla stuck to his mustache.

"I got an email from Michael. So we talked about that," I said, trying to sound like it was just another day at some boring job.

"Yeah? What did Michael want?"

"He wanted some money to feed some kids."

He turned to look at me, his eyebrows raised. "So what'd you say?"

"I sent him $250."

"Really?" he said surprised. "Even after all that. Wow," he said in a higher register. "You're still shelling it out."

"Technically you're shelling it out," I said. "The only reason I have any money is because you're paying my food, housing, and therapy bills."

"True." He sat back, seemingly satisfied to be at the financial center of the equation. "So what did Paul tell you to do?" After a year of asking me questions and hearing me respond "Paul told me to…," he had learned to just go straight to the source.

"He didn't tell me what to do."

We sat silently looking out at the boats cutting back and forth as the orange sun dipped behind the trees. "You know, alcohol makes people do stupid things," he said.

"It certainly does."

"My dad used to drink." He said.

The fact that Grandpa was an alcoholic was one of the few things I knew about my dad's childhood. He never talked about our grandparents and I never got up the courage to ask him about it.

"My dad was a traveling shoe salesman. He'd be gone for weeks at a time. Then he'd come back for a few days and take off again. When he was home, he wasn't really much of a father." His voice was detached, as if he was talking about an obscure historical figure. "So one day he decides he's gonna start driving this mentally handicapped kid from the hospital in town up to this tiny town on the Canadian border. He did this every month. Every month. I couldn't figure it out. He wouldn't take me to hockey games, drive me to school, take me shopping, and here he was driving this disabled kid clear across the state. Well your grandma started heralding it around like she thought her husband was Gandhi."

He turned to me with a knowing glance. "But I knew something was up. That fall we spent a week deer hunting in that town on the Canadian border. And one night we go into the bar for dinner. And I'm sitting there, I'm sixteen years old, mind you, and he walks up to me with his rifle on his shoulder and a middle-aged woman on his arm. 'Mike, this is my girlfriend,' he said. I could smell he was drunk."

He scoffed, "That's when I realized what was happening. That handicapped kid was his excuse to visit his girlfriend." My heart sank as I imagined my father in rubber overalls sitting on a bar stool glaring at his drunken father. "I wanted to punch him," Dad said. "Not for cheating. I didn't care if he was cheating. I wanted to punch him for telling me about it."

I sat there quietly watching small lights from the boats hovering over the dark water, hoping he'd finished telling the story.

"That's when I moved out. I couldn't stand to live another day in that house."

"So that's when you started smoking pot," I said, recalling the conversation we had the day I moved into my freshman dorm. I remembered his Bible-study leader, Bill, in a pink polo, his daughter's pillow under his arm.

"No," he chuckled. "I started smoking pot way before that."

We sat there for a while in the dark, licking our ice cream cones and swatting mosquitos. It felt good to talk to him without arguing. "You know why we moved to this city?" he asked. "I wanted to get you away from all the crap—the drinking and the drugs and the lies and the endless secrets." He said each word with distinct disgust.

I stared out at the lake, still trying to imagine my father as a teenager smoking a joint.

After a long pause he spoke, but his voice had regained the tone he used to set me straight, somewhere between patronizing and exasperated.

"I got a job at that corporation you hate so I didn't to have to be on the road three weeks of the month. And we started going to the Evangelical church so you wouldn't have to be around drunk people. You know, they pretty much kick you out of that church if they catch you drinking or cheating on your wife. It's like a little world out here." One by one, my childhood memories began inverting themselves: Sunday school, camp, my Christian college. My parents weren't close minded; they were retreating. They had intentionally raised me in a bubble.

"And when I went to Greece, I broke out of the bubble," I said, putting the pieces together.

My dad sighed. "You looked terrible when you got back."

We sat for a long time in silence, watching the lights on the last few sail boats bounce up and down on the waves. I took the final bite of my chocolate ice cream cone, picturing Tom sitting on the floor, the bong between his legs.

"It wasn't supposed to turn out like this," Dad said, with a defeated tone I had never heard before.

"Parents are people too," I said.

"I suppose they are." He looked out at the dark water.

"So what are you going to do about Michael?"

"I'm going to give him another chance."

"Well, good luck with that," he shrugged.

15

A SEMI-TRUCK-SIZE JESUS

The $250 I sent to Michael was enough to feed the thirty kids for two weeks. Michael sent me a list of a dozen random people he'd met at college, his odd jobs, or churches dotted across Minnesota. But they all had one thing in common. At one point they had all told him he could call if he was ever in an emergency. And thirty orphans sleeping on the floor of your house seemed to qualify as an emergency.

Over the next few weeks, I nervously sipped coffee across from half of the people on Michael's list, a picture of smiling black kids resting between us. "How's Michael doing?" they would ask.

"Yeah, good," I'd respond, fumbling for the words that steered the conversation from small talk to their hand-writing a check with multiple zeroes. "He asked me to get in touch with you because he said you had met at _____ and that you said you would be willing to help him if he ever needed it."

By the look on their faces, it was clear they didn't remember making any statements of the sort. After exhausting the list along with a dozen of my parents' friends, it was clear people were not thrilled at the idea of writing a check to Nathan Roberts with "Kenyan Orphans" in the memo. I had even resorted to calling the Feminists, most of whom were unemployed and living in their own parents' basements. I only managed to raise $150. So I quit trying to fundraise and got a job at the local elementary school, teaching reading to kids with autism. With a theology degree and nothing but a failed church internship on my resume, it was the highest paying job I qualified for.

A month later, I was driving the last stretch of highway between the school and my parents' house. The spring grass was finally tall enough to hide all the garbage that had been tossed out the windows of passing cars. My first paycheck was resting against the steering wheel. I stared at the light-blue paper, the square, cold, computerized numbers, doing the math in my head. My jaw clenched when I realized that after gas and a new muffler for my car, there would be next to nothing left to send to Michael. That's when the numbers started to blur and crystalize through my tears.

"It's not gonna work," I shouted at the steering wheel. "What the hell am I supposed to do?" I shouted at God. I had long since given up on hearing any answer. "If you're out there and you have some sort of idea about how this is supposed to work, well, now's the time to speak up." I punctuated the prayer with my fist on the tan plastic dashboard. Then I caught a sun flare off the hood of a semi-truck that had pulled up close beside me.

I swerved back into my lane and I looked up to wave an apology, but my hand hung frozen in the air when I saw a blue cartoon outline of Jesus, fifteen feet tall, painted on the side of the white semi-trailer. It was the smiling face I recognized from my Sunday-school coloring sheets: fluffy beard, shoulder-length hair, a long robe draped off his outstretched hands. And in block letters above him were the words "Jesus will lead you and guide you." A small cluster of children stood in front of the cartoon Jesus, and behind him was a medieval-looking castle I assumed was the Kingdom of God. The truck hung in the lane next to me for a moment before passing in front of my car as the highway merged into a single lane. I wiped away the tears and drove the rest of the way to my parents' house in an elated fog. I took my seat at the dinner table between my mom and dad, silently eating bacon-topped macaroni and cheese.

"You look concerned," Dad said. After spending a year paying for medical bills, he was understandably hawkish about my emotional state.

"Huh?"

"Nathan, your dad asked you if you were feeling alright," Mom responded, translating his comment into a softer tone.

"Yeah. I'm just worried about what I'm going to send to Michael this month. I already met with everyone we could think of."

"You didn't ask me," Dad said, taking a long drink of milk.

"Oh." I paused, trying to figure out what he was getting at. "Do *you* want to donate?"

"Sure," he said eagerly, as if I had just invited him out to the movies. "Put your mom and me down for five hundred dollars a month."

I eyed him for a second, trying to figure out if he was kicking me when I was down. "Really?"

"Sure," he smiled back. "Why not?"

"Thanks." I felt my jaw release as I chewed the macaroni, still wondering what to make of the last twenty minutes.

That night I lay in my childhood bedroom trying to figure out how to tell Emilie that Jesus had spoken to me from the side of a semi-truck. When my depression spiraled out of control Emilie had put herself in charge of "filling my empty love buckets," as she put it. That was her diagnosis of my depression. Smiling at me with her head on my shoulder after I came home from work early because of a panic attack, she would walk into my bedroom lay next to me, and tell me she wasn't going to stop hugging me until my love buckets were at least three-quarters full. Strange as it sounds, I could actually feel the love flowing through her arms and filling me up. And after months of this, as you can imagine, I fell in love with her. And she reluctantly agreed to give *us* a chance.

By the time I saw her, I had convinced myself that my conversion was going to push her over the edge. Her boyfriend was already an anxiety-wracked mess, and now he was seeing visions. She sat on the couch listening to my story, her eyes narrowed on me like I was explaining a complicated math problem. After I finished, she breathed in deep and exhaled slowly, the way my mom would when I sent a baseball through the window.

"No, it's not a problem for me," She stood up and started to pace, her hand on her forehead. "I mean, I'm happy for you. That's what you wanted, right?" Her eyes narrowed even more. "Now you can be a pastor like you planned." The way she said *pastor* made my heart sink. She was clearly disappointed that her life was repeating itself. The daughter of a missionary accidently falls in love with a pastor. Then her expression flashed with fear. "Unless you're breaking up with me."

"No. No. I'm not." I assured her.

Her head tilted: *Don't lie to me.*

"I swear. This just happened to me all of a sudden and I'm still trying to sort it out."

She smiled with the corner of her mouth. "So after four years of theology classes, a semi-truck with a smiling Jesus did you in?"

"I guess so," I shrugged.

I started calling myself a Christian again. But the word felt different coming out of my mouth. In high school I had paraded the title around like a merit badge, but now I only told close friends, hoping they wouldn't assume too much. The next week Amanda and Billy invited Emilie, and by association me, over for a bonfire in their tiny urban backyard. I sat in a lawn chair listening to the mariachi music coming from the Mexican family's house next door.

Emilie told the story of my conversion like it was a soap opera with a surprise ending "...and THEN he saw Jesus on the semi-truck and he decided he was a CHRISTIAN again!" Her hands waved in the air.

A mixture of laughter and booing erupted from the listeners. "Whatever," I shouted at them, half smiling, realizing I would probably do the same thing if I were in their position. "You're all just pissed it was Jesus on that semi-truck," I smiled sarcastically. "If it was a picture of a cross-legged Buddha up there and now I was calling myself a Buddhist, you'd be totally into it."

"Yeah, that's because Buddhists don't suck," Amanda scoffed from across the fire. She rarely spoke to me, but my conversion clearly pissed her off enough to break her wall of silence.

"Whatever. You always go on and on about Martin Luther King Jr. He was a Christian."

"Seriously?" She stood up, shouting, "This is unbelievable! Now you're comparing yourself to Martin Luther King Jr.?"

"No, that's not what I meant," I said.

"Hold on, Amanda," Billy said. "I'm sure he wasn't trying to compare himself to MLK." Billy looked at me. "Right?"

Before I could answer, he continued. "And Nathan, no one is saying we don't *like* you. You're one of us, whether you're a Christian or not." Billy's voice took on a motherly tone. "We just don't approve of your choices right now."

Everyone laughed and the banter drifted onto another subject. I stared into the fire wondering if I should keep arguing my case or just let it go. Sensing my deliberation, Emilie put her head on my shoulder and whispered, "Don't worry about it. It's just really unexpected."

"It was unexpected for me too," I said, kissing her forehead.

* * *

Michael called me a few days later. "Thanks for sending the money, buddy. That's really something."

I hadn't spoken to him in over a year and his accent was thicker. I could hear little kids playing in the background. Hearing him say "That's really something" melted away the tension.

"Yeah, my parents gave most of it."

He asked me to send his greetings to my mom and dad, and laughed as he told me Kellen's comment about Kenyan food tasting like dirt was now his children's favorite bedtime story. It was clear from his tone that Michael wasn't holding anything against me. His political and now parental roles

174

seemed to have swallowed up all his emotional resources. Before he hung up, he slipped in one more request.

"So I don't have so many minutes on my phone to talk, but I just wanted to call and say thanks for standing beside me, buddy."

The word "buddy" released the tension from my shoulders. *Parents are people too*, I said to myself. "Thanks. It's good to hear your voice."

16
BLOOD SOUP

While I was begging people for money, Michael was putting together a school. His family of six was living in a three-room cement house across from the Catholic boy's high school he had attended a decade before. Thirty multicolored cups were strewn about the dirt yard. Long grass sprouted up around a dripping spigot near his red Nissan SUV.

After he lost the election he went to the desert to inform the elders. But when they had heard he was coming, they rounded up all the orphaned children in their village. As he pulled into his mother's homestead he saw Keu and a dozen elders flanked by thirty children. "Now that you are the leader of this village, they have decided that you should take care of the orphaned kids," Keu told him in the shade of a thorn bush. "But I don't have any money," Michael said matter-of-factly. "That's why I lost the election." Keu put a piece of dead grass in his mouth. "That's not how it works. You were chosen to lead. And no election can take that away from you," he said, taking a long drink of the Coca Cola Michael had brought him. "They think you have money because you're so fat." He smiled, pointing at Michael's belly. "And you know white people." Michael knew he couldn't convince them otherwise.

Michael spent the afternoon sipping tea with his mom and the elders and listening to stories from the village—who married who and where the

Karamoja were grazing. Michael tried to stay focused but he was distracted by the thirty children playing in the dirt behind his mother's hut. As the sun began setting, he carefully loaded each child into the red SUV. As he pulled onto the main roads that lead out of the desert, Michael rolled down the windows hoping to flush the smell of car-sickness.

The next day, he scheduled a meeting with the pastor of a church near his home on the edge of the desert. It was a one-story red-brick sanctuary with three Sunday-school classrooms. The pastor wore a dusty oversized suit and listened to Michael from behind a peeling wooden desk. There was a cross on the wall above him, and a square hole in the wall was the only source of light. Michael assured the pastor that he had money coming from America every week. But it was barely enough to feed the orphans lunch, let alone educate them.

The next Sunday, the pastor and Michael stood in front of the sanctuary giving a rousing sermon on Christian duty to a congregation of farmers and shopkeepers. The thirty nomadic orphans, unable to understand the pastor's language, stood on stage smiling. And at the end of the service, each orphan went home with a family from the church. It was decided that the children would stay with church families until Michael could build a dormitory to house them. The kids returned on to the church on Monday morning for their first day of kindergarten in the adjacent red brick Sunday school classroom.

With the kids in foster homes and classes underway, Michael was convinced of the next step. "It's time for you to come to Kenya," he said. I could hear him smiling through the phone.

"We don't really have money for that," I said. We hardly had money to feed the kids. And I was still in no shape to travel. At work I spent every fifteen-minute break I could scavenge on my back, counting my breaths, trying to keep from myself from spiraling into a tear-filled mess of anxiety. I was still spending every Thursday morning in Paul's office listening to him calmly insist that I "focus on all the progress we've made."

"We don't have enough money for you *not* to come."

* * *

In December 2009, I was sitting in the passenger seat of Michael's red SUV bouncing my way through a washed-out desert road trying to protect my sun-scorched forearm from the Kenyan sun. I stared out the window at the landscape. It looked like the New Mexico desert, the dried red earth dotted with naked thorn bushes. An hour into the trip, we stopped by the side of the road to pee and I noticed the spindly tangled bushes were protected by millions of toothpick-sized thorns.

The air was drier than I had imagined. Growing up in Minnesota, I'm used to a humid heat. But the desert wind filled my mouth with the taste of metallic dust. The endless series of hills and valleys felt like the set of a Clint Eastwood movie. I had run out of sunscreen two days into the trip and none of the corrugated-tin shops in town carried any. I had resorted to cutting off a sock at the heel and wearing it as a wrist guard. But the morning sun was already burning through the cotton.

Michael's daughter Chelimo sat in the cargo area atop a massive plastic bag of corn flour. A mix of body odor and starch filled the vehicle. Before we left for the desert, we had gone to a church called Winner's Chapel. The sermon was given by a tall man who seemed like the Kenyan version of Joel Osteen. He stood on a stage for two hours declaring that "God will provide to those who have faith," while the congregation in their dusty Sunday best nodded along.

After the service, Michael and I sat across from the pastor, a ten-year-old computer resting on the desk between us and him. "The villagers expect anyone driving from over the farthest mountain to come with food." Michael said.

The pastor repeated his mantra "God will provide" in a dozen different ways before ordering his secretary to load up our vehicle with fifty pounds of cornmeal. As we drove away, Michael turned to me. "Say what you will about the prosperity gospel in Africa, but they always have extra food on hand."

A grey-haired nomadic elder named Lokadamuk was sitting quietly in the backseat. He wore a tattered sports coat and faded-green fishing cap, his weathered skin cross-hatched with scars left by the thorn bushes. His left eye was glossed over with white like a desert Captain Ahab. Two weeks prior, Lokadamuk had walked two hundred miles to ask Michael for money after raiders had stolen his family's cows. But Michael didn't have any money. So the old man had stayed at Michael's house to see for himself. He had been to one of Michael's political rallies at a village and couldn't believe a future leader of Pokot couldn't afford to buy him three cows. After two weeks of watching Michael's family eat meager meals inside a three-room cement house, he began to see that Michael was not as rich as he had originally assumed.

But I was a different story. He had never met a white man but he had begun to suspect that if he was going to get any cows, they were going to come from me, a suspicion I had confirmed by taking the entire caravan out for lunch at a small café on the edge of the desert. Lokadamuk couldn't understand the waiter. He only spoke the tribal languages of the desert. So he laughed with surprise when a steak and Coca Cola were placed in front of him twenty minutes later.

The main road winding its way through the desert was marred with sink holes, the occasional slab of concrete sticking sideways from the sunken dirt. The British had constructed it a hundred years ago as a trade route to Somalia and Ethiopia, but the Kenyan government had since abandoned it to the elements. As I nauseously bounced in the front seat, I looked back at Lokadamuk staring out the window with his walking stick resting between his legs. He was smiling, hands folded. He seemed content to sit and watch as bushes along the road blurred past him.

We drove over a dry river bed and I pointed out the window at a pair of monkeys resting on a short acacia tree. "Nathan," Michael said firmly. When I looked at him confused, he softened his tone. "Okay, buddy, you need to keep your arms and legs inside the car. Across this river is a warzone. And behind any bushes could be men with so many guns, and your skin color could arouse their suspicion."

My heart rate started to rise and I turned on the radio, hoping to find some music to distract me. But after scanning the entire FM and AM bands, the only channel still audible was broadcasting a recorded sermon from Rick Warren, his slow pastoral drawl rattling off the marks of a purpose-driven church.

"You've got to be kidding," I said in disbelief. It seemed like a sick joke, sending an English sermon on church-planting to starving people. I reached to turn it off.

"Hey, you. Leave it," Michael said, brushing my hand away from the radio dial. "He's a pastor. So today we will be his congregation."

Warren slowly enunciated the words: "Don't try to do what you're not good at."

"Hey, that's good advice, by the way." Michael smiled. "Don't try to do something you're not good at. Anyways it's better advice than missionaries usually give."

"Oh, yeah?" I said, turning the radio down.

"Okay, I have to be honest," Michael warned. While Michael does his best to understand and appreciate the differences between whites and blacks, whenever he says "I have to be honest," it's followed by a scathing critique of white people. "There are two kinds of missionaries who have been in Kenya since I was a boy," he said, two fingers in the air. "One kind is walking around helping people, and living with them in the villages and shacks. This one I very much like. Like John and Sarah. But," he said, wagging his index finger, "there is another kind that live in massive houses in Nairobi." He said "massive" as if they were palaces. We had driven through a mostly white neighborhood where Michael said the western missionaries lived. And while their houses did seem big compared to the single story cement houses most Kenyans lived in, it seemed like a stretch to call them massive.

"These missionaries have like two servants who cook and clean for them. And to be honest, I have *no* time for them. You know, I went to their big homes one by one and every missionary I visited had two cars." Michael's tone made it sound like they were stockpiling nuclear weapons. "And not one nice one and one junk like our car." He pounded on the cracked dashboard, under which were fuel lines held together by duct tape and prayer.

"After college, I was the principal at Kiwawa, just over that mountain." He pointed to a blue hill on the horizon. "And we so desperately needed a car to deliver the food to the kids. So I traveled two weeks down to Nairobi. And I went to that neighborhood knocking on door after door asking the rich missionaries from the city for one of their cars." Then his anger turned into a devilish grin. "I stood on their doorstep and I explained to them that I was the principal at a bush school and then I asked them to give me one of their cars. And if they refused, which they always did, by the way, I would pull out my Bible and read them Luke 3:11." His finger pointed at the Bible that was resting on the console between us. "Anyone who has two shirts should share with the one who has none, and anyone who has food should do the same. And I would add, 'Anyone who has two cars should do the same also.'" He burst out laughing. "Those missionaries were so mad."

"Well, you did ask them for their car," I said, chuckling at the absurdity of the situation.

"Their car." He scoffed. "That's the problem. They thought of those cars as *their* cars. If you come to Africa as a missionary then *your* car becomes *our* car."

"Fair enough," I said, turning the radio back up. Rick Warren's voice filled the car with the words "Every church is big in God's eyes..." I closed my eyes and fell asleep as the sermon faded into white noise.

I awoke at sunset to a gun barrel clicking on the tinted passenger-side window of our SUV. A sixteen-year-old held the assault rifle in his hands. He was wearing a frayed green army jacket and what looked like a picnic blanket wrapped as a skirt. After attempting to look through the glass, he motioned for me to roll down the window.

I looked at Michael. "We found them."

"Actually they found us," he corrected. "And now we are their prisoners. Or their guests," he added with a grin. "That remains to be seen. Either way, they will bring us to the camp." He reached across me to roll down my window before shouting at the teenager in his mother tongue. Two more teenagers with AK-47s emerged from the desert thicket. Michael reached out of the driver's side window, shook their hands, and asked them where their camp was.

"So do these guys know who you are?" I asked, trying to sound calm. We were out of cell phone range. The radio stations had buzzed into white noise hours ago. "Oh no worries, buddy," he said. "These are just some young herdsboys from my tribe, the famous Pokot." He pulled down his lower lip and pointed at a gap where his bottom two front teeth should have been.

The boy at the window smiled with the same missing teeth. "Don't worry." He patted me on the leg. "They are just taking some precautions. In fact, when I was a herdsboy we were always on the lookout for spies. You know so many people out here are trying to steal cows. So they have to make sure. They want to take us in for a bit of questioning."

"But they know you, right?" I asked, my voice losing confidence with every emerging detail. Michael shouted to the herdsboys and then said to me, "Okay, you shake this guy's hand." He pointed at the teenager who had his gun pointed at me. The boy leaned in the vehicle, and as I shook his hand, he smiled at me for the first time. I could smell the acidic sweat coming from his dehydrated armpits.

"Okay, do they know me?" Michael said. "That is a good question. These boys do not know me. But the older men in their camp will. This I am sure of. Because I am pretty much one of the most famous Pokot in Kenya. Between the bigness of my belly and our work with children, most nomads have at least heard of me. But these are just some young herdsboys and they are being a little bit cautious." We locked eyes and he quickly amended his explanation. "But no worries, buddy. No worries at all."

Everyone in the vehicle started discussing our situation in a language I couldn't understand. But their pointing assured me I was the topic of debate. The boy motioned to a path barely wide enough for two cows to walk side by side. Then he shouldered his semi-automatic, and stepped onto the SUV's running board as Michael pulled off the broken desert road and down the path. As the vehicle navigated the rocky terrain, I could hear the boy's brightly colored beads bouncing around his neck. I rummaged through my backpack and found the plastic bottle containing my anti-anxiety medication, shook out a single pill, swallowed it, and started counting my breaths along with the rattling beads.

One of the boys must have run ahead and warned of our arrival, because at the end of the path, a dozen men stood wearing what I had begun to suspect were Pokot military fatigues: green army shirts and wraps around their waists, each holding the same Soviet-era AK-47s. Behind them, thousands of emaciated cows with humps above their necks and ribs like xylophones stood grazing on short greenish-brown grass in a valley dotted with short thorn bushes. When the vehicle stopped, I noticed flies swarming around piles of cow dung. I rolled up the window. The travel nurse had told me to avoid all contact with African insects.

"You better stay in here, buddy," Michael said, stepping out the vehicle. "These boys told me that they have never seen a white person before, and you people can be a pretty scary thing to behold for the first time."

As Michael and the others began speaking to our captors, a group of half-naked kids waddled out of the thicket and rushed to the vehicle. They tucked their hands around their faces and tried to catch a glimpse through the tinted glass. A boy in only a blue tank top and beaded hoop earrings caught my eye. He pointed to his mouth and cupped his hands. I could see big horseflies were drinking the liquid from the corner of his eyes. Then another landed on the snot trickling from his nose. But he didn't seem to notice. I opened the window and handed him a lemon candy as flies poured into the vehicle. The boy laughed, his eyes wide, pointing at his mouth, like he was acting for a TV commercial.

Michael shouted to me, "That's good to give out the candies. The children most probably have never tasted one." At the sight of food, the other kids rushed to my window. Muddy hands cupped one on top of the other as I placed a lemon drop in each palm.

One of the men started shouting and shaking his gun the way terrorists do in the movies. Michael frantically motioned for the men to calm down, pointing at himself, then at me, and then at the children. I rolled up the window and reached into my backpack for another anti-anxiety pill.

I counted to sixty and waited for my neck muscles to relax. I watched the kids, who were sitting in a circle, taking turns spitting the candy into their hand to look at the shrinking yellow dot, their hands getting stickier and stickier, attracting more and more flies.

After the cattle rustlers started shaking their guns, Lokadamuk got out of the vehicle and approached the group. They stopped shouting when he raised his voice. He looked to be their elder by twenty years at least. I watched as he pointed at Michael, then at himself, then at the children eating candy, then at me. Then he pointed at the cows grazing behind them. At that, the younger boys went back to their cows while the older men walked up to the vehicle. Michael ran ahead of them, smiling.

"Michael, what's going on?" I sounded more worried than I intended to.

"Oh, no worries, buddy." He put his hand on my shoulder. "That old man won the day. You see, these nomads have been fighting with the Kenyan government. Only last month the Kenyan army killed hundreds of Pokot and took away their guns. So when they saw our truck pull up, they suspected we were a government scouting party looking for them. And when they saw a white person in the car, they thought you were a British."

The euphoria from a second dosage of medication had set in and the whole situation seemed much less dramatic. "But the British haven't been out here in forty years," I said with an atypical calm.

183

"Well, nobody told these boys," Michael said, wiping the sweat off his forehead. "Anyways, the old man told them that you had bought him so much food at the restaurant. And he convinced them that you were here to help." Michael paused, thinking of how to say it in English. "Which was good, because they were probably going to kill you."

I looked over at Lokadamuk seated on a rock next to a dozen kids who were still sucking on lemon drops. He smiled with his few remaining teeth. He seemed quite satisfied to have held my life in his hands.

I got out of the vehicle and the men slowly walked up to me, a mixture of excitement and suspicion across their faces. They regarded me in the way a kid at the petting zoo might reach out to touch a snake. I noticed the nomads' hands were thin and boney with dust-stained callouses on their palms. It was strange to feel callouses on small hands, having grown up associating them with the muscular hands of Midwestern farmers.

A few of the children refused to touch me, hiding behind the bushes the way I imagined Michael had when he first saw John step out of the truck. But we were eventually able to coax them out into the open with lemon drops. And after the hands had all been shaken and the lemon drops were all deposited in mouths, Chelimo and I spent thirty minutes trying to find a ten-foot-by-ten-foot section of ground without a bush or cow pie where we could put up our small orange tent. We fastened the last tent poles as the sun slipped over the hills and the air turned cold.

Soon hundreds of campfires dotted the surrounding hillsides, the flickering flames mirroring the stars in the night sky. I hadn't stopped to think that there were nomads herding cows all around us. I heard laughter and turned to see a group of teenagers hunched over boiling pots of milk eagerly adding the sugar and tea Michael had brought for them. The smoke rose into the air before the wind changed and sent it drifting towards me. To escape the cloud, I unzipped the tent door and lay on my sleeping bag. I felt my head settle deep into the pillow and I closed my eyes.

I woke to Chelimo's voice. "Nathan, wake up. Father wants you." It was dark and I rifled through my bag and found my flashlight. I shined it through the tent mesh window at her. She had changed into a bright pink shirt. She smelled like smoke and I could see a charcoal hand smudge on her side. The boy from the car window stood next to her looking into the tent with his hands still cupped, hoping for one last candy. It was colder than when I had fallen asleep. I put on a sweatshirt and followed them down a small footpath. I stared up at a collection of stars I had never seen before, looking down occasionally to free my sweatshirt from the thorns. As the path opened up, I could see cows standing around a few hundred seated nomads. In the center, one man was shouting and jumping, a red plaid blanket tied over his shoulder. The others seemed to be nodding in agreement.

"What is he saying?" I whispered to Chelimo.

"He's sharing the scouting report." She said, motioning for me to sit down on the edge of the crowd. The man standing in the center pointed at the nearest hill.

"He must have found something important," I whispered back.

"Yes, a scouting party found a Karamoja raiding party on top of that hill. And he is telling the young men that they need to be brave." Then she paused to listen. "Now he is reminding them of the morning they got their teeth pulled out and how they did not cry. And how they fought the Karamoja and the government and they kept surviving."

The seated men started shaking their guns and blowing whistles. "What are they doing now? Aren't the Karamoja going to hear them?" I felt my heart rate climbing back up. Chelimo shook her head. "They are calling a cease-fire because you are here."

"Wait. Not six hours ago these people had tried to kill me as a British spy. So why wouldn't the Karamoja do the same?" It was clear my sentence structure was too complicated for her to understand. But she gathered that I was upset. Her face was calm and reassuring. "They are calling a cease-fire, so you don't need to worry," she repeated.

The entire group stood up. For the next twenty minutes, they jumped and whistled. You would have been hard pressed to find a living thing in a two-mile radius who hadn't heard about the cease-fire. Finally, after a few final loud blasts, the men sat down and Michael stood up to speak.

"Now Michael is telling the men to send their children to school," she said. "He says he is fat and safe because he can read and write."

The men shouted, "Oee!"

"Now my father is explaining that these men should send the children to school, that it will bring peace between the Karamoja and Pokot."

But the nomads didn't say "Oee." Instead, they turned to discuss it among themselves.

"Why didn't they say 'oee'?"

"They do not understand how school can bring peace. They think school is for cowards who don't want to fight," she said with a seriousness beyond her age. "They aren't sure how reading and writing will end the war. That's what they are talking about."

The talking went on for an hour with so many opinions flying around that Chelimo quickly gave up translating and I went back to the tent.

The next morning, I woke to the sound of Chelimo brushing her teeth outside. When she heard me roll over, she looked into the tent. "Psst, Nathan. Nathan, are you awake? The elders want to speak with you. Come quickly because after your meeting we must be going."

A minute later, I was winding my way through a herd of cows. Up close they looked more like wide dogs than the cows I saw in the Midwest.

The cows' ribs pressed up against their short slicked-back fur. I ran my hand along a brown and white heifer and my hand returned covered in dirt and hair.

Halfway down the path, I felt a tap on my shoulder and turned to see a bare-chested teenage boy holding a steel bowl of pink soup up to my face. Chelimo stepped in front of me and gently pushed the bowl away. The morning air was already hot. I stopped walking and I felt two flies land on the back of my neck.

The teenage boy stood with his pink soup in hand and repeated his question in Pokot. They were the about same height and were probably distant cousins. It was strange to see them standing face to face, two children separated by a string of unlikely events thirty years ago. Michael had found John. That was the reason why Chelimo was wearing a clean dress, could read and write, and had a Facebook account. And this boy's father had wandered the desert, taken a wife, and now his child was wrapped in a thorn-snagged cloth living on whatever was in this pink soup.

"He wants to know if you want to see him make blood soup," she said to me. "You can't drink it, but it's fun to watch." Before I could answer, she took me by the hand and led me to a cow pen made of wrapped thorn branches.

Inside the pen, three boys hunched over a struggling cow. They waved at me. The expressions on their faces reminded me of the look kids have on the playground when they shout "Watch me!" before doing a summersault.

One of the boys held a bow and arrow drawn taught, the second held the cow's head, and the third stretched the skin from the cow's neck. Then the first boy released his arrow and sent it plunging through the cow's neck.

Instantly, the cow bucked and the boys struggled to steady it. Blood poured from its neck like water from a hose. When they finally steadied the cow, they filled a half-gallon jug with ruby liquid. Blood soup.

"Why is it pink?" I asked, shaking an anti-anxiety pill into my dirty palm.

"They mix it with milk." She chuckled as a boy who had been bucked into a cow pie stood up with a look of disgust. "But don't drink it or you'll get sick. My father drank it last night to prove that he was still a Pokot warrior, but he has been throwing up this morning." Then she burst out laughing the way all teenage girls do when they talk about the silly boys in their lives.

We walked down the same path we'd taken the night before until we got to the SUV. A few feet from the vehicle, a circle of elders squatted on short wooden stools, their colorful garments hanging loosely on their bones. In the morning light I could see they had the same look as Lokadamuk. Their gaunt faces were weathered from years of walking the desert, a few teeth left in each mouth, tiny orange, blue, and white beads hanging around their necks. Behind them a camel was tied to a bush eating the final leaves off the top branch of a thorn bush.

This is what the Israelites must have looked like after 40 years I thought.

Michael sat in the circle in his jeans and polo shirt. "Good morning," he shouted to me. "This is your big moment." He waved me over. "The elders want to hear what you have to say about education."

I sat down and Chelimo put a hot cup of tea in my hand.

"Don't worry, buddy, I will be translating your words. I'll explain any difficult concepts they may encounter," Michael reassured me. This was what we had waited for. For months I had rehearsed my speech on the importance of education for the future of the tribe. I had decided to retell the story of the Native Americans, how their land was stolen by missionaries claiming to be Christians; the history of broken treaties and natives forced at gunpoint into desolate reservations. This would lead into a discussion of violence with the Kenyan government. I was going to tell them this same story was being repeated in Kenya. But if they educated their children, they could perhaps change the ending. If they learned to read and write, they could advocate for their rights, maybe even get back some of the government money Potea had stolen over the last fifteen years.

But sitting in the circle, my mind went blank. I took a long drink of the hot milky chai as two flies landed on the edge of my cup. I smiled at each of the war-beaten old men, an AK-47 between each set of knobby knees, their eyes looking at me expectantly.

I couldn't remember what I had planned to say. After a minute, it was clear I wasn't going to remember. I steadied myself and then, like most of my more memorable statements, I started talking with no idea of what I was about to say. "Elders, thank you for inviting me and my friends into your camp," I said. Michael translated as the elders nodded in response. "I come from a country over those mountains called America. It is a big country where a black man is president." Michael chuckled as he translated. The men turned to one another and spoke in hushed tones.

An old man wearing a green-and-black checkered blanket tied over his shoulder spoke in Pokot. "Yes, we have heard that a black man from this land has conquered a tribe of white people. We hope he rules you fairly," Michael translated with a smirk. The other elders nodded in agreement. I stood there waiting for the elder to say something else. "Okay, go on," Michael said. "You are doing so good already, by the way. They really liked what you said about a black man ruling the white people." He smiled. Another elder stood up. "We would like to know more about this land you come from," he said, pausing to deliberate how best to phrase his question.

"Do they have grass there?" Michael translated. I looked down and saw that their grass looked like the stuff that grew alongside the gravel roads at my uncle's farm in Iowa. I nodded, "Yes. We have grass like you do."

He made no facial expression except to nod and ask, "And cows?"

"Yes."

"And sheep?"

"Yes."

"And camels?" the old man said, pointing at the camel lying asleep under the sparse shade of the now barren bush.

"No, we don't have camels."

He smiled, and a few of the elders started laughing. It was clear they liked having something that I didn't have. The elder seem satisfied and sat down. Then another old man with wrinkled, ashy skin cleared his throat. I could hear decades of phlegm rattling around his lungs. "How long does it take for a child to learn the white man's magic?"

I looked at Michael. "I don't understand the question."

"He wants to know how long does it to take for a child to learn the white man's magic, by which he means to learn to read and write. The Pokot believe that writing and numbers are like a magic power behind the creating of trucks, buildings, cell phones, and paper money."

"So what should I tell them?"

"Tell them twelve years," Michael said. "That way they won't be asking for their children back before they are done with high school."

I looked at the elder who had asked the question. "It takes twelve years for a child to learn the white man's magic."

The elders shook their heads in disbelief. Then another man spoke up.

"Will our children become fat like you?"

Michael burst out laughing as he translated. I glanced down at the outline of my pot belly under a thin layer of white poly-cotton. One of the side effects of the anti-depressant medication was that I spent a year putting on pound after pound. I was easily thirty pounds overweight but hadn't worked up the courage to commit to the move from large to extra-large t-shirts.

Michael could see I wasn't laughing and put his hand on my shoulder. "Don't feel bad. They like that you have lots of food to eat. They want fatness for their children too. They are always telling me how much they like my fatness." Michael grabbed his belly and shook it, and the elders burst into another round of laughter.

It was strange watching them joke around like old men in a bar. I had assumed nomadic life was more serious. The National Geographic specials I had seen never showed any indigenous people laughing. I looked at the elder who had asked the question. I could see the outline of his skull through his smiling cheeks. I smiled back at him. "Yes, their children will have food to eat and water to drink at school."

I waited for a moment for another question, but the elders sat in their chairs sipping their tea. The meeting seemed to be over. "Is that it?" I asked. Michael put his arm around me. "You did good, buddy. In fact, most missionaries do so much talking, but they liked that you just listened to their questions."

"So the meeting went well?" I asked, not sure what a successful meeting would even be.

"It went very good, buddy. In fact, they are considering the importance of school for their tribe, which is good progress. Right now we have thirty children and I think that soon we will have a few hundred. But convincing a family to give up their child for twelve years takes so many meetings. You know these children are their livelihood. They are the ones who are supposed to herd their cows and later they will hopefully give them grandchildren."

Michael stood up. "Okay, now it is time to be going." Behind us a group of kids had gathered around the vehicle kicking the mud-crusted tires and looking at their dusty faces in the mirrors.

"You know we could just steal some kids and take them to school," I said sarcastically.

"Oh man," he shook his head. "That would be so bad for a guest to be invited into a camp, and make off with the children. They would find you and beat you, surely." Michael climbed into the driver seat. I got in the back seat and started swatting flies off my face. Chelimo wandered up to the truck trailed by ten more kids. Then she turned to hug each one before she climbed in next to me.

Michael sat for a moment looking out at the men who were smiling and waving at us. Then he turned on the car. "Wave goodbye," he sighed, "because most of these men will have died by next year." I looked at the nomads' faces. Young kids with bald heads stood at attention, old men with squinting eyes, deep lines echoing the contours of their dark faces. One young man brushed his teeth with a stick, an AK-47 slung over his naked shoulder, his stretched earlobes swaying. As I waved, an emotional nausea set in.

"Okay, let's go," Michael said, a resignation in his voice. I made eye contact with Lokadamuk and forced a stoic smile. He stood stone faced, his green fisherman's cap now browned with dust. It would be the last time we saw him. Eighteen months later, Michael would receive a call that Lokadamuk and a dozen of the other herdsboys had been killed by a Turkana night raid.

The vehicle lunged out of park and slowly crawled back down the same small path out of the camp. I watched as a cloud of red earth enveloped the crowd. Chelimo relaxed into her pillow and fell asleep. I looked out as the survivor guilt settled in my stomach. We got to drive away and they were staying there. Tonight they would probably call off the cease-fire and the war would resume. As we pulled back onto the road, we picked up speed and soon the last of the flies were sucked out of the window. Within a mile, we were driving on an empty desert road. I looked back into the bush and saw nothing but the mountains, thorns, and the occasional monkey swinging from the branches. And yet we were surrounded on all sides by thousands of people grazing cows and drinking blood.

A silent war was being fought with guns from a foreign land. A strange world, lost in time, and we could have easily driven right past it.

I shook out a pill and counted to a hundred, breathing deeply between numbers. *Dear Jesus, don't let these people die*, I prayed as the medicated euphoria set in.

17
PUTTING MARY ON THE MOON

For hours we lurched up and down sandy river beds, navigating around eroded slabs of British concrete. Dust clouds blew through cracks in the window. The water in my canteen was hot and filled my mouth with dirt and rust. As the sun moved directly over the car, I moved into the front seat, and Chelimo uncurled across the back seat, the upholstery still covered in corn flakes.

After a long stretch of silence, Michael pointed at a trail like the one we had taken to the cattle rustler's camp. "There is a village in that valley," he said. "During the election last year, Keu and I had a meeting with his cousin Potea and a number of village elders."

This was the first time he had mentioned the election since I landed in Kenya. I hadn't brought it up, partly because I wasn't sure how sore he was about the loss and partly because I was worried the conversation would lead back to Michael's DWI.

"Potea left his helicopter at home and came to the meeting in a jeep. I think he wanted to seem like a man of the people," Michael scoffed. "At the meeting he promised to bring wells and food and doctors, the same things he always says. But this time the elders didn't believe him. And after he spoke I asked him to show the elders one well he had dug in the last ten years, which he couldn't do, of course." Michael chuckled. "So when it was my turn to speak, I told the elders that Potea had abandoned us and I was going to finally make good on the promises he had made years ago. And the meeting went on like that a long time, Potea making up stuff and me refuting him. And by the end of it we were talking in the dark with only a small fire in the center for light. So one of the elders invited us to stay in his homestead. You know, it's not good to be driving around the desert at night," he said, pointing at a few pot holes further down the road. "Not on these roads. And so Keu and I agreed, but Potea absolutely refused to sleep in a mud hut. So he told his driver to take him back to the hotel. And the old man got so furious…"

"Wait, what hotel?" I said, cutting him off.

"The hotel we are driving to right now," Michael said. "It's not far from here. There's a British power plant that turns a waterfall into electricity for the capital city. And they have really good chicken." He smiled.

"There is a waterfall out here?!" I shouted with righteous anger. "And the government is using it as a power plant while people are literally dying of thirst!"

Over the last two days we had driven over a dozen dry riverbeds. Earlier that morning Michael had stopped the vehicle by a hand-dug well. I watched a herdsboy, maybe ten years old, climb a ladder twenty-plus feet into the sand and come back with only a gourd full of water.

"That's just how it is out here," Michael shrugged, having come to terms with the absurdity years ago. "So anyways, the old man in the village shouts at Potea for not accepting his offer to sleep the night. 'You think you're better than us!' the old man shouted at him. But Potea just got in his jeep and drove off. So the next morning, Keu and I get in our truck and drive to the next village for another meeting. But about a mile down the road we see Potea's jeep stuck in a hole. Now, Keu wanted to just drive past, leaving his own cousin stranded in the ditch." He smiled, wagging his finger at me. "But I convinced him that even though Potea is a cheat and a liar, he was still our leader and at the very least our fellow Pokot. And that meant we were required to help him. So we pulled up beside the jeep and Potea's driver leaned out the window and said we probably needed six guys to get them out."

"What did Potea say?"

"Nothing. Not one word. Potea just sat in the back seat, arms folded like a spoiled kid. So finally we brought six guys back from the homestead, which took no small amount of convincing, by the way. It took us two hours to push him out and the whole time Potea just sat there."

"That's unbelievable," I said, indignant.

"I'm telling you. That's just how it is out here. The desert makes people do crazy things."

"I guess." We picked up speed for the first time all morning as the neglected road transformed into well-maintained gravel. In the distance I saw what looked like the kind of military bases you see in movies about Roswell, miles of desolate landscape punctuated with a chain-link fence and short military-style pole barns surrounded by bright green lawns. Men in starched uniforms were walking around with bottled water. When we got to the entrance, Michael waved at the gatekeeper, who had his military fatigues tucked into high leather boots. As we drove the paved road, I could see businessmen strolling around on freshly mowed lawns in slacks and dress shirts, a bottle of water in each hand. I felt another wave of nausea crash on me. From blood soup to bottled water in a single morning was too much.

"Park the car," I shouted frantically at Michael. I stepped out of the vehicle and a server dressed in a tie and slacks handed to me a bottle of water. I rifled through my bag, and shook out another pill.

"What is that?" Michael said, watching me disintegrate in front of him. I started counting my breaths as I tried to decide how much to say. "It's brain medication," I said.

"Like for cancer or something?" Michael asked concerned.

"No," I sighed. "Do you remember how I got so mad about your accident?" I didn't wait for him to answer. "Well, I started having what doctors call panic attacks, where your brain stops working correctly. I just got so mad that my brain sort of broke for a while. So I had to start taking this medication."

"Is that why you stopped talking to me?" He seemed like he wasn't buying it. "Your brain *broke* as you say?"

"Sort of." I felt my heart rate slow down. "It's really complicated and I don't fully understand it myself." I looked at him for a second, but then realized I couldn't bear to watch his face as I apologized. So I stared over the chain-link fence and into the desert.

A few days after the DWI Amanda had taken me to the site of Michael's accident. There was a tangled mess of chain-link fencing at the top of the hill where Michael's car had gone off the road. Standing on the side of the highway, I looked down the hundred-foot hill, a path of cut prairie leading to shards of broken ice. "Can't you at least tell Michael you're happy he didn't die?" Amanda had asked, pointing down the path of destruction. I hadn't talked to him since the accident.

I looked down at the plastic pill bottle in my hand. I had disowned Michael for drunk driving and yet here I was two years later furiously popping pills trying to manage the stress of crisscrossing between the desert and the modern world.

"I'm sorry that I abandoned you," I said. "It's been a really tough year for me. I've had to go to the doctor every week to try and put my mind back together."

Michael took a long drink of water. "It's a lot to take in," he said. "You know, after our village burned down, my father's brain broke." He threw the empty bottle into the nearby garbage can. "When I found my family, I found him shouting at goats." His voice sounded detached. "I guess it's something that just happens." He patted me on the back and walked over to a lawn chair under a canopy. I didn't answer him, but his words brought a strange confluence of relief and exhaustion that made me feel like I was going to cry. I kicked off my shoes and followed Michael onto the lush lawn. But before the tears breached my ducts, the weight of two days of over-medicating hit me. I stumbled a few feet and collapsed. I fell asleep, my face resting against blades of grass that felt indistinguishable from the lawn at my parents' house in the suburbs of Minnesota.

Chelimo woke me up late in the afternoon and led me to a tiki-style café with a faux thatched roof bar and a bleached white tile floor. Twenty black men were sitting around wrought-iron tables watching a soccer match, empty bottles of beer resting next to assorted pieces of fried chicken. Behind them was a rusty playground and an empty swimming pool with a large palm leaf blowing around the sky-blue bottom. I sat down at the table next to Michael and a server put a Coca Cola and a plate of fries and roasted chicken in front of me.

"Are you feeling better?" Michael asked as he watched the soccer match.

"Yes. The medication just made me really tired."

He ate the last few fries on his plate. "Well, you did so well at the camp, better than I had imagined."

I thought back to the night in college when we watched the child soldier documentary. I had melted into a puddle. It was easier to let my emotions run free when the kids weren't staring back at me. "Thanks," I said, devouring the food before ordering a second plate.

"Do you have beer?" I asked the waitress.

"No, don't order that one. It's not good to be drinking in Kenya," Michael said. "It's not like in America. People here don't have one or two beers. If you drink, people think you are getting drunk," he said, his head motioning towards a group of red-eyed men talking loudly at a nearby table cluttered with empty beer bottles. "Besides, alcohol has already gotten us into enough trouble."

I looked over at the men. The waitress stood next to me watching the European soccer game on the TV across the bar. "Three Coca Colas," I said to her, putting three fingers up.

"I think it's better that way," Michael smiled.

The waitress came back a few minutes later with a sun-warm bottle of cola. Even warm it still tasted like home.

"So what did you do this afternoon?" I asked Michael, the familiar taste raising my spirits.

"I met a woman named Mary."

"Yeah. So what's her deal?" I assumed she worked in the compound.

"She told me she spends her day sitting by the grocery store begging for food. She said the people of her village forced her to leave because she is struggling with a woman's issue." He pointed to his groin. "Chelimo, why don't you go get us a couple more sodas?" It was clear he didn't want to talk about Mary's issues in front of his daughter.

"You see, when Pokot boys become men we get our teeth pulled so we can never defect to the Karamojan army." He pointed at his missing bottom teeth. "We are Pokot for good. Well, young girls have something a little bit different. They get their lady part circumcised off." He pretended to clip off the tip of his pinky finger. "The thinking is that if they don't like the process of making children, then they won't be tempted to abandon their husbands for another man." He shook his head. "Nomads unfortunately believe that an uncircumcised woman will be driven mad with lust. So they cut them. They say it's for the good of the tribe, but it's such a horrible procedure. Because sometimes it gets so infected or the women get improperly stitched up, it causes so many problems during childbirth. So I told her we would take her to Keu, and then decide what to do after that." It was becoming apparent that Michael had a reputation for solving people's problems.

We finished watching the soccer game as the sun set. Then a woman dressed in a uniform walked us to a hotel room that looked like a freshman college dorm with a small TV on the dresser and a sink and shower in the bathroom. I lay in bed for the next hour wondering if Michael's comment about his father meant he had accepted my apology.

The next morning, I woke up to Michael yelling from outside my hotel room door. "Hurry up," he repeated as I threw on some clothes and finished brushing my teeth outside the car. Chelimo was sitting on a pile of luggage, having lost the back seat to three women in traditional nomadic clothes. Each woman had a plastic bag of various food items they had bought at the compound grocery store resting on their laps. I got in the passenger seat and we navigated the maze of grey cement buildings with forest-green tin roofs as men in military, waiter, and mechanics' uniforms waved at our passing vehicle. When we got to the front gate, Michael parked the SUV. A teenage girl wearing a lime-green dress dotted with red flowers hurried to the front seat, her plastic bag in hand.

Michael reached across me and opened the passenger door, motioning for her to get in. I scooted over until I was straddling the gear shift. The girl sat next to me in the passenger seat, and Michael pulled out of the complex. As we pulled away, I saw the waterfall—a white cloud falling down the four-story rock face and into a white factory. Out of the side of the factory, a pipe wound around the complex and disappeared into the ground.

I imagined the electricity flowing under the desert and re-emerging in the capital city as neon lights illuminating billboards alongside four-lane highways.

We drove all morning toward Keu's homestead, dropping off the women and picking up new passengers along the road. At dusk Michael pointed up at a trail that circled a small mountain or big hill, depending on whether you were walking or driving. As the vehicle crawled up the trail, I watched robed nomads clearing the path of logs and rocks, moving in and out of the large thorn bushes. Finally we pulled into a homestead with nine circular clay huts. Each had a small rounded doorway wide enough for an adult but too narrow for even a starving cow. On the far end of the dirt clearing was a long, rectangular mud structure with a corrugated-tin roof.

"Keu finally got his tin roof," I smiled at Michael.

"Yep. It was a big day at his homestead. He was so happy."

Seeing the tin roof felt like the first time I saw my mother's childhood home. Seeing her point at her childhood bedroom changed the stories I had grown up with, as if being there proved once and for all that my mom had actually been a little girl.

In the center of a cluster of huts, a group of women were jumping and singing while a dozen camels sat listening behind them. When I opened the window, I could hear the woman in the center leading a call and response. We sat there for a moment listening as the smell of cow dung and smoke filled our car. "That is how we welcome people," Michael smiled. "I would say these women have most probably been on this mountain having church all day just waiting for us to come. In fact, you have to start in the morning because you simply have no idea when your guests will be coming and you don't want to be unprepared."

After their song was done, Mary slowly got out of the car, lifting herself with one arm on the dashboard and the other on the door. Her teenage face contorted in a pain beyond her age. When she was back on solid ground, her bright smile resumed as she scurried over to join the singing women. I noticed a dark brownish-red stain on the seat upholstery where Mary had been sitting.

"What the hell is this?" I asked.

Michael looked down at the stain, and then at me. "Okay, buddy, I will explain later. Just cover it up with a blanket for her sake and we will talk later."

Soon we were surrounded with women wearing dangling beaded earrings and bright-colored tank tops. As the women in the center began another song, we were pulled into a round of jumping.

"Why are we jumping?" I shouted to Michael, sweat pouring down my face.

"That's what we do," Michael shouted back. "We are a jumping people."

Our jumping session lasted until the toddlers started crying for dinner. I finally sat down, my legs burning. That's when I saw Keu standing next to Michael. I knew it was him. He had a striking resemblance to his cousin Potea. He was built like him, tall and barrel chested. But instead of a suit, Keu wore a dirt-stained plaid shirt and khaki pants. His sandals were made from cut-up car tires. His cousin had been flanked by Washington elites. Keu stood in front of four of his wives, each one wearing a tank top with an infant strapped to their back. The youngest wife looked like a teenager. The oldest had crow's feet gathered around her eyes.

"This is the famous Keu," Michael said, presenting him like a trophy.

Keu extended his hand and smiled. "Hello, Natan. These are my wives," he said as Michael translated their names, "Chemkan, Chepurayi, Chemrio, and Chepotineu." As he introduced them one by one, they stepped forward and shook my hand and smiled, then wandered back to their separate huts. Keu pointed across the valley where I could see a few fires burning on the silhouetted mountainside. "Four more there," he said.

"I tell you, the man is an empire in the making," Michael laughed, slapping Keu on the back. "The UN needs to get another desk ready for Keu's mountains."

I stood in front of Keu wondering what to say, my usual round of introductory questions all seemed trivial in comparison to Keu's adventures. "You have beautiful wives," I said word by word. Keu smiled and looked at Michael. Michael took a few minutes to translate. I remembered Michael and Emilie talking about how Pokot women were celebrated for being strong and not for being pretty. "I mean strong," I cut in. "Michael, tell him I think his wives are strong."

Michael turned back to me. "No worries, buddy. That is exactly what I already told him. I translate the word beautiful as strong so that you would be saying the right things to him on your first meeting."

"Thank you, brother," Keu said clearly choosing each English word. "Thank you for school with Michael." I nodded and waited for him to continue but he just stood there for a few minutes. Then he reached down, grabbing a long piece of grass and putting it in his teeth. He motioned for us to take a seat around the fire. As soon as I sat down, Chelimo handed me a blue plastic mug of chai. It was much thicker than any I'd had since I'd been in Kenya.

"Good," I said to Keu raising the mug.

"Camels make the best milk. It's a sweet milk," Michael translated.

As the sun set, I watched Keu's wives milk the camels in a pen ten feet from me. "Michael, tell Keu I want to ride his camels before we go."

"Oh, man." Michael shook his head. "I'm *never* gonna tell him that. You can't ask that one."

"Why not? People ride camels."

"I know that. But we don't ride them like the Arabs. In Pokot, camels are so sacred. It is our belief that the camel already does enough work by providing us with milk. That riding it also would be expecting too much. In fact, if someone saw you riding a camel, they would beat you until you cried, then they would beat you for crying," he laughed. "Then they would beat us for helping you up there," he added, pointing at the nearby camel.

He took another drink of chai. "Ride a camel. Sheesh."

I watched the ten-foot-tall camel eating leaves off the top of the bushes. "You know," I said, "I think that's probably the biggest difference between Americans and Pokot. In that pen over there I see ten perfectly good modes of transportation, but tradition is holding people back from using them to their full potential."

Michael looked at me and sighed. "So you are partly right. Americans are able to invent things like internet and space ships because they don't think so much about tradition. But that's not the biggest difference between Americans and Pokot. No, I think that the difference between the West and Africa is something else. When we look at that camel, we see something sacred, something with a purpose in our community. And when you see that camel, you see a possible slave."

He wasn't just talking about the camels. Michael knew the pattern: the Africans we took to America in chains and the American factories across his continent paying a dollar a day.

"You see that woman sleeping over there?" He pointed at one of Keu's teenage daughters sleeping on a blanket. "She is so exhausted because she spent the whole day knee deep in a nearby river panning for maybe two so tiny specks of gold." His fingers pinched together. "And when I am in America and I see so much gold jewelry just sitting on the shelf in people's bedrooms, it makes me wonder why this girl even bothers. Why work so hard trying to find it at the bottom of a river, if no one is even going to bother wearing that gold?"

I sipped my tea and thought of my mother's jewelry collection, each piece made from a million tiny specks of gold sifted out of a sandy river bed. For a long while, I stared into the fire, hoping the light from the flames would mask my cheeks flushed with embarrassment.

In the dark Keu's wives scraped the burnt tea and porridge off the blackened bottoms of the cooking pans. They used just a dash of water with a care that comes from having carried jug after jug up and down the mountain.

"Michael? Is it okay for me to ask Keu why he has so many wives?" I asked quietly, having depleted the majority of my cross-cultural confidence after my last two comments.

Michael rubbed his chin. "Yes, you go ahead. In fact, it is a very interesting story."

After Michael translated my question, Keu looked at me. "My father…" he began. Michael nodded to Keu that he had used the correct English words. Then Michael turned to elaborate: "You see, after the drought that sent us to the feeding camp, there were so many raids by the Karamoja." Michael's hand circled the air. "By the time the rains came back, Keu's father was the only male left alive in the Sun clan." He pointed his index finger at Keu. "So you can imagine the Sun clan was not shining very brightly. So his father told Keu to rebuild the Sun clan. He was to have so many children and wives and cows and camels that the Sun clan would shine forever. And he has done pretty much a good job. Now he has sixty kids, eight wives, ten camels, and a thousand cows. The man is a country unto himself." I was sitting beside a modern-day Abraham.

Michael started chuckling. "A while back I asked Keu if he wanted to be like Jesus. I told him he already has eight wives, so he just needs four more to be like Jesus and his twelve disciples. But Keu said 'No way,' that one of his wives 'would make like Judas' and betray him to his death." Michael doubled over with laughter as he translated the joke to Keu who burst out laughing.

I wasn't used to people making jokes about women's rights. Amanda didn't have a sense of humor about the issue and she didn't allow anyone else to either. But Michael had decided long ago that laughter was the only way he was going to make it through the tragedies that surrounded him.

"Chelimo, what do you think about polygamy?" I asked. She was poking the fire with a long stick, clearly un-amused by the banter.

"I don't like it. I will never agree to be a second wife." She had grown up in the city and educated at Christian schools where they spoke against polygamy.

Michael immediately stopped laughing as if he had just remembered that Chelimo was there. "Very good, Chelimo," he said, switching to his fatherly voice. "And in fact you won't have to because you are educated. You can get a job and provide for yourself. Then you can wait for the right man to come along."

"Michael, ask Keu if he wants his daughters to be polygamous," I said.

"Okay, that is another good question, buddy."

Michael asked Keu, who shook his head.

"He says that he had so many wives because of his father's request. But now he wants his daughters to go to school. He knows now it is so un-Christian to have so many wives. But it is also so un-Christian to leave your family. And if it is a sin to stay married and a sin to divorce, what can he do?"

Mary walked out of the darkness and carefully lowered herself onto a blanket near the fire. She was wearing a different skirt, which reminded me of the stain on the car seat.

"Michael, you said we would talk about the car."

His eyes narrowed in confusion. I tilted my head towards Mary, and Michael shifted uncomfortably before glancing at Chelimo.

"Okay, Nathan. Let's go for a walk." Michael stood up to leave and I followed him down a path that opened up to a rocky ledge. A mosquito buzzed in my ear, distracting me from the beauty of the moonlit valley and plumes of grey smoke rising from hundreds of fires.

"Mary is from a homestead on the far side the valley." He pointed to a cluster of fires a few miles away. "But now she lives alone at the power plant because she's unclean." Michael sighed. "You know, I have often wondered if the Pokot are in fact one of the lost tribes of Israel. I first suspected it when the missionaries told us of Moses and the Israelites crossing the sea. You know this story is a very common children's story in Pokot, from times well before the missionaries came. Small kids are told the story about a man named Morse who separated a great river to bring the nomads to the green hills on the edge of the desert." He pointed back towards Kapenguria. "And I realized that the Pokot were speaking of the Bible story of Moses. And since then I have found so many similar laws and customs between the Bible and the nomads." He pointed north. "You know, it's not so far a walk that way to Jerusalem." He smiled.

"Anyway, one of these ancient customs is the belief that a woman is unclean during her monthly time. They say the blood makes her unclean. And as I told you before, she was circumcised a few years ago. So when Mary had a baby, due to all the cutting and stitching, her skin was not able to hold. And during the birthing, her insides came out with the baby. And the midwives were so horrified and they frantically tried to push it all back inside. But her guts could not be forced back. So she has been bleeding slowly by slowly since that day. And that blood is what you saw on the seat." I felt my stomach turn. "She was told by the elders that she was unclean and that she had to live outside the homestead. So now she sits alone in town begging for food while her baby son lives with her husband and his new wife."

I stared down at the cluster of fires in the valley, where Mary's baby was sleeping with a new mother. When I was a child, I nearly lost my own mom. I remembered washing my small hands in the porcelain sink of our family bathroom. I turned to dry my hands on the towel before catching a glimpse of the wicker garbage basket full of toilet paper stained red. I ran out of the bathroom yelling for my brother Kellen, assuming he had cut himself. But as I ran down the hall, I heard my mom crying and I stopped outside my parents' bedroom. I leaned in the doorway and saw her lying face down on the bed as my dad rubbed her feet. That's when I knew it was serious; my father only rubbed our feet when we were really sick.

"Dad, what's going on?" I asked. "Where's Kellen?"

My mom looked up quickly, wiping her tears with the corner of the pillow case. My dad stood up, took my hand, and walked me to the dinner table.

"Is Kellen okay?" I asked, still looking around for him. "I think he cut himself, because the bathroom garbage is full of bloody Kleenex."

"No, Kellen's fine." Dad put his hand over mine. "Nathan, your mom is bleeding a lot and needs to have surgery right away."

I stopped looking around and stared at him. I wasn't really sure what a surgery was but I knew enough to know it happened with special doctors.

"It's nothing to worry about, but you and your brother are going to spend the weekend at Brad's house and I'm going to need you to be extra nice to your mom for the next couple of weeks."

Brad's mom came to pick us up the next morning, and two days later, mom had her uterus removed. As my mom lay in a hospital bed, I was wrapped in my sleeping bag on the carpet floor of Brad's bedroom telling him that my mom was having surgery.

Brad stared at the ceiling, his hands under his head. "Is she gonna die?" he asked matter-of-factly. Until that moment I had never considered the possibility that moms could die.

"So what's going to happen to Mary?" I asked.

"I'm not sure. She just asked for help. You know, this happens so much. That old man Lokadamuk walked 200 miles to my house to get money for just one cow. And this happens all the time. Almost every day someone will come to my house asking for malaria medication, or money for a new piece of tin to patch their roof."

I could hear the exhaustion in his voice. "Everyone thinks I have money because I went to college with white people." He kicked a rock over the ledge and looked up at me.

"When I was campaigning for parliament, there was a moment when I thought I might actually win the election. That was before Potea started flying around the desert in his helicopter. After that it was all over," he trailed off. "But for like one week I thought I might actually win. And I remember talking to a group of women who were showing me how far they have to walk for water every day. And I realized that as the parliamentarian I could just snap my fingers," his fingers clicking in the night, "and a hundred men would drive from the capital city and build a well for those women the next day. And then I started imagining building hospitals with ambulances to pick up women in labor, like they have in America. I would put a school for kids to learn in every valley. And not just a few tin sheets, but a proper school with computers and Facebook. It could have been

201

done in like ten short years." His voice carried a hope that defied all rationality before he exhaled it all out. "But when I saw Potea's helicopter flying overhead, I realized that it wouldn't happen through the government. Not in my lifetime." He paused for a long time before adding, "Now I'm just a poor millionaire."

I looked back across the homestead. Mary was sitting between two of Keu's wives sipping tea, a blanket wrapped around her waist. I swatted the mosquito as it landed on my earlobe.

"Yeah?" I asked. "What makes you a poor millionaire?"

"Because I am the richest poorest person in Kenya." He smirked. "I have a master's degree from America and I live in a cement house on the edge of a desert with a leaky tin roof. But by the grace of God, we run a school for children. And even you are a poor millionaire too," he said, slapping me on the back, his words winking at the absurdity of the desert. "Because you don't have so much money in America, but you can always find some when you need it." He smiled wide, "And more importantly, when I need it. We are two poor millionaires, putting kids on the moon."

The first time Michael had asked me to help him put kids on the moon I was in my college apartment. I had invited him over for dinner, and when he walked in, he was captured by the poster of JFK hanging on the living-room wall. Kennedy was wearing a white shirt and staring into the middle distance, his hair wind-sculpted like he had spent the day at a beach in the Hamptons. Below were the words "It's time for a new generation of leadership... For there is a new world to be won." Michael sat below the poster mimicking Kennedy's pose. He had insisted I take a photo. I turned on the lamp beside him, hoping to get enough light on his dark skin to capture his expression. I asked why he liked Kennedy so much.

After I snapped a few pictures, Michael stood up. "You know that before Kennedy was famous for putting a man on the moon, in Kenya he was so famous for something called the Student Airlift of 1959." He said the words "Student Airlift" as if it were common knowledge.

"Oh, yeah?" I said, having never heard of it.

"When Kennedy was still a senator he went to Kenya to meet in secret with a group of black freedom fighters. He was so passionate about ending colonialism and spreading democracy across the whole world. The young freedom fighters told Kennedy their plan to organize a democratic Kenya, free of British control. And after the secret meeting, Kennedy held a press conference where he told the world, 'Education is, in truth, the only key to genuine African independence and progress.' Which is true, by the way. And in the fall of 1959, Kennedy gave those young Kenyan freedom fighters each a full-ride scholarship to an Ivy League school in America, like the scholarship I was given to come to our college.

And in 1963, the year these graduates returned home, Kenya declared independence from the British."

I watched the fires below go out one-by-one as the homesteads drifted off to bed. "Putting kids on the moon" collapsed Kennedy's two great achievements into a simple mantra. That was Michael's plan for his people. He was determined to airlift as many children of the desert as he could. He didn't care if they were Karamoja, Pokot, or Turkana. He sent them all to school in hopes that they would become doctors, lawyers, teachers, and architects. He was raising an army of children to bring the desert into the modern world. He was training a generation of nomads to bring modern medicine, human rights, education, and infrastructure to their villages.

That was the plan, and now we had a classroom with thirty kindergarteners, hoping one of them would grow up and build a hospital for women like Mary to have their babies in. Maybe they would even convince the elders to stop circumcising girls altogether.

But that was years away, and Mary needed help now.

"How much would it cost to help Mary?" I asked.

Michael rubbed his chin. "Hmmm, I'm not so sure, but a while back I read something about this problem. And the article said it usually takes a surgery that costs a few hundred dollars."

"Okay, let's put Mary on the moon," I said. "I'm a poor millionaire. I'll find some money somewhere."

"I'm glad to hear you say that," Michael said, slapping me on the back. "I will tell Keu to arrange things with Mary's father and we will bring her back to a hospital."

Before sunrise, it was decided that Keu would accompany Mary on our drive back to Michael's house on the edge of the desert. And after we said goodbye to Keu's wives and hugged each of his kids, our vehicle began its crawl down the mountainside.

We drove all day. Keu and Mary silently bounced up and down in the back seat, a rubber floor mat lodged between Mary and the seat cushion. When we arrived at Michael's two-room cement house, I sent an email with Mary's story to a small church in Minneapolis I recently joined. The following Sunday the pastor read Mary's story to the thirty people in attendance, explaining they would be taking a donation for her surgery. Following the service, a wicker basket was placed between the regular and decaf coffee and within an hour the money was raised.

On Monday, we drove Mary to a gynecologist fifty miles from Michael's house. Michael's wife, Angelina, came along for support. After Mary was examined by the surgeon, we were called into a small office. The surgeon sat behind a shiny wooden desk in a bleached-white lab coat. He calmly explained that he was confident he could stop the bleeding and even hopeful that she would be able to have more children.

Angelina translated the surgeon's words to Mary, who sat still seemingly unable to process the surgeon's prediction. Angelina rubbed her shoulder, assuring her that the surgeon could be trusted.

On the drive home, Mary stared out the window. When we arrived at Michael's house, she quietly walked into the house and lay on the bed.

After dinner, Mary asked to speak to me. I walked into her room. She was lying on the bed under a wool blanket, a glass of water on the wooden bed stand. I sat on the plastic chair beside Angelina. Mary turned towards me and smiled, speaking slowly in Pokot. "I don't understand where you came from," Angelina translated. "But Michael tells me you are going home. So I want to say thank you because I may not see you again. And if we don't meet again before heaven, I will see you there." My tears blurred her smile. "And if I get to heaven and find that you are not there, I will walk up to God and tell him that he has made a big mistake. I will tell him the story of how you saved my life. And then he will come get you and we will surely meet in heaven."

I smiled as hot tears rolled down my cheeks. "Thank you" was all I could get out. It had been a long time since anyone had told me they thought I was going to heaven.

18
LINES, NOT CIRCLES

The next day I sat in the front seat of our vehicle as it hobbled down the main street of Kapenguria, the engine's death rattles rousing barking dogs. After two weeks of gunning the engine through sand dunes, re-duct-taping exhaust pipes, and dumping gallons of bottled drinking water over the smoking radiator, we had one final stop to make before the SUV was sent to the mechanic for hospice care. We were headed to our school.

"This is it," Michael said, struggling to turn the wheel through a swinging metal gate, the tires squealing like a kicked pig. I read the words "Kapenguria Baptist Church" painted on a short red brick wall. Behind the sign I could see a series of single-story, matching brick buildings with blue tin roofs spread across an acre of short green grass that was surrounded by a barbed wire fence. Michael parked the car in front of a hand-painted sign reading "Daylight Center and School Headmaster Michael Kimpur" with our school logo painted below. The logo featured a drawing of a man standing next to a cow underneath a yellow sun.

Michael got out of the vehicle. After a month of driving from homestead to homestead, I was getting used to being met with a group sing-a-long followed by an hour of jumping and dancing in a circle, humming a melody without understanding any of the words. So my heart sank a little when thirty children marched out of the brick building in a single-file line. Gone were the beads and robes. Each child was dressed in a student uniform—a mishmash of fraying orange and blue shirts, skirts, and shorts. Their teacher, a tall woman in a white blouse and black skirt, organized the kindergarteners into two rows just like my kindergarten teacher had done to me on the other side of the world. Michael and I clapped along with the class singing, "We are marching in the light of God...," first in Swahili and then in English. The kids were smiling wide, clearly proud to show off their ability to sing in two new languages. Their cheeks were fuller and their hair was darker than the children I had seen in the desert. They smiled when I waved at them, no longer staring at me like a curiosity.

I thought of the conversation I had with my brother, Kellen, before I left for Kenya. He had recently started teaching at an inner-city school in Minneapolis. The week after he got hired, I invited him out for coffee, hoping he would make a donation to Daylight. "You know, the pioneers already tried what you and Michael are doing," he said, sipping coffee. "They rounded up Native kids and put them in western-style schools dressed like tan Europeans." He paused with the face he makes when he is about to say something he knows I don't want to hear. "They tried to make the Native kids white. But it didn't work."

"Well, they didn't have Michael," I snapped back at him.

"Oh, they had people like Michael," he said dismissively. "I'm not saying it's impossible. I'm just saying it's gonna get messy."

"So you think we should just leave orphans to die out in the desert?"

"I'm not saying that," he said, putting his hands up as if I had pulled out a gun. "I'm just saying it's complicated. The Native kids at my school have the highest suspension rates of any ethnicity, and it's not 'cause we are racists about it. It's just that the sit-down-shut-up-and-listen-to-the-white-lady model doesn't seem to work very well for them."

"But we don't have any white teachers."

"Well, that's a good start," he said, pulling out his checkbook.

Michael and I clapped as the children finished singing and filed back to their desks in the classroom. I asked Michael why they weren't jumping in a circle like in the homesteads.

"Oh, they do that one sometimes," he said, leading me into the classroom. "But they also need to learn to stand in lines. The modern world is divided up into lines, not circles."

"We could use a few more circles in America," I said, entering the cool cement classroom. The walls were covered in hand-painted posters of addition and subtraction problems and pictures of the alphabet with small drawings—M is for Milk and C is for Camel. The building blocks of their nomadic culture now reduced to reading lessons.

Daylight Students at Kapenguria Baptist Church
in January 2010

I stood in front of the class. Each child was seated at his or her desk waiting for me to speak.

"This is English class, so you should greet them in English," Michael whispered.

"Hello, I am Nathan," I pointed at myself.

"Hellow, Natan," they repeated in unison.

Michael told the class in Swahili that I was the man who helped pay for their food and books.

"Thank you," the children said, smiling.

Their English teacher, Joseph, was dressed in a beige sweater and slacks. He looked to be about twenty years old. "Thank you for saving these children," he said to me. "Without this place they would have surely died in the desert."

Then he led them through the alphabet song. Afterwards I asked the class to sing a song from the desert. Michael put his hand on my shoulder. "Don't worry, buddy. We won't let them forget those songs." When we started the school I had told him that I didn't want our kids to forget their traditional values. "If they are going to help the desert, they have to remember it," I told him over the phone.

A young girl with a bald head and thin lips stood up. She was a head taller than the other kids and her dress was already a little too small for her. She opened her mouth and a cold piercing melody cut through the classroom. The other children responded in a slow, rhythmic cadence. I recognized the song from Keu's homestead, but I didn't remember it sounding so tragic.

Before I could ask Michael what the words meant, the lunch bell was rung and the kids rushed out of class in a whirlwind. Ten minutes later they were sitting in the grass, a plastic bowl of beans and rice resting between each of their legs.

Joseph sat on a plastic chair sipping tea and I sat down in the chair next to him. "What are primary schools like in America?" he asked. I looked around for Michael. I never knew how much to say. I didn't want to lie, but sitting on a lawn chair next to kids eating beans and rice on the grass didn't seem like the right time for a lengthy description of suburban American schools.

Before I left, Emilie had given me a copy of *Little House in the Big Woods* by Laura Ingalls Wilder. "Something to remind you of home," she said, handing me the paperback as I packed my bags. She had traversed enough countries to know it's always good to have reminders of home. "I decided to come to Minnesota for college because I wanted to experience the winters that Laura was always going on about in her books."

I looked at the red-brick building and tried to put together a complimentary but honest response to Joseph's question. It was small and dark, but it was a classroom. The essentials were all there: books, a chalkboard, eager students, and their teacher. Behind was a small grass field where kids were playing soccer, a cow grazing near the goal post. It was a beautiful place for a school. It was perched on the top of a hill, overlooking a lush green valley dotted with tall evergreens. A small stream wound its way through the small farms sectioned off with short wooden fences.

I looked back at the red brick buildings. Laura Ingalls Wilder had probably studied in a classroom like this one, and so had Shakespeare and the Apostle Paul for that matter. The majority of children throughout human history had been taught without florescent lights and high-speed internet. After a long pause, I looked back at Joseph. "Schools in America are a lot like this one, except they usually have electricity and computers. And they usually don't have such a nice view."

He sighed as if he had expected that answer. "The public schools in the capital city have electricity and computers as well," he said, taking the final bite from his bowl. "That is why our children are so far behind in the national testing." He took another glance at the valley before shepherding the children back to class. "But only the richest men in Nairobi have views like this one." He shouted over the hum of the children.

Michael sat down in the chair Joseph had occupied. "So what do you think of it?" he asked, excited.

"It's a beautiful school," I said, watching the clouds move across the valley, their shadows alternating the grass from light to dark green. We sat quietly, bathing in the cool afternoon sun, listening as the class started another round of singing on the lawn at the far end of the property. I remembered the young girl's haunting song. "What was that girl singing about in Pokot?" I asked.

"That young girl was singing a very important song in Pokot. It's called *The Land Question*," Michael said, clearing his throat. "When something important happens in our culture, we write a song. We don't have books to write our history so we write songs, which are a bit easier to remember, by the way. So when our Pokot ancestors were kicked off their land by the British, they sang a mournful song as they walked. It is a call and response as you heard. The leader sings 'Our land is' and then the name of a place that was stolen by the colonists. 'Our land is Kapenguria,' 'Our land is Kitale,' 'Our land is Mukatona...'" He listed off a dozen cities that dotted the edge of the desert. "And then the group responds with the question, 'Why are you taking the land of our ancestors?' So that girl is singing about the great tragedy of our people. That our land was stolen and now we struggle in the desert."

Michael pointed to a mountain several valleys away. Its massive base was dark, the top lost in blue rainy air and clouds. "You see that mountain? That was Tororot's original holy mountain. It's called Mount Elgon. But when the Pokot were forced away from these hills and into the desert, they felt that God lived too far away. So they asked him to move to Mount Mtelo near where I was born."

I looked at Mount Elgon, its peak shrouded in clouds. It seemed believable that God lived on its summit. "Do you think the Pokot will ever get this land back?"

"Nobody knows," Michael said with resignation. "In 1963 when the British left Kenya, they gave all the land to the new Kenyan government. And our politicians divided all of Kenya between the tribes. But the problem was that there were no Pokot or Karamoja leaders to represent us there. So the politicians gave our land to other tribes. In fact even most of the farmers in town are not Pokot, they are from other tribes. And they bought the land with their money. So it seems a bit unfair to take it from these humble farmers who have been living there for some fifty years now."

"That sounds like huge a mess," I said.

I remembered my dad telling me a similar story as we navigated his small aluminum canoe down a creek near our house. It was our Father's Day tradition, the one afternoon of the year where we agreed not to fight under any circumstances. "They're putting together a lawsuit to get this land back," my dad said after fifteen minutes of paddling in silence. He sounded as if he had just started talking mid-thought.

"Who is?" I asked.

"The Native Americans. They are suing us for the land." Dad had been a school teacher on a Native American reservation on the Canadian border for a year after college and would occasionally update me on the latest news from the reservation.

"Us? Like our family?" I asked, surprised.

"Well, not just our family. Everyone in town."

It wasn't a big secret that our town was built on Native land. The town library was literally built on Indian Mound Street East. There was no doubt that the land had been stolen, but it seemed odd to sue my family for that.

"Isn't there a statute of limitations on land stealing?" I asked.

"That's what the courts have to decide." My dad sighed. When he said "courts," I imagined a room full of white people with formerly Native American addresses on their licenses.

I told the story to Michael and afterwards his eyes narrowed on me. I waited, wondering whose side he was going to take.

"It's a huge mess," he repeated. "That's why these kids have to go to school, so they can buy back their land or build a new city in the desert or some other solution I haven't thought of yet." He grinned. "But the Native people suing for their land back is a creative idea, by the way."

We played a game of soccer with the boys that lasted until the sun turned orange and the air began to cool. Then we said goodbye to the teachers, thanking them for their hard work, and slowly drove back to the Kimpur home across town. Angelina and Chelimo were waiting for us in the grass outside the house, sitting on identical plastic chairs washing potatoes under the outdoor spigot. Michael and Angelina's one-year-old son Joshua bounced on Angelina's lap. He wore a tiger-striped onesie, and a single tooth was emerging from his bottom gums. I took my seat on a stray cinder block and began peeling potatoes with them. "Chelimo, do you wish you grew up in the desert or at school here in Kapenguria?" I asked. Sixteen seemed old enough to conceptualize what her life would have been like as a village girl. She paused, putting the sentence together in her head. "I like to visit the desert to see my grandma and stay with her. But I want to live here where life is easier."

Then Chelimo translated the question to her mom. "Here is better," Angelina said firmly, her index finger pointing at the grass. It could have been an unintentional result of her poor English skills, but her tone made me feel like an idiot for even asking. I quickly finished peeling the potatoes and walked back into the house. Keu and Michael sat on the couch drinking sodas and talking quietly in Pokot as Mary slept in the next room. After the sun set, Angelina and Chelimo turned on the single overhead light bulb and handed a plate of potatoes and greens to everyone. As we ate, I could hear Keu's lungs rattling.

"It's the altitude," Michael said, hitting him on the back a few times. "His lungs are not used to the moisture after the hot and dry air all this life." Kapenguria was high enough above the desert that my ears popped when we reached the top of town.

"Hard for breath," Keu said, wiping the spit from the corner of his mouth.

After five generations exiled in the desert, Keu's physiology was rejecting his people's native land. Keu and Michael embodied *The Land Question* on a single couch. Keu was incapable of living in the green hills of Kapenguria and Michael couldn't keep down a bowl of blood soup.

That night I woke to a banging on my bedroom door. "Nathan. Nathan get up," Michael shout-whispered. "Get your pants on. Keu must be going to the hospital now." I reached for the gym shorts and an undershirt next to the bed. The air was cold and heavy as I ran towards the shining headlights. Keu was sprawled across the back seat, his shirt drenched in sweat, his head rocking back and forth, his massive chest moving with shallow, quick breaths. I felt Michael's hand on my shoulder. "Get in the car. We have to be going."

The paved road to the hospital gave me a sense of hope that we were driving Keu to modern medicine. Keu descended into a coughing fit before groaning in pain. "This is how people die," Michael said, revving the engine. "They die like this all the time."

My seat started vibrating as the engine struggled to maintain the speed. My mind emptied with panic. I heard Michael's words echo as the mix of adrenaline and sleeplessness pushed my heartbeat into my throat. I had left my medication in my bedroom. I counted the trees as we drove by them. "Last month my youngest son Joshua got malaria. We gave him medication but it wouldn't take. So after two days we drove him to this hospital. But the doctor at this hospital said the fever was close to breaking, so he sent us back home." I looked back at Keu who was doubled over with hard dry heaves, as if his lungs had given up and his inexperienced stomach had taken charge of oxygen distribution.

Michael shouted something back to Keu in Pokot ending in *"Kidogo, kidogo." Slowly, slowly. Little by little.* It was the rallying cry of Kenya. As if to say, we defeated the British, it took us two hundred years, but we did it. So whatever you're facing, remember that it will be done slowly, but it will be done eventually. Lord willing and the creek don't rise.

"But on the drive home Joshua stopped breathing," Michael continued, his fingers pointed just around a bend in the road. "Right here he went into a coma and in Kenya that's pretty much it. People don't come back from that side of things. Angelina couldn't take it. She was crying and shouting for me to drive back to the hospital. And I tried to drive as fast as I could but the car was shaking so badly. Then Joshua stopped breathing and she shouted for me to stop the car. Then she started hitting me from the back seat to let her out. That she wasn't going to stand in the hospital and listen to the doctor tell her that her son was dead."

Listening to Keu's lungs bubble with fluid in the backseat as Michael recounted his son's near death was too much. I tried to block out all of the sound, stare at the dashboard, and count my breaths. When I got to one hundred, I remembered I had put an EpiPen in the glove box. The travel nurse had given it to me in case I discovered that I was deathly allergic to something in Africa. I pulled the eight-inch syringe out of the dash. "I could give Keu this. I forgot I had it. It's a shot of adrenaline. It will give him a burst of energy."

"Then give it to him," Michael shouted, irritated that I had held out for so long.

"Actually, I'm not sure," I said frantically. "It could make him worse."

Michael looked at me "Don't waste time. Just do it." His voice was firm and measured.

"But what if it kills him or something?"

"Listen to me, Nathan!" Michael shouted, slamming his fist on the steering wheel. "I call it the paralysis of analysis. People don't help because they are afraid that it might turn out to be the wrong choice. But I say at least do something, even if it's the wrong thing."

212

Then he softened his voice. "Because then when you are standing in front of God you can say *at least you tried.*"

That's how Michael has lived his life. Bring a nomadic kid to school, dig a well, take an American out into a desert war-zone, and go to the moon. Do something. And if the children you educate grow up more like Potea than Kimpur or you dig and dig and never hit water, at least you went down swinging. I popped off the cap to the EpiPen, prayed for God to save Keu and forgive me if I was about to kill him, and stabbed the needle into his thigh.

I sat watching Keu's chest move up and down in short, erratic bursts for five minutes. As soon as we reached the hospital driveway, I ran towards the painted, one-story cinderblock building. Glancing in each room along the open-air hallway, I hoped my white skin would curry some favor with the doctor who was working the night shift. The cement walkway opened up into a lobby, the walls lined with short wooden benches. A father in a leather jacket and a young girl holding a crying baby sat outside a florescent-lit examination room. Inside, a grey-haired man sat at steel desk writing on a pad of paper, a stethoscope sticking out of his white jacket.

"Excuse me, sir," I said. "I think my friend is dying and I need you to come right away."

"Do you have his file?" the grey-hair doctor responded, not looking up.

"What?" I was shocked he hadn't burst through the door at the word "dying." "No, just come out here and check him out. My friend will go find his file."

The doctor looked up. I could see purple skin gathered under his tired eyes, like old sandbags around a swollen river. "I cannot see patients without a file," he said matter-of-factly.

Michael walked into the doorway with Keu slumped over his shoulder. He shouted something at the doctor in Swahili. The doctor pointed back towards the hospital entrance and then returned to his notepad.

"Help me put Keu on the bench," Michael said as we lowered him onto his back. Keu stopped wheezing for a moment before rolling over as milky liquid poured out of his mouth and onto the concrete floor. The girl, no older than ten, pulled up her feet to avoid soiling her dress. Then Keu bolted upright and ran down the hallway shouting to Michael. When he got to the end of the building, he doubled over and threw up again. "He says he has so much strength all of a sudden," Michael laughed.

"It's the adrenaline," I said watching him run back towards us.

"Your needle is really something." Michael whistled. "Okay, he seems alright for now, but let's be going to find his file." We returned to the entrance of the hospital and Michael stopped at an illuminated window with a white curtain pulled shut, the word "In-take" written in red on the door frame. I had run past it hoping to find a doctor instead of a receptionist.

"Excuse me," Michael said into the crack in the window. A man flicked the curtain aside before scooting his rolling chair over to the window and speaking to Michael in Swahili.

"He wants three hundred shillings for the file," Michael said, clearly disappointed at the turn of events.

"But you told me that Kenya has free healthcare," I said, winded from running.

"Free is a relative term here," he said curtly. "You give him something and he gives you something." I pulled out a few small bills and the receptionist slowly counted out change before handing me a red ticket, the kind kids win at a fair.

"What the hell is this?" I said, pressing the ticket to the window.

"That is a ticket for the file," the receptionist said.

Michael took the ticket out of my hand. "We have to walk to the other end of the hospital to retrieve it."

"We don't have time for this bullshit," I shouted, my hand balled in a fist. Michael saw the flash of anger and grabbed me by the arm pulling me down the hallway. "I nearly lost my son to men like these. I'm not losing my best friend to these tax collectors."

We walked past Keu, who was lying on the bench wheezing and crying into the corner of his unbuttoned shirt. A puddle of red and orange vomit beside him was working its way down a crack in the cement. I could see the doctor was hovering over a blue-vinyl examination table pressing his finger against the now-silent baby's naked chest. The father and daughter were seated on chairs beside the steel desk.

At the far end of the building, a young man in a long white lab coat was watching a soccer match on a small black and white TV, his back turned to the window. I could see bottles of pills lining the wooden shelves and a metal scale on the table. I slid the ticket through the slot under the window and Michael shouted at the man to bring Keu's file.

"He wants money for a handling fee," Michael said.

I looked at the clerk, then at the ticket. "What would happen if I couldn't pay?" I asked Michael, my anger swelling into my voice.

"He knows you can pay because you are a white man."

"What if you had come alone?"

"Then that would have been something else entirely," Michael sighed. "Just pay him, we are wasting time."

"Two-hundred-fifty shillings," the clerk replied in English, glancing back at the TV.

"Fine," I said, tossing two bills and three coins through the slot under the window. When we returned to the lobby, the family was gone. Keu was laying on his back in a fit of coughing as the doctor wiped down the vinyl examination table with a hand towel. I slammed the folder on doctor's desk.

"Keu Limon" was written in black ink on the edge. The doctor opened the folder. Inside was a blank pad of yellow lined paper. I realized Keu didn't have a file. The file was just an excuse to scam an American out of the price of a burger and fries. This doctor had listened to his patient dying for forty-five minutes outside his office waiting for a cut of the profits. I was frozen with rage as the doctor wrote Keu and the date on the top of the first page.

"So what is the problem that Keu is experiencing?" the doctor asked as if we had never spoken.

"I need to leave or I am going to punch this doctor," I whispered in Michael's ear.

"This is the same doctor who nearly killed my son," Michael whispered back. "But he is the only doctor available at this hour so you should wait outside, buddy." The doctor closed the door behind me and I sat on the plastic chair as tears began running down my cheeks. I sat crying for a long while, pulling myself together enough to listen whenever I heard talking or coughing from inside the examination room.

What seemed like an hour later, the doctor stood silhouetted in the doorway. "Keu had a serious asthma attack." His voice was deadpan, as if he was announcing the soup of the day. "That is why he is having such trouble breathing. We will give him some medication to help."

Five-hundred shillings later, steroids began to massage Keu's lungs. And as we pulled out of the hospital parking lot, I could hear Keu begin to snore in the back seat as Michael drove in silence. I looked back at Keu, watching his chest now rising and falling at regular intervals. It was hard to believe a man who had survived for thirty years on blood soup, stood his ground as a tank rained fire down on his family, a father of sixty children, had nearly died of an asthma attack four feet from a doctor.

"This whole country is a mess," I said, disgusted. As the words came out, I realized how arrogant it sounded.

"We're still a young country," Michael sighed, "not even fifty years old. Kenya still has some growing up to do. Now you sleep, buddy. It's been a long night." He reached for the radio dial and turned on the BBC.

I stared out the window watching the white lines along the highway as a smug British man droned on about unseasonable weather. Somewhere along the drive home my anger gave way to exhaustion and I fell asleep between the rhythmic cadence of the news reel and Keu's snoring.

19

IT'S NOT EASY BEING GREEN

Michael spent the next day leaning over the SUV outside a smog-stained repair shop haggling with the local mechanic. I was across the street in the café drinking soda watching him going back and forth over the price of every rusty limb the mechanic dug out of the car graveyard behind the shop. Michael had insisted I stay out of eyesight. "If the mechanic sees you, this is gonna cost a fortune. They'll charge me the white price, which is double what they will charge a black man."

After the vehicle had been put back together and the engine had been re-duct-taped, Michael waved for me to come over. When I walked up, the mechanic's lips pursed in frustration as I handed him the Kenyan price for the repairs. We drove back to Michael's house in the dark, listening to the BBC news as the Frankenstein engine maintained fourth gear at a dull roar.

At two o'clock the next morning, Michael pointed his cell phone light at my face. "We must be going, buddy," he said over me as I lay in bed. I could hear the vehicle engine idling outside. "Keu says you are to become a Pokot elder today."

"What do I have to do to become an elder?" I pulled the sheets over my head to avoid the cell phone light.

"They just paint you green and say a blessing on you." He threw a pile of clothes at me. "Get dressed. Angelina has the tea ready for you.

217

A minute later, I was leaning against the vibrating vehicle sipping scalding-hot chai as I grinned, imagining my face on the cover of *National Geographic*, my face painted with green and white lines, holding a long wooden spear, and a necklace of bones wrapped around my sunburned neck. The words "A New Village Elder" in white bold letters hovered above my photo.

I tossed the tea into the grass and lay down in the back seat. Soon I was dreaming of running around a roaring fire, my necklace of bones shaking like a maraca.

I awoke when flies started landing on my hot skin. Michael tossed me a bunch of bananas he had picked up from a roadside vendor. I ate one and fell back asleep.

Then the vehicle parked and I woke up again. This time I was covered in sweat, my mouth dry with the taste of dusty air.

"This is my mom," Michael said to me through the backseat window. I had to sit up to see her behind the car door. She was half his height and wore a faded floral skirt and tank top. A necklace of yellow, red, and blue beads hung around her neck like the rings of Saturn. Her eyes were pushed closed from her wide smile. Behind her was an acre of hard-packed red dirt with a hut in the center. The homestead was shaded by green bushes and a dozen cows were standing in a sunny corner of the thorn-wrapped pen. A small cooking fire with a steaming pot was being tended by laughing women in their late teens. Michael had told me his mother's homestead was deep in undisputed Pokot territory. "No Karamoja will come this far into our land," he had assured me. "That is why I told my mom to build her hut there. I have enough to worry about without wondering if my own mom is safe."

I rolled out of the backseat and shook Kama Kimpur's sandpaper hand as she whispered something in Pokot. "She says she can hardly see you because her eyes are so old," Michael translated, "but that she can still see that you are the white man who has been helping me, and she is very grateful."

"Tell her I have heard so many stories and it is wonderful to finally meet her."

She nodded as he translated. I half expected her to ask me the standard-issue suburban mom questions. "So what do you do? Where are you from? How many brothers and sisters do you have?" But she just stood there for a moment squinting at me. Then she turned around and walked through a waist-high thorn gate and disappeared into her thatch-roofed hut.

I noticed a dozen elders were sitting around the homestead drinking tea on a wooden bench in the shade of a thirty-foot baobab tree. "They have been waiting for us all morning," Michael said. "So that they can stand witness as you become an elder. We call it *Sapana*, and in fact we are already so late in the day for it."

"I didn't know Pokot had a word for *late*," I smirked, stretching my cramped legs.

"Sapana must be done in the morning, so it's good they don't have watches or they would know it is already a little past noon," Michael laughed under his breath.

I shook hands with the elders before Michael motioned for them to follow him down a path. We walked a quarter mile in silence, winding our way down a slope as thorns grabbed at my gym shorts and poked through my rubber sandals. The path opened to a green shaded clearing where Keu stood bare-chested with a long spear in one hand and a rope tied to a large brown and white goat in the other. A few younger men stood around him. The elders sat down cross-legged in a half circle facing the noon sun. The younger men who had been standing with Keu took their seats behind the old men. I walked past the roaring fire, which was being fed by a serious man in a blue and green robe who I assumed was the werkoyon.

"Why do they want to make me an elder?" I said to Michael as we walked past the young men seated around the elders. They looked like teenagers. A few of them had AK-47s lying on the short grass beside them. Seeing them made me feel painfully inadequate. I hadn't gotten my teeth pulled, or been publically circumcised as a ten-year-old. I hadn't spent long days herding cows without water, a rifle over my naked shoulder. I had skipped all the suffering and went straight to elder.

Keu handed me the spear, its smooth wooden shaft the width of a broom handle, a long steel rod sticking from the end like a giant syringe. I looked at Michael. "Are you sure this is a good idea? I mean, I'm honored that you wanted to make me an elder, but I don't really deserve it."

"Who gets to be an elder is not for you to be deciding," Michael said, brushing aside my question.

I felt like an imposter standing there in gym shorts and a white t-shirt with a spear in my hand. I looked at the teenagers. Their faces were serious but not angry. *I wonder if they hate me. I would hate me if I was them.*

"Okay, buddy," Michael said in the same tone my childhood baseball coaches used. "Now the first step to becoming an elder is slaughtering that goat for lunch." Michael whistled and Keu yanked the reluctant goat towards me.

This wasn't how I expected it to go. Over the last few weeks I had eaten a dozen recently deceased animals. But I had always walked away when it came time to kill them. Most Midwestern boys had grown up fishing but I refused on the grounds that I couldn't bear to stand by and watch as the fish flopped around the bottom of the boat, suffocating violently.

"You stab here," Keu said, pointing to a white tuft of fur where the goat's chest bone met its throat. The goat was shaking its head and barking, clearly sensing that something was very wrong. I pulled a pill out of my gym shorts and tried to swallow it without enough saliva. I felt it stick at the bottom of my esophagus.

Keu looked at me. "Be man. Leader of children." He laughed, flexing his bicep.

"You must be killing it quickly so the werkoyon can cook it," Michael said, holding the bucking goat by its legs. "These people have walked all day and they are ready for lunch."

"Okay, I'll kill it," I said, coughing down the pill. "But you're gonna skin it."

"Oh definitely, definitely we will be skinning," Michael nodded. "But first you stab it." He pointed at its chest. I touched the end of the spear with my finger; it was flat steel in the shape of an arrowhead. "It is definitely sharp enough," Michael reassured me.

I took the spear with both hands and thrust it at the goat's chest. The spear hit the goat's chest and bounced off. The goat screamed and jumped out of their hands. Once it was free it darted around the clearing looking for an escape. Michael and Keu chased after it as the rest of the elders erupted in laughter and shouting in Pokot. I saw the teenagers pointing at me and shaking their heads. Michael and Keu finally managed to wrestle the yelping goat to the ground.

"Okay, buddy, let's try it together," Michael said when he had recovered from a fit of laughter. I felt small and alone.

"Michael, maybe this isn't a good idea." I was sweating in shame.

"No worries, buddy." He picked up the spear lying next to me on the ground. He placed it in my hand and placed his hand over mine, tightening his grip. "Do it like this," he said, slowly rotating the spear in the air.

"Okay." I sighed. Keu held the goat's head and steadied its body between his thighs. Michael moved the spear to the goat's chest and slowly screwed the metal into the white fur. The goat let out a short bark as blood matted the white hair and ran along the spear handle and over our hands. The goat stood still, struggling to breathe but unable to move. When the spear had gone six inches deep, Michael screwed it back out and Keu stepped back from the goat. It struggled to get its footing, taking two steps and then collapsing as a teenage boy grabbed a bucket to catch the falling blood.

I handed Keu the spear, my heart racing. Michael put his hand on my shoulder and walked me back to the elders, who watched me with a hint of amusement on their faces. "Sit down here and eat this until the goat is ready. It will make you calm down," he said, handing me what looked like a handful of cilantro.

The bitter greens tasted metallic in my dry mouth. I tried to hand the bunch to Keu sitting next to me. "No, no, you eat. Boy walk far," Keu responded, pointing at a shirtless teenager who smiled from across the clearing. "That boy climbed so far to pick them," Michael shouted as he and the werkoyon tossed the limp goat onto the roaring bonfire. "It is traditional medicine for fighting hunger during droughts. It can be a bit bitter so take it with some sugar." Michael picked up a ceramic bowl of cane sugar and handed it to me. I waved at the smiling boy and threw a handful of sugar in my mouth, followed by the entire bunch of greens.

The elders gasped, glancing at each other before bursting into another round of laughter.

"Yes, they liked that," Michael said enthusiastically. "They liked seeing you take it like a man."

My eyes began to water from the combination of smoke rising from the burning goat hair and the acidic greens filling my mouth. I gagged. This sent the elders over the top. A few held their sides as if their bones were going to break from laughter.

I was determined to make a good impression after the goat debacle. I smiled and forced a laugh out to make it seem like I was in on the joke. Then I doubled down as my jaw methodically broke the leaves into a mush before choking them down. The effect was almost immediate.

"Michael what is this stuff?" I said, watching my fingers slowly move as if they were no longer under my control. I had been drunk before. Tom had bought me two pitchers of beer and a plate of lasagna as a twenty-first birthday present. I had returned his gifts to the toilet two hours later.

"They call it *mirah*. But don't worry, buddy." He turned the flaming goat over on the fire. "Just relax. You ate quite a number of them with not so much to eat before, so you are really going up."

My head began to slowly rock from side to side. Next to me Keu was munching on his own bunch of mirah, his eyes glazed over like a cow. I closed my eyes and felt the sand under my crossed legs swell and fall like a boat on a quiet morning.

I may have fallen asleep for a while. Because the next thing I remember was a slurping sound. I opened my eyes and the goat was laying a few feet in front of me, its ribs splayed open, three men on their knees, hunched over the carcass drinking the dark blood pooled in the empty chest, blood dripping off their chins.

The cocktail of prescription medication and mirah had somehow trapped me inside a cerebral aquarium. I sat watching the ceremony from under glass. The grey-haired man next to me was gnawing what appeared to be the goat's lungs. On the other side, a bald man was pinching his fingers along the goat's intestines, forcing the small brown pellets onto the ground in front of him. I stared at their faces, their ashy cheeks chewing the translucent fatty tissue like bubble gum, the sound of slurping echoing in my mind.

I sat entranced by the two old men devouring unwashed goat organs, staring at their jaw bones through their hollow cheeks.

Michael tapped me on the shoulder. "Okay, buddy." He placed a plate of greyish fatty meat covered in flies on my lap. "Your goat is ready." His voice sounded like he was shouting under water. "You eat, man. It's good." He popped a chunk into his mouth, a fly leaping off just before his teeth crushed it. "See? No problem."

"No, no, thank you," I said slowly annunciating each word. "The flies. I can't eat the flies."

Michael laughed. "No, you don't eat the flies. The meat, it's so good a goat. A strong he-goat."

Under no circumstances are you to eat any food from street vendors or food cooked outside of a restaurant. The travel nurse's voice burst into my head. "No. I'm sorry, but no." I pushed the plate aside.

"Just eat one," Michael demanded. "It's required for Sapana."

I picked the smallest piece I could find. *I'm at a celebration*, I told myself, placing the grey meat on my tongue. *They are inducting me into their tribe. This is a huge honor.* I looked back at the carcass. The intestines were laying on a pile of green leaves, the werkoyon hunched over it whispering a prayer under his breath.

As I chewed the sinewy rubber meat, I felt my mind settling back into place. The mirah was wearing off.

"What did he prophesy about me?" I was finally able to get full sentences from my brain to my mouth.

"The elders didn't ask him to prophesy," Michael said, lifting me to my feet. "He is from another village and no one has ever heard of him, so they didn't know if he was a true prophet."

"You're serious?"

Michael's polo shirt and khakis were spattered with blood. He was wearing the same outfit he had worn when I met him three years ago in the college cafeteria. In a vivid moment of clarity I saw Michael Kimpur: Michael, the man who was educated by American missionaries, and Kimpur, the Pokot boy who was born in a mud hut. A man who traveled not just between continents, but back and forth through time, from pizza to blood soup, wooden church pews to mountainside bonfires. And somehow I had fallen into his time machine.

"Now it's time to paint you," Michael said calmly. He handed me the spear. "It was decided that from now on your Pokot name will be Natun, meaning Lion, because they think your hair looks like a lion's main." He said running his fingers through my curly hair. "And it sounds like Nathan so it will be easy for you to remember." He smiled.

"Natun," I said, gripping the spear, the goat's wet, veiny intestines at my feet.

"Natun. Good name. Strong," Keu said.

"Okay, now for the painting part. We need you to strip down to your underwear and cut the stomach open," Michael said, patting me on the back. "Don't worry, buddy. We are almost finished."

I stood in my boxers and white sandals as Michael once again put his hand over mine. And together we pushed the spear through the goat's white stomach. Green feces spilled through the punctured organ. That's when I realized, there wasn't going to be any paint.

I felt Michael's hand on my naked shoulder. "If I said you were going to be covered in goat poop, you would have never come. And it is important the elders know you are committed to us one hundred percent."

An old man took a handful of green feces and slapped the grassy soup against my chest. As the acrid smell of grass and bile enveloped me, I closed my eyes and thought, *So this is how I die, in plaid boxers, covered in goat shit.*

I felt Michael's cupped hands run up and down my left leg and handfuls of mushed feces rolling down my calf. I tried to pull my lips into my mouth as an old man painted my forehead with his index finger. My nose was assaulted by the smell of warm vomit and lawn clippings.

"Don't worry," Michael said to me. "It won't hurt you." I looked down at him. He smiled at me as he tossed a clump into his mouth.

"I'm gonna die out here," I said to Michael. "And it's gonna be your fault."

"No. You won't die," Michael chuckled, a bit of grass stuck to his front tooth. "You are a Pokot now and Pokot don't die so easily."

Soon Keu and Michael were down to their underwear as the elders began covering them with feces.

"Wait. You two are already elders," I said as my green chest began to crust and flake in the sun.

"In Pokot we do things together. And normally you would have a group of boys with you, but today it was a little short notice so Keu and I will stand beside you," Michael explained with a clump of grass on his forehead. After the goat's stomach had been emptied, Keu, Michael, and I sat in a line facing down the hill, Michael's green legs tucked around me, the way my brother's had on our family toboggan.

The elder began shouting, as the rest of the group responded, "Oee."

"He is praying for you," Michael whispered in my ear. "He is praying that the people of your village will hear your stories and come dig a well and build more schools."

"Oee!" the men shouted

"And now he is praying that you will build a church here so that it will rain." Michael paused, thinking how to explain the situation.

Keu, a Pokot Elder, Nathan, and Michael
at the Sapana ceremony

"Like the Israelites," I said, flicking a clump of dried grass off my sunburned forearm.

"Very good buddy," he said, patting me on the back. "Just like the Israelites."

After the prayers, I stood up and Michael poured a basin of brown water over my head.

"How did I do?" I asked, looking over at the elders sitting around the goat carcass picking for scraps of meat.

"You did very well." Michael smiled, then took me by the hand and led me back up the path. Michael's mom smiled and waved at me from the shade of her hut. I waved back. The sun had dried most of the feces into a cake and as I waved I felt flakes crack and fall off my skin. I smiled at her, wondering if she thought of me differently now that I was a Pokot elder. I saw two small kids squatting around a pot of boiling water. It reminded me I hadn't drunk anything all day. A wave of exhaustion overcame me when I saw it. I walked through the thorn gate and collapsed into the back seat of the SUV.

Keu leaned inside the open window. "Natun. Lion." He smiled.

"Lion," I said, putting my fist in the air.

"Good bye, Natun," Keu smiled, putting his fist in the air.

I saw a beaded hand wave in the window. I sat up. It was Michael's mother. "Goodbye, Kama Kimpur," I said. She nodded and turned to walk back to her hut. I lay back down. I was soaking wet and smelled like death. Michael got in the driver's seat "Ready?" he said, looking at me through the rearview mirror before the vehicle lurched out of the homestead.

We drove all day across the desert. I fell in and out of consciousness as the wheels banged against shards of concrete or the engine revved as the tires searched for traction in the sandy riverbeds. I felt my ears pop on the switchbacks up the farthest mountain, and as the sun was setting, we pulled into Michael's dirt driveway. Chelimo and Angelina waved from the bedroom window of the concrete house.

The next day, the mechanic told us there wasn't enough duct tape in all of East Africa for our engine to survive the eight-hour drive to the capital city. With one day until my flight back to Minnesota, Michael and I stood in the tall grass alongside the paved road to Nairobi, waving our arms for a ride. After twenty minutes, a rusted fifteen-passenger van rattled to a stop in front of us, the driver pointing to the way-back seat where two grown men, a mother, and her baby squeezed close to make a seat and a half for Michael and me to share.

I stared out the mud flecked window at herds of zebras and antelopes galloping across lush prairies, the bones in my knees clacking together over each bump in the paved road. My chest hair had been washed and rinsed several times but still radiated the smell of dead goat up through my shirt collar. I slid the window open a few inches hoping to freshen the ninety-degree bus. But the mother next to me shook her head pointing at the bundle of fuzzy cloth that had swallowed her child. "She doesn't want her baby to catch cold," Michael said, shutting the window.

Over the course of the day, Michael and I gained seniority over the waves of new passengers and eventually made it to the front row. A lifeless flat-screen TV surrounded by rope lights—both of which I assumed died along with the van's muffler—were now the only things separating us from the driver. But as the sun set, the driver turned on the multicolored flashing rope lights, and MTV music videos began playing on the flat screen. I watched the two-lane road open into a four-lane highway, the flashing interior of our van now echoed by the illuminated billboards lining the highway. The smiling two-story-tall faces advertised dish soap and cell phone rates. At night Nairobi's skyline wasn't all that different from Minneapolis'.

As the van pulled in to the airport, the music video changed to Rick Astley awkwardly gyrating in denim. *"I'm never gonna give you up. Never gonna let you down. Never gonna run around and desert you."* I smiled, unloading my backpack from the trunk of the van, wondering if this flat-screen TV was sending me the message the werkoyon hadn't been allowed to.

"I'll call you when I get back," I said, hugging Michael. "And thanks for not killing me."

"No, there was no worry of that," Michael said, stepping into the passenger seat of the van. As they pulled away, he shouted, "Remember, you're a Pokot elder now!"

I thought about the series of fragmented moments from my induction. But any pride I felt was overwhelmed by the smell of goat feces seared into my chest hair.

20
A PUBLIC RACIST

Two years later in October of 2011, I was standing, microphone in hand, on my old campus chapel stage looking out at two thousand empty chairs, feeling an orchestral swell of emotions. The nostalgia was palpable. I was standing right where the evangelist in pinstripes had declared a war for the cafeteria lady Joanne's soul. I looked back at the section of chairs hidden in the shadows of the balcony where Emilie and I ate popcorn, watching the Purity Group bring hundreds of students to tears over masturbation. There was the front row where I hid under my orange Save Africa shirt next to Michael during the documentary on child soldiers.

"Ah, the video's not working," a man's voice echoed through the PA. I squinted through the spotlights at the sound booth, the epic swell replaced by my stomach-twisting anxiety. "So—can you go on without it?" the voice asked.

Before I left Kenya I had filmed a two-minute video of Michael telling his story: where he was from and why we had started a school. And at the end, Michael gave me a ringing endorsement to speak on his behalf. I showed it any time I asked someone for a donation to Daylight. Over the last year, I had sat down with hundreds of people trying to raise money and I noticed they always seemed more comfortable after hearing Michael speak. When Michael pointed at me and said, "Nathan and I are here in Nairobi, excited as ever to reach out to the children of the nomads in northwestern Kenya," it brought the reality into focus. I wasn't there to parade around pictures of frowning hungry kids from some faraway land, lay on the guilt, and then hit them up for money.

I was sticking my neck out because Michael was my friend and he needed help. And friends helping friends seemed to make a lot more sense to the people I talked to than trying to solve a desert war they couldn't really wrap their heads around. Michael wasn't just another cause with a 1-800 number. I would watch them sit back in their chairs and chuckle as Michael explained the first time he stepped onto the frozen Minnesota lakes. "Yeah, I had a cousin from Florida who said the same thing," one wealthy businessman had told me.

But without the video, I was just some suburban kid with a cause. "So can you go on without it?" the voice from the sound booth repeated. I felt my armpits liquefying and my lungs constricting as I stared at the silhouetted man wearing headphones waving at me. "Sure fine, I'll talk without it," I said into the microphone as I loosened my tie.

The previous winter, the college had published an article on Michael and me in the alumni magazine. It wasn't *National Geographic*, but it felt like a good place to a start. When I told Michael about it, he said, "This is it, buddy. People will read this and we will be building a hundred schools in no time." I had learned to just smile and nod. After everything Michael had accomplished, who was I to tell him what was and wasn't possible? "That'd be great," I said, trying not to throw water *or* gasoline on his fire.

The writer of the article was a young woman who had recently graduated with a journalism major. She interviewed me by phone and I told her our story: Michael's journey from mud huts to director of a school and how I went from trying to save souls at Bible camp to trying to help feed kids in Kenya. "Anything else you'd like to add?" she asked. The magazine was cover-to-cover puff pieces, something for the college to show the alumni that their alma mater was still on the right track. I hadn't mentioned my agnosticism, Michael's DWI, and my subsequent spiral into depression. "No, that's about it," I said. "But you should call Michael and get his side of the story."

Michael called me a few days later. "I asked her if she wanted to put kids on the moon," he laughed. When the journalism major emailed us a copy of the article to review, the title was "College Values Bring Light to Kenyan Darkness."

"That is colonialism," Michael said with disgust. "Darkness? I can't *believe* that."

"I know, it sounds pretty bad. She probably doesn't understand how racist it is. I mean, she seemed nice over the phone. She's probably just trying to make a play on the word 'daylight.' You know, daylight, darkness."

"Well, she's not doing a good job playing with words," he said, sounding a little less irritated. "Anyways, you call her." He paused. "But it is good word is spreading anyhow. However you make sure you figure something else out for a title." He wrapped up the call with his usual flurry of updates. "All in all, things are going pretty well here. Keu said their cows have enough grass in the villages. And the kids here are learning and they are so happy. And say hi to your mom and dad. Okay, you take care, buddy."

I called the author back and profusely thanked her for helping spread the word about the kids, before giving her a brief history lesson on the word *darkness*. How Africa had been named the Dark Continent after European Colonialists equated the inhabitants' dark skin with their sinful and savage souls. "...like *Heart of Darkness* by Joseph Conrad," I concluded. She said she hadn't read it. "Well, all I'm saying is that you probably don't want to use the word 'darkness' to describe any Africans—or black people in general."

The magazine article came out in the winter of 2010 under the title "Lighting the Way." It was a glowing description of our work alongside a dozen smiling students in blue and orange. The next year, Michael and I were invited to preach at the campus chapel. "Oh, man, that is incredible," Michael said over the phone before yelling the news in Pokot to everyone in his living room. I could hear a flurry of excited responses. "Keu is so excited. Here, you say hi to him."

"Good job, Natun, Lion," he said, shouting each word as if a phone call across the ocean required him to talk louder.

Michael took back the phone. "Okay, buddy, everyone here is really encouraged. I will go to Nairobi next month and get a visa to return to America. We will be the next U2 Bono for sure," he laughed.

But like so many of Michael's plans, an East African drought stood in his way. After a month without a drop of rain falling in Kenyan's northern neighbor Somalia, a national disaster was declared, and soon waves of Somali refugees began pouring into Kenya in search of food and water. By the time Michael reached the U.S. embassy, there were a million Somalis living in tents outside the capital city and the embassy was swamped with a backlog of refugee visa applications for America. To make matters worse, two Somali mothers were currently standing trial in Minneapolis on charges of aiding terrorists. Local news was parading around an image of the two women wearing long burkas shaking their heads *no* as the white lawyer asked them if they knew their Somali sons were card-carrying members of Al-Qaeda. It was a perfect storm of reasons for the U.S. immigration officer to deny Michael's visa.

When I called the campus pastor to tell him Michael wouldn't be coming, I could hear his disappointment through the phone. "We can cancel it," I offered.

"No, no, it'll be fine. You'll still do great," he reassured me.

"I can show a video." I said.

I sat in the front row of the chapel watching the first students wander in. A student with a blonde ponytail approached me and said, "It's time to pray." She motioned for me to follow her into a side room. Backstage, six college kids stood in a circle holding hands. They had left a spot open for me. I wiped my sweat-covered hands on my jeans and joined the circle. "Dear Jesus, this morning we want to magnify your name..." the student next to me began. Another student continued praying that "God would speak through Nathan," followed by a whispered chorus of "hallelujah" and "amen" from the others. Their whispers reminded me of the elders shouting "Oee" as I sat on the ground covered in goat feces.

I used to have to take meds to get through church services. But over the last two years I had come to terms with my faith. I had stopped expecting to feel any spiritual elation. I hadn't heard anything from Jesus since I saw the semi-truck. I kept my eyes open but I had stopped expecting to see or feel any messages coming directly from God. But it did feel good to know these students were rooting for me. The guy next to me squeezed my hand, the sign it was my turn to pray. "Dear Jesus," I said, grasping at straws. "Thank you for these young people...And help us to clearly communicate the work we are doing. Amen."

"Amen," they repeated in unison.

I walked back to my seat in the front row and remembered the video wasn't working. I started flipping through my notes as the students from the prayer circle shouldered guitars for the opening song. On the first page of my notes I crossed off the words "Video finishes." Next I had written, "As you can see, Michael is a very intelligent and funny guy." The next line was "But I didn't know that when I met him. I just wanted to have a black friend..." I had no idea how that was going to go over without the video. I scanned down to the middle of my sermon and jotted down the story where Michael goes back and tells the elders about eating smart and refrigerators.

Following a glowing list of my accomplishments from the campus pastor, I walked up and stood behind a black-metal music stand, staring out at a thousand students waiting in silence. I could see my mom and dad in the back, Brad seated between them. I took a deep breath.

"When I was a student here, I was one of those kids who was always protesting something. You might still have students like that. I was always holding a sign and shouting at people about the mistreatment of animals or the wars in the Middle East or whatever issue was in the news that week. And while these were issues I really cared about, and still care about—," I paused. The students' faces had no visible signs of agreement. "But it wasn't until I met my friend Michael, a former World Vision sponsor child from Kenya, that I began to really understand that relationships are more important than the causes we fight for." A few people began to nod, and one girl scribbled something down on her note pad. "I realized we can't just say we want something to change and then write it on a poster board, march around the campus thirteen times, and expect the problem to fix itself like the walls of Jericho tumbling down."

I saw a few more heads nodding and got the feeling the crowd was on my side. "I was in the cafeteria when I first met my friend Michael and he told me his story. How at five years old he had escaped through the night as raiders burned down his village, and his adventures going to school by becoming a World Vision sponsor child. He told me that his picture hung on someone's refrigerator in Portland. And as amazing as his story was, after listening to him talk for an hour, I remember thinking, 'I hope Michael will be my friend, because it would be really cool to have a black guy standing next to me at the next Save Africa rally.'" The crowd nervously laughed, as if white people wanting to have a black friend was a secret I wasn't supposed to tell.

Then I continued with the story of Michael working at the cafeteria and his nightmares trying to get food to his people. The students' gasps and hums of agreement were all coming on cue. It felt like they were right there in the palm of my hand. I looked down at my notes and saw the words "Michael with his tribe. Eat Smart/Refrigerator" scrawled in the margin. I had heard Michael tell it a hundred times and I plunged in headlong, recounting the story just as I remembered him telling it. The crowd laughed when I told about the woman saying how fat Michael had gotten. I was on a roll when I looked down at the campus pastor's hand practically chopping his head off in the air, mouthing the words, "Stop it!" And at that moment I realized I was enunciating the words "re-frig-er-a-tor" in Michael's African accent. I had told the whole story in Michael's East African voice.

I froze, realizing the mess I was in. "Oh my goodness," I said, laughing nervously. "Sorry about that. That must have sounded kind of racist." And when the word "racist" left my lips, I could feel the air leave the room. That's when I realized that the students hadn't thought it sounded racist until I said it. I looked back at the campus pastor. He was holding up a piece of paper mouthing the words "Your notes." I stared down at my outline trying to read the words. My mind went empty with hot panic. When I looked up, the students were searching each other's faces trying to figure out what was going on. The blood drained from my face. My momentum was lost.

The pastor's face was in his hands. "So…" I tried to restart. "As you can see when Michael told me this story I realized that I had a lot to learn about his village." My voice was slow and unsteady. "That his people needed help." I was drowning in sweat. I adjusted my papers before finding the

231

final point. I read the last line unable to look up from the page. "So now I share what I have with Michael and he uses the money to help his people. Not because he's a cause but because he's my friend. It's got to be about relationships, not causes."

I looked up and heard some scattered applause as the band came back out for the final song. I sat down in a daze, staring at the polished cement floor, the tension penetrating my back muscles. After the service, a few students came up to me and thanked me for my talk, explaining about how they had met a friend from this or that country. I nodded along, barely listening. I was too focused on my dad standing in the back of the line wearing a suit and tie. I was dreading the *I told you so* that I was sure was coming.

After the students left, he shook my hand. "I'm proud of you. It was a great talk." He sounded sincere.

"Yeah?" I was waiting for the rest of the lecture.

He rubbed the back of his neck and looked at the floor. "You know, we haven't always gotten along. I don't really understand what you believe or why you do what you do." He looked me in the eye and smiled. "But seeing you up there, I knew you were on the right track, that God had an important job for you to do. And I'm proud of you." He pulled me in for a hug. And for the first time in years, I let my head rest on his shoulder.

"Thanks, Dad," was all I could get out. It took every facial muscle I had to keep from crying.

Brad hung in the back until the room cleared. "Oh man, you did great." He paused, grinning. "Until you said you were a racist." He burst out laughing. "I mean, who does that in front of a thousand people?"

"Me?" I said, the embarrassment flooding back over me.

"Oh, my gosh. I thought that was incredible, I mean why would you call yourself a racist?" Brad chuckled devilishly the entire ride home.

"I said it *sounded* racist," repeating my position for the hundredth time.

"Oh, yeah, that's a big difference," he said sarcastically.

I got a call from the campus pastor the next day. "I'm calling you because the administration would like you to issue a formal apology for the racist remarks you made to the campus yesterday."

"Any particular remarks?" I asked, wincing.

"The part where you dishonored the African elders with your impression." I thought about the elders' hands covered in goat feces rubbing up and down my chest. I thought about telling him, "I'm pretty sure they're not offended by my impression. They're more offended by you hearing my talk and worrying more about saving the college's image than saving people's lives." I paused taking several deep breaths. At this point it was about damage control. "I understand your concern, and I'll write something up."

I called Michael. "How did the talk go, buddy?" His voice sounded eager for details. He had been expecting to build a classroom with all the donations from the sermon.

"Not so good, Michael."

"Hmmm, did you tell a joke?" Michael replied suspiciously. He had spent the last week warning me over email and text not to tell jokes. "This is serious business," he had told me an hour before I spoke.

I had only felt anger until now, pissed at the sound guy for his incompetent handling of my video, at the campus pastor for throwing me under the bus rather than asking the school to rethink its priorities, furious at Brad whose retelling always ended in wide-eyed laughter. "I'm sure it's not that bad," Emilie had said after hearing Brad tell it four times over dinner.

"No, it wasn't a joke, Michael. I didn't tell any jokes." I sighed. The shame of public humiliation coupled with disappointing Michael settled in my stomach. "I told the story of you going back to the tribe and explaining what a refrigerator was. But I told it in your voice." Michael was silent on the other end. "Are you still there?" I asked.

"Yep, I'm here," he said. "Okay, go on. What did you say after that which was so offensive to the people?"

"Nothing. That was it. They said my impression was racist." Adding quickly, "I did say that it might have *sounded* racist, but I don't think it actually was." I was hoping to breeze past the more incriminating details.

"Hmm. Maybe I'm not understanding what they mean by racism. In fact, you sound so much like me when you are impressioning me." He paused. "But never mind about it. Anyways, these were the same people who said they were bringing light to Kenyan darkness. So perhaps their perspective on racism is a bit different than the rest of us."

"Sorry, Michael," I said, feeling relieved that he didn't seem mad.

"It's no big problem," Michael reassured me. "We will still find a way. Kidogo, kidogo. Slowly, slowly."

The next week, I got a call from the college. I braced for impact before hearing "Hello, Nathan?" It was the blonde-haired girl from the chapel prayer circle.

"Yes?" I said, preparing to apologize.

"So I'm from the World Prayer Team."

"Yep, I've heard of you." It was the group Amanda had reluctantly joined forces with for the Save Africa march. The *Christian* kids. "So I wanted to call and tell you that this last week we prayed for you and Michael and Daylight. Our group heard your talk and we were really inspired. And I was wondering if you could come to our meeting next week."

"Sure. That sounds good," I said, hoping it wasn't some kind of elaborate trap.

The following Wednesday I parked right outside a red-brick dorm building wearing my baseball cap pulled low, hoping to avoid being recognized by anyone who might be holding a grudge from my sermon. The blonde girl smiled and waved at me through the glass doors. She looked sincerely excited to see me. With renewed confidence, I followed her down a cinder-block hallway and inside a small apartment where twenty kids were seated on the floor. After introducing myself, I showed the video of Michael and me, the one I had tried to show the entire school the week before. Afterwards I passed around a few pictures of the kids at Daylight and thanked them for their prayers.

"So, Nathan, we have something for you," the blonde girl said, handing me a white envelope with the word "Daylight" written in pen across the front. It was thick and heavy. I slid open the sealed flap and inside was a collection of green bills and a half sheet of paper with "$1,200" written on it. I felt tears welling in my eyes and goose bumps running down my neck. "We went door to door asking for change and people were super generous." She smiled.

Before the chapel sermon, Michael and I had talked about how the wealthy Friends of the College were going to invite us to steak dinners in order to inform us that they were connecting Daylight to their family foundations. I stared down at the white envelope. "Thank you," was all I could say without crumpling into an emotional mess. It wasn't enough to build our own school. But $1,200, combined with the $500 check I got in the mail from preaching at chapel, was enough to feed the kids next month.

21
A BOY NAMED CORN

In December 2011, I was seated cross-legged on a dried brown-and-white cowhide next to Emilie. Four cows loomed over us, basking in the morning sun. Emilie was fingering the six brass bracelets around her wrist, which Michael's sisters had pounded into circles with a thousand taps of their grinding stone. Michael's mother leaned over us smiling, her calloused left foot caked with mud.

Michael had missed our wedding ceremony in Minnesota and he insisted that Emilie and I be remarried at his homestead. "Your husband is a Pokot elder," he explained to Emilie over the phone. "And besides, it's not so bad as Sapana. A wedding is a short ceremony by the oldest woman in the village," he assured her. "It's no big deal."

The smell of warm cow dung was a sharp contrast to the mix of cake and perfume that marked our first marriage ceremony. Michael's mother raised a dried squash jug to the sky before pouring a half-second's worth of fresh milk on both our heads. It was the first milk to come from the black-and-white spotted cow a few feet behind us. I felt the liquid slide off the side of my greasy unwashed hair and watched it disappear into my t-shirt. Then Michael's mother pointed at the cow.

"You have to grab a handful of the cow's poop and then rub the poop on its back," Michael laughed from outside the thorn-walled pen.

"Seriously?" Emilie shouted at Michael before glaring at me.

I shrugged. "I fell for the same thing."

Michael rolled up the sleeve of his buttoned shirt. Then he disappeared behind the thorn fence and re-emerged with a dried dark-green pile, a hundred flies swarming its hard surface. "Here use this one," he said, holding it with both hands. Apparently, nothing important happened in the village without a little dung.

Emilie took a deep breath, stood up, and took a palm-sized ball of grassy poop. "Is this enough?"

"Fine, no problem," Michael smiled, dropping the rest of the pie on the ground. His brother stood on the far side of the pen holding the spotted calf by the neck. "Now you just rub it on the cow's back and you and Natun are married for real."

Emilie rolled the ball of dung quickly back and forth against the calf's back, her hand bumping along its visible spinal cord. "Very good," Michael said, throwing her a small, clear bottle of hand sanitizer, which Emilie poured up and down her arms. I had told Michael we needed hand sanitizer if we were going back to his homestead.

"Okay, now we have to be going," he said.

After a dozen hugs between Michael's sisters, brothers, aunts, and several nieces and nephews, we pulled out of the homestead. The worn out shocks tumbled down the pock-marked path that traversed the valley.

We drove all day before we saw the next nomad, a woman in a dirt-stained wool sweater leading a camel twice her height along the side of the road, her bright beaded necklaces in stark contrast to the endless brown landscape. It had been months since it rained and the clay earth had dried into jagged tiles. We found her by following two sets of footprints fracturing the otherwise untouched ground.

Michael pulled the truck up beside her and her camel bucked. She yanked on its bit with her full weight and the camel bent down low enough to sneeze on Emilie through the open backseat window. From the front seat, I could see flies drinking the goo collecting around its ink-black eyes and long feminine eyelashes. Michael asked the woman a few questions in Pokot before she pointed down a trail and into the next valley. "She is saying the child is this way," Michael pointed.

Michael had received a call from a local elder a month ago. They had identified a boy they wanted to send to Daylight. After seeing Michael's first crop of Pokot students, the village elders' position on education had moved from suspicion to grassroots activism. Michael had brought several of the now second-grade students back to their home villages. And when their aunts and uncles saw them, they noted the children's full cheeks and dark black hair. They were equally impressed that the children had already learned so much of the white man's magic.

"They can already read and write," Keu exclaimed. "Kimpur, these kids are learning faster than you did in Kiwawa," he teased.

When Michael returned three months later, there was a group of thirty children assembled for him to take back to school. But this group wasn't just Pokot. The Pokot elders had sent messengers to the Karamoja and Turkana elders about Michael's school for orphans. Michael smiled as he saw orphaned children from both sides of the war, all eager to go to school, standing side by side. Michael called me the next day. "Natun, I think I have an idea about how we can end the war." He said smiling through the phone. "We will educate children from all the tribes. They will become friends at school. And when they grow up they won't fight one another. When the Pokot children see the Karamoja they will remember that the war took both their parents. They will remember the humanity in each other."

"That sounds amazing," I said.

From then on Michael would return from each trip to the desert with the SUV crammed with as many kids as could fit in an eight-passenger vehicle. By the time Emilie and I arrived to Kenya, Daylight was educating 200 kids from every tribe in the desert. Michael was so overwhelmed by the number of children waiting for school that he decided he would only accept kids whose parents had died. He knew all too well the fear of being a parentless child in the desert.

But Michael had made a special exception for the child we were looking for. We followed a path across the hot, desolate valley to a cluster of mud huts. A woman with short dreadlocked hair stood in front of the unprotected homestead wearing a wide-beaded necklace of red and brown. Perched on her hip was a boy with a calloused stump where his left foot should have been. "His name, Pembe, means corn," Michael said, parking the car thirty yards away from the woman.

"When Pembe was a baby, his homestead was attacked by raiders in the middle of the night. And his mother picked him out of bed to escape, but it was dark and she tripped over the logs that were still smoldering from the dinner's cooking fire. She accidentally dropped Pembe into the still red-hot embers and his foot was burned so badly that they cut it off."

I stared at the child, who was covered in dust. His mother waved at Michael in recognition. "After the raid, their family was left with no cows, walking from village to village looking for help. But it was a drought, like this one," he said, pointing at the dry dirt surrounding our vehicle. "It was so hot that none of their neighbors had any cows to spare. They finally ran into a USAID truck that gave them two bags of corn. So they named that baby Pembe, meaning corn." He pointed at the boy with one foot. "So they would remember the men who gave them the food in their time of need." He smiled at me and unbuckled his seatbelt. "Anyways, Pembe's mother has been carrying him ever since. But now he is four years old and he is too

Pembe and his mother

big for her to carry and he can't keep up with the other boys, so she requested us to bring him to Daylight."

I watched as six naked children emerged from the hut and huddled behind their mother. "Okay, Nathan, get out. Emilie, you wait here." At the sight of me, the children fled in every direction. Pembe started hitting his mother, trying to escape. When it was clear he couldn't get away, he began shouting and buried his crying face in her shoulder.

"What's he saying?" I asked Michael as we shook hands with Pembe's father, a grey-bearded man in a tan blazer with several buttons missing. "Pembe is begging his mother to protect him. He thinks you are going to eat him," Michael said to me casually. I looked at Pembe, whose small fists were pounding on his mother's shoulder. Then I looked at Michael.

"I'm an ogre." I realized we were reprising the roles of the ogre and the black man from Michael's childhood.

"Exactly," Michael said, putting his arm around me. Pembe's mother smiled at me and put Pembe down, pushing him towards me as the rest of her dusty, half-naked children peeked their heads out of the interior of the huts.

"Is this what it was like when you met the missionaries?" I knelt in front of Pembe with my hands outstretched, my palms up. Pembe looked at me for a moment with terror. Then he turned and hobbled away as fast as he could, favoring his calloused stump with each step. His mother slowly followed him, her voice quiet and reassuring.

"Yes, buddy," Michael said. "He thinks he will be eaten for sure. But his mother is trying to calm him. She keeps telling him it's going to be alright."

Emilie got out of the vehicle when Pembe started to run away. I could see she had been crying. "We are *not* taking him," she shouted at me, wiping the muddy tears across her face. "We can't force him against his will. We just can't."

I ran up to her. "Shhh...," I shout-whispered, hoping she wouldn't scare Pembe any more than he already was.

"I can't sit back and watch this happen," she mumbled through her tears.

I knew why she was upset. When I had told her Daylight was building a dormitory for the orphaned nomadic children, she told me about the boarding school for the children of missionaries where she spent several years growing up. She had grown up watching parents drop off their crying kids so that they could spread the gospel to some village in Mongolia or the slums of Ghana. She told me how she watched the kids sob into their pillows late at night as their dorm mothers rubbed their hair and explained in soothing tones that their missionary parents weren't coming back this Christmas; that they were spending the holidays in a distant land saving other children's souls. "They would cry for the first few years until one day they realized their parents weren't coming back. Then most of them stopped missing their parents and started hating God."

She cried beside the vehicle. She was dressed in a Pokot skirt and tank top she was given as a wedding present, her greasy hair pulled back into a ponytail. I ran to her and hugged her. "I'm sorry this is difficult for you to watch," I whispered in her ear. I could feel every muscle in her back was clenched tight.

"I don't want to take him away." I could feel my shirt absorbing her tears as she buried her face in my shoulder.

"This is the best option we have," I whispered.

"We can't. You don't know what it's like," she sputtered through the sobs.

I hugged her tighter. "Pembe can't live out here. He can hardly walk," I said, holding her face in front of mine. "I wish the nomads didn't have to live out here. I wish the British would have never come to Kenya. I wish Pembe still had his foot. But this is what Michael and Pembe's mother decided. And we have to trust that they know what's best."

Behind me, Pembe started screaming "Yoo, yoo," begging his mother to save him as Michael carried him, arms outstretched to avoid Pembe's swinging arms and kicking legs. Michael forced Pembe into the back seat, strapped the seatbelt across his chest and shut the door. Pembe pulled at the straps shrieking "Yoo! Yoo!" His mother tried to hide her own tears as she rubbed his head goodbye through the open window.

"Get in," Michael shouted to us. Emilie looked at me, took a few deep breaths, and got in the backseat. I watched her trying to force a smile, rubbing Pembe's back as he shouted for his mother with increased desperation.

"Nathan, give him some candy," Michael said, opening the glove compartment full of sweets. I unwrapped a watermelon-flavored lollipop and stuck it in my mouth. Then I looked back at Pembe from the front seat. I held a second cherry lollipop in front of him as the vehicle began rumbling away from his homestead.

I acted out putting the lollipop in and out of my mouth and licking it with my tongue before handing it to Pembe. He sat transfixed by what he quickly realized was food. I handed him the red lollipop and he carefully placed it in his mouth. His eyes widened with the same look of elation that had marked every child's face when they tasted their first piece of candy.

Michael looked back at him through the mirror. "Oh man, he likes it," he laughed. "Everybody likes candy."

Emilie looked at Pembe, who was now quietly sucking on the lollipop, and smiled before sniffing through her nose. "Nathan? I need a lollipop too," she said. "A peach one."

As we pulled out of the valley and back onto the main road, we picked up speed and Emilie and Pembe both collapsed in the back seat, exhausted from emotion. Their bodies were held upright by the seat belts, their heads bouncing in unison as the vehicle struggled over the rocky terrain.

We drove for an hour in silence as I watched the sun set behind Tororot's holy mountain, the first stars slowly punctuating the darkening sky. "Up that path is my school, Kiwawa," Michael said, pointing up a washed-out road lined with short green trees. "Someday I'll show it to you," he said as we drove past.

"I'd like that," I said, remembering all the stories he had told me about John and Sarah. I wondered what had brought them to the desert, what kind of church they grew up in. If it was anything like mine, I imagined they had been sent out here to save lost souls. I wondered where they were now, how the desert had changed them, if their family and friends had accused them of going native.

I was spending eleven months a year in America and one in Kenya. But I still felt like I was living in two worlds, and I was beginning to feel like a stranger in both. I tell stories around the dinner table about the villagers I've spoken to like they are families living just on the other side of town.

Back home, standing in line for a latte and scone, I'd get a call from Keu, his slowly pronounced English words coming out more like a collage than a sentence. As I repeated his words, "Tin sheet, shillings, cows, wives" (plural), I'd feel the stranger in line behind me zeroing in on my unusual conversation. Sitting at a table a half-hour later, I finally realized he was asking for a new tin sheet to repair his leaking roof. "I'll try to find something to help"—"find" being the operative word. It was my programmed response for the weekly requests for cows, medicine, or a spot for one more kid at Daylight. I had stopped saving money; it was almost impossible to keep anything in the bank once the villagers started passing out my cell phone number. After each request, I would hang up, take a deep breath, and then start making calls asking friends and family for help. "Roof repairs," I'd repeat over and over. "He's my friend in Kenya, the one with eight wives and sixty children."

But as the two cultures blurred, I found that the words of Jesus came into an unexpected focus. "Sell your possessions and give to the poor." "Give to the one who asks you, and do not turn away from the one who wants to borrow from you." "Do not worry about tomorrow, for tomorrow will worry about itself." His words no longer felt like a stump speech on economics from a homeless man. They felt like reminders from the desert, proverbs around the campfire spoken by a Pokot elder.

We drove late into the night, across valley after barren valley, the vehicle's shocks groaning with exhaustion. I looked back at my sleeping wife, Pembe's head on her lap. His missing foot was hidden under a wool blanket she must have put over him. "What do you think is going to happen to him?" I asked Michael.

"Who?" Michael asked, lost in his own thoughts. "Pembe? Oh, man, he will do incredible. He will grow up to be a poor millionaire." He laughed under his breath, trying not to wake up the sleeping passengers. "In fact, he will most probably be the president of Kenya someday."

I imagined Pembe in a full suit and tie, his long wooden desk covered in papers waiting to be signed into law.

"I wonder if he'll remember me," I said.

Michael smiled. "You never forget your first ogre."

ACKNOWLEDGMENTS

To all our friends in America: Thank you to Mom and Dad Roberts (you filled my life with hope and possibility!), Emilie (I love you to pieces!), Kellen and Marisa, the Herd, the Farm, Soup Night, Joyce Kama Ridley, George and Marilyn, Prof. Samuel Zalanga, Kevin and Carole, Carol C., House of Mercy, Lynnhurst UCC, First Lutheran, Stillwater Presbyterian, and all the Daylight partners who give so generously to make this school possible.

To all our friends in Kenya: to Angelina Kimpur, who has been a mother not only to the Kimpur children but to all the children of Daylight. To the whole Kimpur family: may you go farther than you ever imagined! To the teachers and students at Daylight: you inspire us! Asanti Sana to the people of Kapenguria: Alale, Ombolion, John and Sarah, and all those who helped Michael at World Vision. Oee to the Pokot elders for teaching us so much! To Pembe (congrats on getting to the top of your class!), Limon, and Losengoria for keeping us alive on all our adventures, and to Mary for naming her unexpected baby Nathan.

Thanks to our amazing team of editors: Greg Daniel, Linda Henry and Keith Hanson, JeaNell Krupnick, Luke and Rachel, Ben, Andrew, Brianna, Richard, Andrew and Becca, Rev. Debbie and Rev. Russell, Prof. Eric Baretto, Dr. William Obaga, Rael, Rev. Tom, Edwin, the Emerson House, and the Daylight Center Board of Directors. Thanks to Jeremiah and Alex for making the book come to life in picture. And to everyone who listened to us tell these stories and encouraged us to write them down.

We must take a moment to remember the leaders who inspired us: Mother Teresa, Nelson Mandela, Martin Luther King Jr., John F. Kennedy, and all those who want to put a kid on the moon.

This book was made possible by the generous support of:
Matt Horn, Travis and Chelsea Mann, and all the beautiful people who donated to our Kickstarter campaign.

Thank you.

I am so thankful to Nathan and Michael for writing this book, and for their generosity in donating fifty percent of book sales to Daylight Center and School. I hope this book helps illustrate why Daylight is so important. I hope someday there will be more books like this one, written by Daylight graduates who will become leaders for change in northwest Kenya, like Michael. If this story moved you, please consider making a donation to Daylight. For more information, please visit our website, daylightcenter.org or contact us.

Rachel Finsaas
Daylight Director of Operations